FOOD AND EMOTIONS IN ITALIAN WOMEN'S WRITING

A Reassessment

Food and Emotions in Italian Women's Writing

A Reassessment

PATRIZIA SAMBUCO

UNIVERSITY OF TORONTO PRESS
Toronto Buffalo London

Toronto Buffalo London
utorontopress.com

ISBN 978-1-4875-0683-4 (cloth)
ISBN 978-1-4875-3493-6 (EPUB)
ISBN 978-1-4875-3492-9 (PDF)

Toronto Italian Studies

Library and Archives Canada Cataloguing in Publication

Title: Food and emotions in Italian women's writing : a reassessment / Patrizia Sambuco.
Names: Sambuco, Patrizia, 1965–, author
Series: Toronto Italian studies.
Description: Series statement: Toronto Italian studies | Includes bibliographical references and index.
Identifiers: Canadiana (print) 2024045636X | Canadiana (ebook) 20240456408 | ISBN 9781487506834 (hardcover) | ISBN 9781487534936 (EPUB) | ISBN 9781487534929 (PDF)
Subjects: LCSH: Italian literature – Women authors – History and criticism. | LCSH: Italian literature – 20th century – History and criticism. | LCSH: Italian literature – 21st century – History and criticism. | LCSH: Food in literature. | LCSH: Emotions in literature.
Classification: LCC PQ4053.F58 S26 2024 | DDC 850.9/3564 – dc23

Cover design: Alexa Love
Cover images: iStock.com/Timbicus; iStock.com/Dewin ' Indew

We wish to acknowledge the land on which the University of Toronto Press operates. This land is the traditional territory of the Wendat, the Anishnaabeg, the Haudenosaunee, the Métis, and the Mississaugas of the Credit First Nation.

University of Toronto Press acknowledges the financial support of the Government of Canada, the Canada Council for the Arts, and the Ontario Arts Council, an agency of the Government of Ontario, for its publishing activities.

Canada Council for the Arts
Conseil des Arts du Canada

Funded by the Government of Canada
Financé par le gouvernement du Canada
Canada

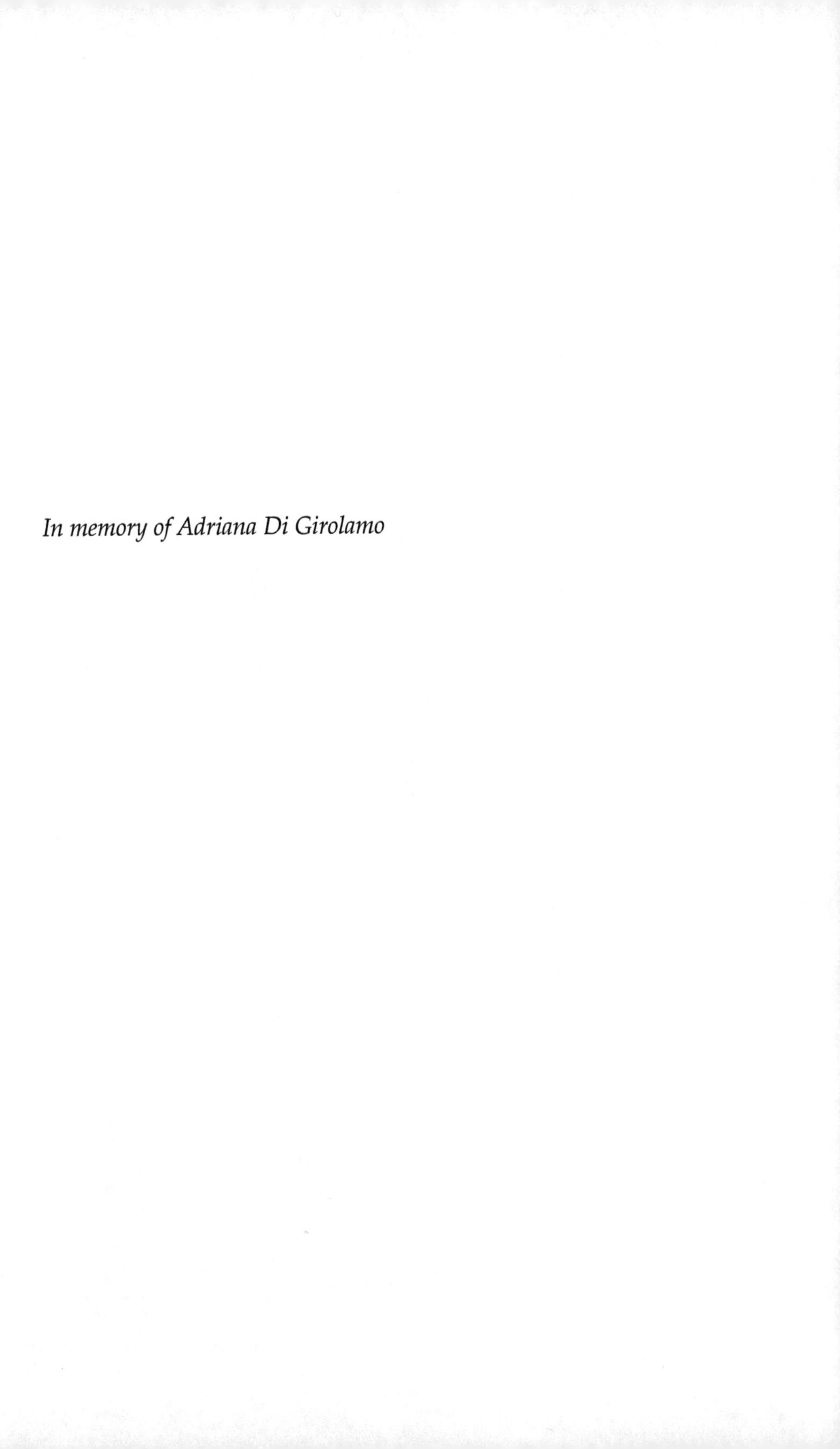

In memory of Adriana Di Girolamo

Contents

List of Illustrations ix
Acknowledgments xi

Introduction 3
1 Fascism, Food, and the Senses 16
2 World War II, Food, and Women's Bodies 51
3 The Politicization of the Everyday 84
4 The Third Millennium: Food as Relationships 119
Conclusion 147

Notes 153
Bibliography 177
Index 201

Illustrations

1.1 Picture of a Black wet nurse attending two white babies published in Giuseppe Lucidi's article "L'alimentazione del bambino in colonia" 39
1.2 Picture of a Black wet nurse holding a white baby published in Giuseppe Lucidi's article "L'alimentazione del bambino in colonia" 40
2.1 Page 1 of the autobiographical notes by Cesarina Bracco 67
2.2 Page 2 of the autobiographical notes by Cesarina Bracco 68
2.3 Page 3 of the autobiographical notes by Cesarina Bracco 69
3.1–3.2 Extracts from the documentary *Libreria delle donne* 114

Acknowledgments

I am delighted to have the opportunity to thank the many people who helped me in this project. First of all, I am very grateful to my editor, Mark Thompson, for believing in this project from the beginning. His professional expertise has been an invaluable guidance throughout my journey. I also thank the copy editor, Barbie Halaby, for her very fine work; the managing editor, Mary Lui, for her gentle and organized approach; the cover designers for their fantastic job; the product marketing specialist, Stephanie Mazza; and all the staff of the University of Toronto Press who contributed to the making of this book.

The first person with whom I discussed the ideas around *Food and Emotions in Italian Women's Writing* was Kathleen Lennon, Emeritus Professor of Philosophy at the University of Hull. Her advice on my very embryonic ideas were useful till the final version of the book, so I thank her for her ever-illuminating suggestions. The fact that she was my PhD supervisor many years ago gives an idea of her lifelong commitment to her former students.

This project was supported by a two-year fellowship at the Centre for the Study of Cultural Memory (CCM) of the School of Advanced Studies (SAS) of the University of London. The fellowship has been fundamental to the planning of my research and exciting for the expansion of its scope and the academic collaborations it generated. I am very grateful to the SAS and the CCM. Katia Pizzi, director of the CCM and later director of the Italian Culture Institute in London, deserves a special thanks. Her support of my research initiatives at the CCM and encouragement for this project have been nothing less than exceptional. I thank her for her unremitting assistance and her friendship.

The conferences I organized during my CCM fellowship, "The Taste of War: Values and Meanings of Food in WWII Italy and France" and "The Diasporic Plate: Food in the Contemporary Diasporic World in

Times of Crisis," the latter co-organized with Professor Bryce Evans (Hope University), were crucial for feedback and to further my work.

I also presented papers at several other conferences and seminars and have benefited from the feedback received at all of them. I was an invited speaker at the Cambridge Italian Research Network (CIRN) Symposium "Food" at Cambridge University and at the Italian Studies Research Seminar Series at the University of Oxford. I presented papers at the "Memories of the Future" conference at the University of London, at the annual international convention of the Institut Européen d'Histoire et des Cultures de l'Alimentation at the Université de Tours (France), and at Seton Hall University (New Jersey).

I am indebted to Seton Hall University and their Italian Studies department for granting me a fellowship that gave me the opportunity to spend precious time at their amazing Valente Italian Library.

Libraries in Italy have also shown their support for my research in different ways. The Biblioteca Gastronomica of Academia Barilla was a treasure trove not least thanks to the useful conversations with its curator Giancarlo Gonizzi. I am grateful to the Libreria delle Donne di Milano and to Stefania Giannotti for providing useful information on Estia. I thank the Archivio dell'Istituto per la storia della Resistenza e della società contemporanea nel Biellese, nel Vercellese e in Valsesia for giving me access to the handwritten notes of Cesarina Bracco and allowing me to reproduce them here. The Biblioteca di storia moderna e contemporanea in Rome kindly gave permission to reproduce images taken from *La difesa della razza*, and I thank them for that. I am grateful to the production company 3DProduzioni, MemoMi, and the Association Chiamale Storie for permission to reproduce images taken from their documentary *Libreria delle donne*. The Istituto Storico Parri in Bologna and the Biblioteca delle donne in the same city have provided access to fundamental periodicals. The Biblioteca Ariostesca in Ferrara and in particular its department of rare books allowed me to immerse myself in the study of some of the most difficult-to-find texts by Pina Ballario.

Sections on the analysis of Pina Ballario's books in chapter 2 were previously published in my article "Pina Ballario's Colonial and Travel Writing: Desserts, Breastfeeding and Pleasure as Opposition to Fascism," *Italian Studies* 73, no. 3 (2018): 257–73, https://doi.org/10.1080/00751634.2018.1487104. I thank Taylor and Francis for permission to republish excerpts of it.

The book is dedicated to the memory of Adriana Di Girolamo, my Mum.

FOOD AND EMOTIONS IN ITALIAN WOMEN'S WRITING

Introduction

Virginia Woolf famously wrote that "a good dinner is of great importance to good talk," and synthesizing in her diary her two 1928 lectures at Cambridge University women's colleges, she noted, "I blandly told them to drink wine and have a room of their own."[1] The remark sustained her argument for an improvement of women's material conditions, needed to foster women's writing. Her food references in the lectures that supplied the basis of her *A Room of One's Own*, with their synthesis of feminist, material, and intellectual connotations, raise significant questions about the relationship between women and food. For Woolf, having a room of one's own and drinking wine are a claim to economic independence and intellectual freedom. Both images suggest something daring. A similar effect was achieved by American food writer Mary Frances Kennedy (M.F.K.) Fisher, who openly suggested that the appreciation of food and wine was an assertion of power, especially in environments where expressions of enjoyment were not considered appropriate, let alone when articulated by women. Revered for her writing by both W.H. Auden and John Updike, in her *How to Cook a Wolf* (1942), published soon after America entered World War II, Fisher argued for the importance of taste and food enjoyment in times of crisis.[2] Sandra Gilbert paints a complex portrayal of Fisher as an intelligent and sophisticated femme fatale, who was brought up in the Anglo-Saxon belief that food should be consumed without enjoyment but pursued the idea that the dread of primal hunger and daily needs are counterbalanced by "the voluptuous fact of eating."[3] As with Woolf's invitation to drink wine, Fisher's reference to the voluptuousness of eating proposes food enjoyment as a transgressive pursuit of happiness and independence. In Fisher's autobiographical *The Gastronomical Me*, the description of her enjoyment of dining alone, and the resentment that this causes in other people, perfectly illustrates how transgression and independence intertwine:

> But if I must be alone, I refuse to be alone as if it were something weak and distasteful, like convalescence. Men see me eating in public, and I look as if "I knew my way around"; and yet I make it plain that I know my way around without them, and that upsets them … I know what I want, and usually get it because I am adaptable to locales. I order meals that are more typically masculine than feminine, if feminine means whipped-cream-and-cherries. I like good wines, or good drinkin'-likka, and beers and ales … And all these reasons, and probably a thousand others, like the way I wear my hair and what shade my lipstick is, make people look strangely at me, resentfully with a kind of hurt bafflement, when I dine alone.[4]

Both Fisher and Woolf suggest that the relationships around food interact with the knowledge, experience, and performance of their gender. *Food and Emotions in Italian Women's Writing* asks why food imaginaries have the power to convey such a disruptive message about women's intellectual freedom and autonomy.

Food and foodways "are integral to making, or 'doing,' one's gender," as the editors of the 2018 special issue of *Canadian Food Studies* dedicated to feminism insist.[5] Hence "doing food" interlocks with "doing gender." Feminist food scholars have amply discussed this topic.[6] For both Fisher and Woolf, expressing themselves through food, either as a food connoisseur dining on her own or in the exhortation to drink and enjoy wine as men do, is about doing gender. The message we can take away from them is that food theorization and practice add meaning to the theorization of women as subjects. I am interested in exploring why food imagery can be significant to represent women's intellectual freedom and autonomy. In *Food and Emotions in Italian Women's Writing*, together with an understanding of women's daily life captured by the study of food policies and domestic literature, I argue that food imagery in each historical period becomes a vehicle for challenging established political discourses by conveying unexpressed, alternative, or transgressive emotions. The analysis of domestic literature written by women shows their active role in the codification of gastronomy, how they participate in the construction of gender, and also how they have managed to express their professional interests. At the same time, I demonstrate how and why, in novels, poems, and diaries, dominant concepts of womanhood, which may have been hegemonically imposed by the culture and politics of each period, appear to be contested through the symbolic use of food stories and the expression of emotions. The book will show that, in each historical period, food imagery has often interacted with gender and politics, national and international. Women's bodies, evoked through food imagery, are central to this disruptive function.

The book illustrates how Italian society at large perceived women's bodies in each historical period; it also shows how the interactions of senses – connected to food – and emotions in the texts analysed are key to the representation of the female subjects as embodied agents. In other words, emotions and their expressions through food imagery are shown to be a relevant way to consider how women experienced their relations with themselves and others. In different ways throughout the decades, the marginality of women's bodies has found in the conceptual domain of food the possibility to express forms of selfhood that push the boundaries of dominant concepts of womanhood and interact with the cultural and political panoramas at the national and international levels. From the 1920s to the present, *Food and Emotions in Italian Women's Writing* reconstructs an alternative history of Italian women and their creativity, one that considers women's contribution to society from the perspective of food, encapsulating experiences and representations that value the interaction between senses and emotions – and hence the corporeal. As Joanne Bourk argues in her analysis of pain in Anglo-American society, to interpret the world, people use "not only existing metaphorical tools but also the ability to imaginatively create other conceptual domains from bodily experiences."[7] In this book I demonstrate that the workings of imagination around food and taste have proved to be a form of expression that, because of the connection to the senses and the body, is suitable to voice alternative conceptual domains. This must be related to the idea of the human being as a combination of flesh and mind, the one that Woolf alluded to when she wrote that one cannot think well if one has not dined well – "The human frame being what it is, heart, body and brain all mixed together."[8]

Anthropologists have long considered the interlocking relevance of food and identity. As Claude Fischler's seminal work explains, food consumption is a powerful means to look at the relationship of an individual to the outside world.[9] Carole Counihan has clarified how, from the anthropological and sociocultural point of view, the relationship between food consumption and the body is always gendered. In her examples of past and present civilizations, the representational values of food consumption – that is, the cultural and emotional charges that we attribute to the food we decide to eat – do not exist outside a gendered view of personal reality. Self-control around food consumption for American women and the pursuit of a plump body for Fijian women are views based on different images of an ideal female body.[10] For

Counihan a sense of perfection, as could be the case for contemporary anorexic women or medieval holy women, and rituals such as mixing menstrual blood into the food cooked for women's abusive husbands, a practice of eighteenth-century Mexican women, are all exemplifications of power over the body.[11] Feminist critical constructionists who analyse power structures over food as a dynamic of imposition and resistance have revealed the impact of the food market on women's bodies, adding another point of view to the analysis of food and bodies.[12] This is the case of Carol Adams's feminist interpretation of the meat market. She advocated vegetarianism as a feminist response to a meat market whose mistreatment of animals and support for a meat diet replicate patriarchal structures.[13]

Deborah Lupton analyses food consumption and embodiment from a poststructuralist perspective, crucial in her view to avoid the oppression/resistance dynamic, which she suggests is not particularly useful in representing the changes in individual and societal food preferences.[14] Lupton is keen to demonstrate that through a variety of food discourses, including medical, personal, and popular culture accounts, "in conjunction with non- or pre-discursive sensual and embodied experiences, ... individuals come to understand themselves, their bodies and their relationship to food and eating."[15] I am interested in pursuing a similar line of enquiry, as I investigate gender discourses about women and food and explore the language of food and taste in texts penned by women. My overall objective is, however, also methodological.

In recent years, while the interest in women's and gender issues has spread beyond specialist circles, new publications have problematized the question of how to narrate or teach women's creativity and history. Daniela Brogi's pamphlet *Lo spazio delle donne* assesses the strategies that have obscured and neglected the traditions and memory of women's literary creativity, and it asks questions about how to develop an inclusive narrative of the cultural work of women. The possibility "di una tradizione, di un racconto e di un dialogo tra le generazioni" (of a tradition, a narrative and a dialogue between generations), she states, is damaged, and even destroyed, when the social and cultural history of non-dominant groups is ignored.[16] Thus, it is not sufficient to study, teach, or organize a conference on a woman writer if she is not studied within a relevant artistic, historical, and cultural genealogy.[17] Borrowing a term from film studies, she proposes a "peripheral" reading of women's creativity, which she calls "fuori campo attivo" (active off-screen), that is a reading able to capture not only what is in focus but also what is off-screen. Silvia Salvatici's edited volume *Storia delle donne dell'Italia contemporanea* is another example of a new approach to the narration of women's history.[18] In her volume, themes and periods are orchestrated in such a way as to widen the angle of observation and present a space of history much more populated by women. *Food and Emotions in Italian Women's Writing* opens up the analysis to include both well-recognized and peripheral authors, while also representing the many women who wrote domestic literature. It shows how the interplay of the senses and emotions is a profitable way to illuminate overlooked aspects of women's subjectivity. It reassesses women's writing, giving value to the marginality of women's bodies and subject positions through the conceptual domain of food.

Literary criticism has not been insensitive to the potential of food themes for addressing questions of women's bodies and subjectivity. Andrea Adolph has investigated food consumption in British twentieth-century women's writing, showing how writers have sustained and problematized the mind/body split, synonymous, from a philosophical perspective, with the devaluation of the woman subject through her association with the irrational, the passional, the unruly. In Adolph's words, food consumption "provides a strong lens through which to examine those links that exist among the interconnected qualities of female subjectivity, agency, embodiment and sexuality."[19] Tamar Heller and Patricia Moran analyse food in women's writing by referring to Hélène Cixous's interpretation of the woman eating the apple in Genesis. On this basis, they interpret the subjection of "female 'oral pleasure' to the regulation of patriarchal law."[20] In perfect unison with Adolph's argument, Heller and Moran contend that women's writing counteracts those cultural taboos by "breaking down the dualism of flesh and spirit that has traditionally devalued and silenced women."[21] Sarah Sceats's approach to food in her study of British women's contemporary literature is similar. She points to a search for wholeness as a common thread in the texts she considers and which, she insists, testify to the wide range of ways women have used food as a means of communication in their writing.[22] But theories about dualism and food are not limited to literary criticism.

Theoretical Framework

Philosophy – the discipline which, from Plato on, argued for the subordination of body and emotions to rationality and the mind and then, through Immanuel Kant, sanctioned the inferiority of the sense of taste – has in recent years been active in casting new light on food. From the 1990s a small but growing number of philosophical texts have developed into what can deservedly be considered a new philosophy of food. Their intention has not been merely to reread those theories that have seen the senses in a favourable way, such as the philosophy of Epicurus or of Emmanuel Levinas, but they have used the idea of food as a means to rethink philosophy. Lisa Heldke and Deane Curtin, in their 1992 reader *Cooking, Eating, Thinking: Transformative Philosophies of Food*, laid the basis for an enquiry that would make food and eating a tool for rethinking the subject.[23] Several years later, and after a prolific academic engagement with the topic of food, in her engaging article "The Unexamined Meal Is Not Worth Eating," Heldke summarized the benefits of the study of food within a discipline concerned until then with the analysis of the disembodied life: "Food might be one topic the study of which could enable the discipline of philosophy to reground itself in the matters of everyday life – matters that Plato took to stand at the very heart of philosophy."[24] That the study of food could help rephrase philosophical questions from a different perspective is also argued by Curtin. He privileges the study of food as promoting a new outlook on personhood because it implies taking seriously "our relations to marginalized aspects of life."[25] Curtin uses feminist and Buddhist theories to propose a relational model of the self that takes strength from the acceptance of everyday life and the celebration of diversity. His theory highlights the moral implications which derive from the codependence between the self and the world.

Carolyn Korsmeyer's *Making Sense of Taste* (1999) criticizes the inadequacy of classical philosophy for an appropriate discussion of food and firmly positions food among the fine arts.[26] The same year, Francesca Rigotti published *La filosofia in cucina*, where she noted that the use of food metaphors in philosophical language contradicts the subordination of eating to thinking, of the body to the mind.[27] More recently, Nicola Perullo has articulated a sophisticated but accessible discussion of the experience of taste, an approach which is particularly in tune with the analysis I propose here.

Perullo examines the experience of taste rather than the function of food as such, and this allows him a greater focus on the individual. Taste, he clarifies, is not only about acquiring an experience and knowledge of the things of the world but also is for the subject a personal, inner experience, from which one learns about herself, about the transformation and enrichment of her self. Just as Curtin developed an idea of the relational model of the subject through food, Perullo shows how the relational function of taste is fundamental. But, because he is discussing the experience of taste rather than food, the implications of his thinking are particularly relevant for the conceptualization of the subject, whom he sees united with the object, that is, with what is being eaten:

> [Subject and object] become a totally intertwined, dynamic, and complex in-between organism. The aesthetic of taste is therefore an aesthetics of relation and implication, an aesthetics that attempts to overcome the stiff and hypostatic resistances and dichotomies that exist between the entities of mind and body, subject and object, or nature and culture.[28]

Perullo's views echo some of the interests of feminist theories, for example, in the paragraph just quoted, the overcoming of the mind/body split. He also writes of the need to embrace marginality when theorizing taste, a topic of crucial importance in feminist thinking.[29] Perullo acknowledges gender studies as among the first disciplines to engage with food studies but does not develop a gender discussion, which is beyond his area of specialization.

The concept of taste is defined by Perullo as "ecologically situated." This means it is part of an environment, a field of forces, where it is continually evolving, in exchange with other elements. Therefore, a professional chef's tasting technique is not to be considered the ultimate knowledge; each taste experience is valid within an environment, within its circumstantial experience. Nature and culture, as he puts it, are "procedural articulations," rather than separate blocks.[30] Perullo portrays a relational and democratic concept of taste where the ideas of "subjective" and "objective" are not relevant anymore.

Perullo's philosophical field is aesthetics, and like other philosophers in his area, he is concerned with the reconsideration of gastronomy as fine art. Yet his relational model at the basis of the experience of taste opens up a reflection on ethics. The gastronomic experience interpreted as a relation between the subject and the object is effectively an engagement with the other and with the world, and it exemplifies an ethical relation, "come relazione all'altro, che comprendo senza poter inglobare" (as a relation with the other, whom I understand without being able to incorporate them).[31] In this sense, taste is very much about responsibility and understanding.

For Perullo, the act of eating is a process that may trigger emotions as well as an understanding of the self: "I do not deny the importance of the satisfaction of hunger, but rather suggest that satiating hunger *can be* a way to awaken feelings, create emotions, and enrich one's own life with meanings."[32] The senses, emotions, and cognition join together in Perullo's argument. His concept of "meanings" deriving from taste seems to come very close to what neuroscience calls mental image production, that is, the mapping and translation of information deriving from the senses into mental images.

In recent decades neuroscience research has set out to demonstrate how incongruous is the dualism of material versus immaterial self, of mind versus body. Contrary to assumptions in neuroscience until then, Antonio Damasio's work on the neurobiology of the brain, following his *Descartes' Error* (1994), has focused on the interaction of body and brain rather than on the singular study of the brain. Within this context he has studied emotions, determining that emotions not only enact changes in the body, as is normal in emotional states, but also produce changes in the brain itself, changes linked to cognition and to mental image production.[33]

Other scientists have emphasized how emotions are determined by the interactions between the sensory, the personal experience of the body, and the external world, as shown by David Linden in his study of the skin and by psychological constructionist Lisa Feldman Barrett.[34] This has encouraged historians of emotions such as Barbara Rosenwein and Riccardo Cristiani to hope for closer collaboration between science and the humanities, given that historians of emotions can, for example, add to the picture specific gender and historical analyses for context.[35] The historicization of the dynamic interaction between the sensory and cognition has been further explored by Rob Boddice and by Boddice and Mark Smith, as we shall see.[36]

From Perullo's theorization, through taste we can also discuss the construction of the self, which neuroscience confirms is linked to an interaction between the brain, the body, and the external world. Therefore, not only does the analysis of food in women's writing aim at re-evaluating everyday life, in which women were protagonists. It also refers to the perception of the self and subjectivity, explaining why literary criticism of women's writing and food has been concerned with problematizing the mind/body split and demanded a rethinking of the woman as subject. In fact, feminist criticism has made the interplay between subjectivity and women's bodies central to its theorization.

In the 1990s, inspired by Luce Irigaray's philosophy of sexual difference, theorists such as Elizabeth Grosz and Moira Gatens originated the branch of feminism called corporeal feminism. Corporeal feminism gave value to women's embodied subjectivity, breaking down the mind/body dichotomy that dominated Western philosophy and associated women with the inferior corporeal.[37] If the expression of the embodied self has been crucial for feminist thinking, so has the discourse on emotions that is also central to food studies.

The analysis of food led to the discussion of identity by Fischler, of subjectivity by Lupton, of embodiment by Adolph, and of emotions, as everybody acknowledges when stressing the emotional charges often connected to food and taste. Studies on food, and on pathological eating such as anorexia and bulimia, have often based their analysis on emotions. Emotions like food nostalgia have become a trope in literature and particularly in writing on migration. As mentioned, both Perullo and Lupton, as well as Adolph and other literary critics, underline the close link between food and emotional experience. Yet they do not claim to be part of the "affective turn," the interest in the study of the emotions that was undertaken from the 1990s on in many disciplines.

Very significantly, in *The Cultural Politics of Emotions* Sara Ahmed tears apart the argument that the "affective turn" represents a new model of enquiry. She addresses instead how "feminist work on bodies and emotions challenged from the outset mind-body dualism, as well as the distinction between reason and passion."[38] She echoes the points of view of Ann Koivunen and Ann Cvetkovich, who also criticize the "affective turn" label, showing how the connection between the subject woman, the body, and the emotions has been central to feminism for a very long time.[39] For her analysis of emotions, Ahmed utilizes the works of feminist theorists not normally considered part of the affective turn, such as bell hooks, Audre Lorde, Elizabeth Spelman, and Arlie Hochschild, among others.[40]

In my reading of texts, the emotions and the senses often intertwine. Emotions are relevant as an expression that, starting from the senses, evokes elements of life as it is experienced. Throughout the book, I refer to food imagery in fiction, poetry, and memoirs written by women using the term "literary food." This expression, which echoes Fischler's theory, is designed to suggest that the communicative and identity function normally executed by food, as an element of the outside world that we take into our bodies, can also be seen on the page in the food imagery chosen by the authors explored here. *Food and Emotions in Italian Women's Writing* shows that literary food is a form of expression of personal emotions used either to counteract dominant views and norms or else to project alternative visions and subject positions for women. My analysis shows that over the decades, literary food is a recurrent form of expression that links the subject's emotions to the body and thereby offers a historicized interpretation of the embodied sense of self.

In his discussion of the history of emotions, Rob Boddice argues that the historicity of human experience is also beneficial to scientific disciplines like neuroscience. In particular, he refers to the social neurosciences that demonstrate the mutability of human experience and how it is influenced by context. Even experiences of pain are both individuated experiences and correlated to culture.[41] On that basis, Boddice proposes the term "biocultural" to indicate a concept of human experience that dynamically includes culture and biology, contextualizing it and avoiding the risk of universalism taken for granted in the natural sciences. This perspective seems very similar to the concept of "ecology," the dynamic environment of taste proposed by Perullo. As a historian, Boddice suggests how bioculturalism can help explain the history of human experience: "The entanglement of culture and biology ... forces us to look at what is non-conscious as well as what is conscious ... It gives us cause to explore the historicism of reality, not as a simple gloss on a biologically stable base, but as an authentically experienced and embodied diachronic process."[42] *Food and Emotions in Italian Women's Writing* historicizes the discussion of food and emotions, creating an overview of women's history over a long period and an analysis of the significance of food imagery in women's writing within different times. Taste and emotions are then seen in the context of social environments and historical periods. What emerges from the analysis is a historicized sense of selfhood, one that rejects rigid norms and evolves inside dynamic relationships with others and the world.

Book Structure

The periods studied have been chosen because of the prominence of public discourses on food due to, for example, governmental policies or the scarcity of food or the availability of different foodstuffs. They have also been selected for the importance of these times in Italian women's history. Consequently, the book focuses on the Fascist era, when autarkic policies made both food and women central objects of governmental policies; on World War II, when hunger, scarcity, and the needs of the family were central to women's daily struggle; and on the post-war transition from the image of the modern and impeccable women protagonists of the new food and home-appliances industry of the economic boom to the 1968 youth movement and its legacy of memories. The book concludes with a study of migrant and transnational works of the third millennium, which shows how contemporary women writers manipulate literary food to intervene in the political discussion around migration and postcoloniality.

Chapter 1 shows how Fascist-era food discourses intertwined with nationalistic values and the regime's constructions of femininity. The government's determination to free the country from its financial dependence on imports brought about several new policies and initiatives that changed agriculture, modified the landscape, and directed people to eat more rice and fish instead of bread and pasta. From the *battaglia del grano* (Battle for Wheat), starting in the mid-1920s, to the autarkic policies of the mid-1930s, Fascism actively imposed a culture of self-restraint with moral and nationalistic overtones. Women represented a vital constituency for the Fascist regime, as they were seen as the essential transmission mechanism if its economic and agricultural policies were to be transformed into practice. Women of all social classes were involved in the nation's gastronomic transformation; cookbooks, journal articles, and food magazines all showed how woman could cook with less.

The chapter also examines how women authors of domestic literature exhorted women to do their nationalistic duty, albeit with a degree of liberty allowed to the different social classes, and how some found in their work a way to express their personal interests. My reading of the travel book and novels by the Fascist supporter Pina Ballario shows how literary food conveys expressions of longing for pleasure that contrast with the Fascist dogma of duty and sacrifice and hence how, in these cases, the senses displaced nationalism. The analysis of anti-Fascist Alba de Céspedes's *Nessuno torna indietro* (*There's No Turning Back*) confirms the function of the senses and literary food in contrasting the dominant views of the times, leaving space for personal emotions. If Fascism aimed to shape Italians' private and public lives in line with its pervading nationalism, these texts articulated forms of dissonance that confirmed just which specific structures the regime was trying to control: food, senses, and emotions.

Ideas of economy and self-restraint typical of Fascist protectionism became an everyday preoccupation during wartime. The problem of food availability during the first part of the war developed into a much drearier and more complex issue in 1943–5, when civil war, German occupation, and the liberating Allied forces all had an impact on the food situation. Chapter 2 reveals how women were again at the centre of food dynamics and national interests. Women's engagement in the war was visible at all levels. Food protests and women's participation in the civil Resistance movement were experienced and presented as reinforcing claims to a new legitimacy.

The Gruppi di Difesa della Donna (GDD) exhorted women to take part in food protests and so become politically active in the anti-Fascist war. Through the analysis of archival GDD documents and a comparison of clandestine and official issues of the journal *Noi donne*, the chapter shows how the organizations at the heart of women's protests prompted women to take action but then would publicly modify the narrative in a more traditional direction as, more than ever, women's bodies had become a site of contention. On the contrary, in the memoirs of the

Resistance, literary food acquires the power to bring women's autonomous bodies back into the story.

Food-related scenes in war narratives often illustrate the hunger and food scarcity suffered by many in the country. In the women's memoirs reviewed here, food scenes appear to have another function – that is to be a metonymic representation of an autonomous self. In Giovanna Zangrandi's and Cesarina Bracco's memoirs, literary food gives expression to an affective body that is disengaged from the rules and conventions of the time. The enthusiastic desire to participate actively in the war, so common in women's memoirs of the Resistance, is encapsulated in food scenes that redeem the image of the female body, which stories of hunger-led prostitution and discourse on women's active participation had transformed into a site of anxiety during and after the war. These food scenes rather appear as a celebration of self-awareness and autonomy. In line with a narrative more closely focused on the family and the nation, Ada Prospero Gobetti's exceptional life and testimony offer a less disruptive sense of selfhood. Through the memoirs of the three women partisans, chapter 2 shows how at a time when traditional gender roles were demolished by the pressures of the war but somehow became re-established after it, the female body is renegotiated to signify the joy of autonomy and independence.

With the social movements of the late 1960s and the rise of feminism, emotions and the body were rediscovered as a site of significance and the language of food acquired new political meanings. In Italy and Europe, as well as in America and around the world, the 1970s saw a widespread rediscovery of the values of nature, genuine food, and a search for authenticity. Concerns about food adulteration, processed food, and well-being produced both a rekindling of regional traditional cuisines and new interests in vegetarianism, macrobiotics, and healthy food. In this period too, women took part in the codification of cooking trends. Chapter 3 places emotions at the centre of the rise of women's self-awareness from the disquiet of the 1950s to the affirmation of the personal as political in the 1970s. If the voicing of emotions is for the feminist subject a means to destabilize traditional power structures, literary food equally acquires a political meaning. In the fiction and poetry of Dacia Maraini, literary food becomes a tool to re-elaborate feminist tenets and reposition the subject woman. A radical rethinking of societal structures was at the basis of the feminist movement and the many neo-feminist groups in the country. Maraini uses food imagery as a form of communication that criticizes the lack of gender equality still existing during the 1968 cultural movement and that conveys jealousy, anxiety, love, and anger. In her writing, literary food turns into a political initiative that gives value to the body while subverting patriarchal epistemological schemes. As we will see, the language of food continues to be appropriated for feminist tenets. Clara Sereni's autobiographical *Casalinghitudine* (*Keeping House*) makes strategic use of food in the definition of the self in a way that leaves out references to taste and instead makes emotions central to the self. Chapter 3 also examines the relational cooking of the Estia group at the Women's Bookshop in Milan, a collective which in recent years has reinterpreted the function of the feminist kitchen as a practice of care.

Mass migration has characterized the most recent decades of social development in Italy. As often happens, bodies and material culture associated with foreign cultures and their hybridizations are evident elements of population movements. However, discourses on food in mass and social media are focused not only on migration. Both sensory experiences and affective discourses dominate communication in the new millennium. Chapter 4 examines this complex phenomenon, which more than ever brings together perceptions of bodies, affect, food, and the senses. The chapter looks at food as a constant leitmotif in migrant literature. This is visible both in the description of the new country of residence and as the material culture of affective value in the representation of uprooted migrant identities. In my reading of the fiction and poetry of Igiaba Scego, Laila Wadia, and Laura Pariani, literary food carries an ethical message of responsibility in representing a contemporary racist and multicultural society, as well as the European heritage of colonialism. Women writers of the new millennium use literary food to provide an understanding of the multicultural and transnational world we live in. In their work, the senses and food create a new language, a form of embodied cognition of the world that emphasizes empathy as a means of understanding between cultures and generations. Contemporary cultural debate opens up new vistas that invariably show the complex meaning of food. A revisitation and an attempt to mend the suffering caused by European colonialism, together with hope for a liveable multicultural future, all emerges from the writing of women who have given full expression and representation to Woolf's and Fisher's exhortation to make visible the disruptive function of food.

Chapter One

Fascism, Food, and the Senses

The construction of Fascist ideology is a process of changes in discourses, that is, of strategies that in text and word effect social change.[1] Barbara Spackman demonstrated with her analysis of the rhetoric of virility that the articulation of rhetorical and semiotic transformations around one key code – virility, in her analysis – bound together, evoked, and represented all the other elements of the Fascist discourse.[2] The will to enact social change through discourse and the expression of ideology through encompassing rhetoric have a common basis in the performance of emotions. Text and word are connoted by affect language in nationalistic ideologies of that period, as of the present, and scholars have discussed the relevance of emotions in Fascist ideology and contemporary right-wing ideology.[3] Historians have already demonstrated that food discourses, rural and alimentary policies, and autarky all played their part in the Fascist strategies to exert power and articulate imperialistic policies. Carol Helstosky asserts that in Fascist Italy, food was a vital element to bind people to the regime: not only through the ideas of parsimony and sacrifice, recurrent throughout the *ventennio*, but also through the everyday tasks recommended for the preparation and purchase of food.[4] Alexander Nützenadel underlines how autarky was part of the political project of a Mediterranean empire ruled by the Fascist regime. With its interconnected vision of population growth and food availability, Fascism saw access to food as a way to ensure its hegemony in the Mediterranean area and as a step towards regaining national strength after the crisis of the post–World War I years.[5] In this chapter we explore how Fascist food discourses mobilized emotions and shaped models of femininity and how women writers put into practice counterdiscourses that gave emotional values to food.

Text and word were conveyed through school education, cookbooks, women's associations, women's magazines, and harvest and food festivals. A corpus of domestic literature authored by women was published for the first time.[6] It helped mould women's sense of duty and sacrifice for the nation and make them active participants in its destiny. Using William Reddy's terminology, the set of practices and normative emotions that governed Fascist food discourses were part of an "emotional regime." As he puts it, "Emotional control is the real site of the exercise of power: politics is just a process of determining who must repress as illegitimate, who must foreground as valuable, the feelings and desires that come up for them in given contexts and relationships."[7] Between the second half of the 1920s and the 1930s, when women became the centre of attention of national politics and were indeed "nationalized," as Victoria de Grazia argued, specific and normative ways to feel and relate shaped their daily behaviour. Within women's culture, however, a reaction to dominant rules was also visible.

Reddy foresees the need for an emotional respite, a venue or relationship that allows the expression of emotions not allowed within an emotional regime. This is what he calls "emotional refuge." For the analysis of women writers' response to Fascist emotional control, it is useful to put Reddy's "emotional refuge" in dialogue with Barbara Rosenwein's concept of "emotional communities." In Rosenwein's terminology, these are social communities that could be unsteady and changeable but share common values and modes of emotional expression.[8] Longing for sensuality and pleasure is, in my reading of women's writing, a response to dominant discourses of femininity and food that opposed Fascist compulsory concepts of duty and sacrifice. In fact, in the Fascist regime, the senses were considered inappropriate, and not only for women. For example, as Simonetta Falasca Zamponi notes, iconographic propaganda used bread in its combination of religious and material meanings.[9] These types of images were meant to generate emotions in the masses, but at the same time, the totalitarian idea of God-like creation alienated the senses, which were seen as negative, female, and to be rejected.[10] Women writers of different political views shared an "emotional refuge" through the senses; theirs, then, could be defined as an emotional community.

Fascist Food Policies and Their Symbolic Meaning

The Fascist government was greatly preoccupied with food propaganda and policies. Already in 1919, as a journalist, Benito Mussolini advocated political and economic independence as the fundamental requirement for national hegemony.[11] Once in power, the government chose to focus on producer-oriented policies, while its association with the landowners generated strong support from the countryside, which became the cradle of the violent *squadrismo*.[12] The first steps of the Fascist government in terms of agricultural policies were all about wheat.

Helstosky reminds us that this was not unusual given that the level of wheat production had increasingly become a bellwether for living conditions in Europe, with Germany and Great Britain taking similar actions.[13] In Italy, many initiatives were taken to support and improve wheat production and many more to make wheat a key element of the regime's propaganda. On 18 July 1925, the government announced the constitution of the Comitato permanente del grano (Permanent committee for wheat), whose task was to study solutions to increase Italy's production of wheat. A couple of years earlier, farmers were invited to take part in the first national competition for the best crop, the Concorso per la vittoria del grano (Competition for the victory of wheat). An agricultural revolution was unfolding. The competition, which became an annual event, offered monetary prizes to farmers who followed governmental directives and technological innovations to obtain the optimum quality wheat. Mussolini intended to make Italy independent from importation and to settle, in this way, part of Italy's foreign deficit deriving from World War I.[14] In July 1925 a systematic approach to reach this target began with the launch of the Battle for Wheat. The strategies implemented by the government were wide-ranging and included the constitution of the Ente Nazionale Risi in 1931, an institution dedicated to increasing rice production and consumption; welfare policies for the *mondine* (rice pickers); the increase of fish consumption; research on the most resistant wheat and incremental use of pesticides; and the reclaiming of marshlands. Days dedicated to specific foods important for the Fascist autarkic regime, such as bread and rice, as well as food festivals dedicated to bread, rice, and grapes, were part of the propaganda to promote and celebrate food considered traditionally Italian.[15] Science was at the forefront of Fascist agricultural policies. Experiments with wheat genetics were an important part of the work of the scientists of the Comitato permanente del grano. One of the most important scientists in the field was the geneticist Nazareno Strampelli, who developed wheat breeds such as Villa Gloria, Ardito, Balilla, Mentana, Damiano, and San Pastore to create resistant and efficient wheat.[16] The impact of his agricultural experiments was significant: the cultivation of the Ardito variety jumped from 3 per cent of the grain-cultivated area in 1925 to more than 50 per cent in 1940.[17]

Such initiatives were supported by a culture of self-restraint and sobriety, deemed a measure of Italy's superiority. Yet the *battaglia del grano* did not produce an economic profit. By focusing on only wheat production, the government did not encourage the cultivation of other agricultural products that could be suitable for export. Moreover, due to the fall in international prices, home-grown wheat was, at that time, more expensive than the imported variety.[18] Still, the *battaglia del grano* was very meaningful as a symbol of Fascist propaganda.

As Falasca Zamponi demonstrates, wheat symbolized the importance Mussolini placed on rural culture for the strengthening of Fascism and its expansionist goals.[19] Anna Ascenzi and Marta Brunelli have reconstructed that school textbooks reported the *Preghiera del pane*, a poem penned by Mussolini himself in 1928. This was used as a text for writing and reading exercises and essay compositions, which were part of the competitions organized for National Bread Day.[20] The *Preghiera del pane* exhorted people to "love," "respect," "honour," and "don't waste" bread, which was seen as a symbol of hard work, sacrifice, life, and homeland and as a gift of God. Along with ideas of the sacredness of the regime, school education was imbued with military metaphors. As Ascenzi and Brunelli state, young women were addressed as little soldiers able to administer the household and cook following the autarkic principles. Mussolini's mottoes, such as "You too, housewife, are a soldier of the Fascist revolution," were reproduced on the walls of school economics classrooms.[21] Women's school education and the alimentary education of adult women intersected, given that well-known cookbook authors such as Elisabetta Randi and Lidia Morelli were also authors of school textbooks.[22]

At the turn of the decade, the national economic situation and, hence, people's access to food deteriorated. Deflationary policies put in place by the government caused salary reductions and a negative effect on imports and exports, which would only worsen during the 1929 world economic crisis.[23] Only a few years later, as Italy faced the embargo of the Society of Nations following the invasion of Abyssinia in October 1935, a period of autarky started, officially from 1936.[24] All the autarkic policies were personally supported by Mussolini, who presented himself as the symbol of frugality. Never depicted in the act of eating, he used to reiterate that ten minutes a day was all that was needed for eating, yet his documented frugality had also much to do with his ulcer issues, as John Dickie reports.[25]

Models of Femininity

Food discourses contributed to moulding Fascist gender politics. The vast production of domestic literature is testimony of this, as we will see. But what were the Fascist models of femininity? It could be said that they were structured along an emotional divide: scorn for the unmotherly woman concerned with the pleasures of life, and praise for the women who, through sacrifice, fed and protected the family and the nation. Some Fascist women took part in the first *squadristi* attacks alongside their male partners, yet Fascism soon forgot that small number of radical women.[26] The traditional values of women's dedication to family and nation became core principles of Mussolini's gender policies once he betrayed his original promise of the women's vote in 1925 and withdrew democratic elections. Culinary skills were then important for the autarkic and nationalistic program as well as for the definition of gender roles, in an ideology that placed virility at the centre of its articulation of power, as Spackman argued.[27]

Groundbreaking works by Victoria de Grazia, Michela De Giorgio, Marina Addis Saba, and Robin Pickering-Iazzi have amply demonstrated how the Fascist regime put in place a thorough system to mould models of femininity that at the same time uncovered new expressions of modern and independent behaviour.[28] The image of the "madre e moglie esemplare" (exemplary mother and wife) coexisted with that of the "donna muliebre" (feminine woman), active, determined, and devoted to the Fascist regime.[29] Youth associations and sporting competitions offered new generations experiences of individual and collective achievement and the perception of active participation in a new society. Fascist women's associations such as the Fasci Femminili and Massaie Rurali were pivotal in addressing nationalistic propaganda and a sense of women's collective identity.[30] These forms of active associationism and modern behaviour were meant to be distant from any appreciation of the sensory and personal pleasure.

Giovanni Gentile, the main theorist of the Fascist regime and its culture, explicitly stated that both men and women had "doveri da adempiere, cioé non beni da godere, ma ideali da realizzare con lo sforzo, con la lotta e il sacrificio" (duties to fulfil, that is not goods to enjoy, but ideals to make concrete with effort, fight, and sacrifice).[31] Enjoyment of material things was then immoral and not contemplated. In Gentile's gender theory, motherhood was a woman's destiny to be accomplished for the benefit of the family and the nation. Both popular media and scientific journals launched a fierce attack against the fashionable woman with short dresses and short hair, the very thin modern woman, nicknamed *donna-crisi* (the crisis woman). In the early 1930s, socio-scientific journals such as *Maternità ed infanzia* (Motherhood and childhood) devoted editorials to the figure of the modern young woman, fashionable and thin, only nourished "by a few cooked greens, coffee and tea – all of which ... dressed in the abundant smoke of cigarettes."[32] The articles scorned the thin female body as anti-maternal and un-patriotic, even as pathological and deviant, and capable of putting society at risk.[33]

The places inhabited by these female bodies were also a great concern of Fascism. In cities, middle-class women could work in offices or as shop assistants and were able to enjoy a night at the cinema or shopping at the new department stores like the Rinascente and Standa.[34] Cities were, then, exposing women to public life and, according to Fascist ideology, to disease and corruption. Paris was consistently epitomized as a place of moral corruption. For Ardengo Soffici it was populated with erotomaniac women, lesbians, opium smokers, and hashish eaters; for historian Arrigo Solmi, French women were the victims of moral depravity and dangerously prone to indulge in pleasure.[35] Clearly, material goods, beauty products, entertainment, and, in general, the enjoyment of the senses were critical concerns in the Fascist construction of femininity.

All these unsettling discourses circulating at the time were crystallized in the demographic campaign started in 1927 with Mussolini's "Discorso dell'Ascensione." Mussolini's demographic project of increasing the birth rate and reaching sixty million inhabitants, to compete with the nations that had already outnumbered Italy, as proposed in his speech, was paralleled by the imposed reduction of women in the workforce and sustained by an appeal to the moral role of women in the family and the nation. Women's domestic role was increasingly presented, through a sustained campaign in the press, as the most suitable for women. Women's work outside the house was seen as one of the causes of the increasing level of unemployment. Catholic magazines like *Il Solco* (The furrow) regularly featured articles on working-class women, motherhood, and women's employment; a 1933 article argued against the biological suitability of mothers, and in particular working-class mothers, to work outside the home.[36] Another article in the same magazine supported the employment of unmarried women for positions "esclusivamente femminili, complementari alle occupazioni dell'uomo" (exclusively female, complementary to man's work).[37] The *Almanacco della donna italiana* (Almanac of the Italian woman) – which, in the early 1920s, had supported pro-vote positions – gradually moved to reflect Fascist views by the end of that decade. In the editorial of the 1939 issue, feminism is defined as a "vecchia mentalità democratica … uno dei più caratteristici prodotti della generazione demografica-individualistica" (old-fashioned democratic mentality … one of the most characteristic products of the demographically individualistic generation).[38] The ethical and social value of women's role, the editorial continues, is assured by Fascism, which "vuol ricondurre la donna alla sua vera, naturale, sublime missione; ... il Fascismo vede nella donna, inanzitutto e sopratutto, la sposa, la madre, ... il centro di gravità della famiglia, la detentrice del sacro retaggio della stirpe" (intends to lead women back to their true, natural, sublime mission; ... Fascism sees women, first and above all, as wives and mothers, the centre of gravity of the family, the holders of the sacral destiny of the race).[39] The reviewers of *Il Solco*, even when criticizing women's writing of the time, appealed to the high moral standards of Italian women. The author of a November 1936 article claimed to be perplexed by the fact that love stories by women writers were dominated by "impulsi sensitivi" (sensual impulses) and refused to believe that the readers of works by women writers could share those views.[40]

In a similar vein, the same journal emphasized the ethical value of the domestic role of women in Italy's colonial expansion in Ethiopia. In a 1936 article, the author Giovanna Canuti supported the government's decision to encourage women to follow their husbands to Ethiopia. Their presence would be essential to prevent moral disorders caused by "la differenza di razza, la possibilità del costituirsi di una generazione meticcia, originata con un popolo in condizioni fisiche e civili assai inferiori" (racial difference, and the possibility of the birth of a race mixed with a population in significantly lower physical and civil conditions).[41] In the second half of the 1930s, with increasingly expansionist politics and the introduction of the 1938 racial laws, the engagement of Italian women in colonial activities – whether in support of the work of their husbands or in the form of assistance to the local population – was presented as indispensable and vital also to limiting interracial sexual relationships.[42] Their duty was to make a home of the place in which they lived and to educate servants in Western habits. This also included cooking practices. In an article titled "La donna italiana in A.O." (The Italian woman in Eastern Africa), the journalist Ciro Poggiali praised the civilizing role of Italian women in adapting Italian recipes to the use of local ingredients and in teaching locals how to cook with them.[43] The result of this transformation is the abandonment of the "nostalgie gastronomiche" (gastronomic nostalgia) that, according to Poggiali, affected many Italian colonizers before the arrival of Italian women:

> C'erano pionieri che soffrivano per la mancanza delle tagliatelle o del salame nostrano come può soffrire il fumatore arrabbiato cui manchi la sigaretta; c'erano stati coloniali cui era parso di non poter celebrare degnamente il Natale, se non ricevevano da Siena, da Cremona, da Milano, come dire da seimila chilometri, il panforte, il torrone, il panettone ... Venne la donna e la situazione mutò.

> (Some pioneers missed tagliatelle or salami as badly as a heavy smoker misses their cigarette; some settlers felt they could not properly celebrate Christmas if they had not received panforte, nougat, and panettone from Siena, Cremona, or Milan, that is from a distance of 3,700 miles … The woman arrived and the situation changed.)[44]

By recreating comfortable homes and cooking familiar food, Italian women established safe social conditions. At the same time, the experience of travelling and living in the colonies gave a false sense of freedom to them while also reinforcing the sacrificial quality of women's contribution to family and nation. In *Ricordi somali* (Somalian memories), Augusta Perricone Violà depicts what she considers the special qualities of Italian women in the colonies. In the passage quoted below, warlike metaphors ("coraggiosamente debellare," "battaglia della vita") (courageously fighting, the battle of life) are expressions of the new energy that, together with the Fascist qualities of strength and sacrifice for the nation and the family, represented Italian women in the colonies as protagonists of history:

> Donne che più delle altre hanno saputo, per mantenere salda e compatta l'integrità della famiglia, mettere a prova ogni virtù ed hanno saputo coraggiosamente debellare ogni debolezza: sono quindi fra le migliori nella battaglia della vita, quelle che hanno saputo con letizia ed umiltà rinsaldare il cuore, elevare l'anima, abituare sè stesse alle rinunzie e al sacrificio.

> (Women who, more than others, managed to maintain a solid unity in their family by proving their virtues and courageously fighting any weakness. They are, therefore, among the best in the battle of life, those who with joy and humility were capable to strengthen their emotions, elevate their spirit, and get accustomed to relinquishment and sacrifice.)[45]

In the divisive perspective towards the much-feared and despised emancipated woman, the reassuring motherly woman, and the courageous and dynamic woman in the colonies, the language of food provided a means to express models of femininity. Scholars have already demonstrated the mechanisms of food discourses to uphold and resist Fascist regimes.[46] Diana Garvin, in *Feeding Fascism*, has illuminated the kaleidoscopic presence of women's food work in Fascist Italy and the significance of the materiality that surrounded their work, from the rationalization of the space of the kitchen to new furniture.[47] Building on such scholarship, this chapter will show how an emotional community, in Rosenwein's terms, emerges from the analysis of a selection of women's writing, and in part also from some domestic literature: personal emotions, and longing for sensuality and pleasure, emerge as a valuable system of feelings for a heterogeneous community of women. Domestic literature reiterated the image of the caring and efficient wife but also allowed its authors to give value to their professional life and identity, while supporting the many aspects of Fascist alimentary policies.

Women's Domestic Literature and Its Many Meanings

Pervasive attention to frugality and self-restraint dominated public discourses and women's magazines. Far from being passive recipients of autarkic discourses, women took an active part in shaping Fascist alimentary narratives and in promoting them among the female audience, but often they moulded their approach to carve out their liberties and protect the lifestyle of their social classes. Domestic literature represented, then, both a space where women articulated Fascist models of femininity and one from where their views and professional desires emerged.

A distinctive voice was that of Elisabetta Randi, a scholar specializing in food science. With her scientific background and researched publications that often made use of technical language and tables of scientific data, Randi exemplified the Fascist approach to gastronomic science. Alimentary discourses were meant to be at the forefront of a rational and modern approach to food.[48] She wrote journal articles on nutrition and diet as well as school textbooks; she is, however, better remembered for her book *La cucina autarchica* (Autarkic cooking) published in 1942. Concerned with the war effort, Randi's book presents alimentary autarky as a fundamental pillar of Fascist ideology and as a continuum that began in the mid-1920s and was destined to reach the post-war period. In *La cucina autarchica* she comments on the successful Battle for Wheat put in place by "l'alta mente del Duce" (the bright mind of Il Duce) and writes about the need to comply with the autarkic regime and the war sacrifice, as all aimed to reach a protracted period of sobriety and economical consumption in the "glorioso dopo Guerra" (glorious post-war).[49] Alimentary autarky was for Randi a way of living necessary for a successful life. Her writing is formal and scientific when she discusses in detail the nutritive values of foods and the exact quantity required to avoid waste. She aims to persuade women to use products of high nutritive value and lower cost. Similar is her intent in an article on alimentation in the colonies published in the *Almanacco della donna italiana*.

Here she lists in detail all the ingredients readily available in the colonies and how best to cook them, also paying attention to the dishes traditionally eaten by the indigenous population. She advises on the best healthy choices for the Italian settler and for his Italian wife, whose culinary skills, she remarks, will be the best reward at the end of the working day.[50] The "healthy" body for Randi is a white body protected from the contamination of the indigenous population. The "white man" needs to avoid a type of alimentation too similar to that of the indigenous population. She warns against the lack of hygiene of the local people that could transmit diseases, for example in the production of milk. She advises settlers against eating traditional local dishes, which she is sure cannot tempt Europeans: "Per fortuna!" (Fortunately!), she comments.[51] Ethnic food is, in this case, similar to infectious diseases; she echoes one of Mussolini's central metaphors of the Fascist state, expressed in the Ascension Day speech, that of the unified healthy body protected from infections by the work of the government. In his speech, before arguing for the need for a radical increase in birth rate, Mussolini reiterates the duty of the state to control disease; likewise, Randi justifies her intervention in food choices as protection from external damage.[52] Her writing contributes to the construction of the discourse of virility at the centre of Fascist ideology. Randi's alimentary approach projects the image of a dutiful Fascist, accustomed to sobriety and self-restraint, whom she protects from the external damage represented by inadequate food.

Approaching alimentary autarky from a less scientific perspective, Lidia Morelli's 1935 *Le massaie contro le sanzioni* (Housewives against sanctions) asks what better way for the housewife to show discipline if not by rejecting certain foods and adopting others. Substituting all foreign products was the duty of the shopper for Morelli, a well-known writer of books of manners and school textbooks.[53] Gin and whisky were to be completely banned; Spanish and Portuguese anchovies and tuna were to be substituted with Sicilian and Sardinian products, while Marmite should be replaced with the now obsolete Italian vitaminic extract Este. English pickles had to be swapped with the well-known brand of food products Cirio, while the Italian tea brand Ati was presented as the only one, in place of all foreign tea varieties – the only acceptable alternative was the karkadè tea from the Italian colonies.[54] Morelli's audience is the middle-class housewife who can afford to buy more expensive items. The naming of specific brands demonstrates that she was aware of the middle class's role in the tertiary industry sector.

Directing middle-class food shopping was one of Morelli's contributions to the promotion of autarkic policies. She also reiterated the very autarkic slogan "Riso, riso, riso" (rice, rice, rice). Emilia Zamara's *La cucina italiana della resistenza* (Italian resistance cooking) too promotes autarkic eating among the middle class. It contains many recipes of regional tradition, fish dishes, and no meat, which is replaced by the section "Piatti che sostituiscono la carne composti di ortaggi e uova" (Dishes that substitute meat made of vegetables and eggs).[55]

A completely different style is that of Amalia Moretti Foggia, alias Petronilla, whose work will also be discussed in the next chapter on wartime writing. It is, however, pertinent to introduce her here, given that her cookery publications covered the whole 1930s and concluded at her death in 1947. Foggia had a solid scientific background which comprised a degree in natural science and a degree in medicine, and she came from a distinguished family of chemists. At the turn of the century, she was close to the Milanese socialist circles and worked as a doctor for the poorest sections of society. Her notoriety became widespread starting in 1929 when the *Corriere della sera* offered her a weekly column on health issues in its Sunday supplement, *La Domenica del Corriere*. For her journalistic enterprise, Foggia chose the pseudonym Dott Amal, pretending to be a man. Given her success, she was offered a cookery column titled Tra i Fornelli (At the stove) and a column on domestic economy, for which she used the pseudonym Petronilla. Her writing is characterized by a chatty, confidential tone. She writes like a wise, welcoming, and experienced woman, able to advise on recipes that, in her words, would make a husband happy or, as in the case of a lemon veal recipe published in 1935, even please the mother-in-law.[56] Her successful journalistic work exercised for the middle class the role she had played for the lower classes in her profession as a doctor, that is, advising on diseases and educating towards a healthy lifestyle. Cooking healthy and simple food is important in her writing not only for the effect that alimentation has on the body, as in Randi's work, but also for its ability to create harmonious relationships within the family. It is in this perspective that her cookery writing was functional for the regime: it emphasized the family and traditional roles within it.

Ada Bonfiglio Krassich's *Le gioie della mensa: Manuale di economia domestica e di cucina per le famiglie* (The joy of the kitchen: Handbook of home economy and cooking for the families) was published by Sonzogno, as were all the recipe collections by Foggia and the gastronomic supplements of *La rivista delle famiglie* (The family magazine) edited by Bonfiglio Krassich. The 1937 special issue of *La rivista*, titled *Almanacco della cucina regionale* (The almanac of regional cousine), was dedicated to regional food, seen as an integral part of the autarkic alimentary plan.[57] Interest in regional cuisine, as Paolo Capuzzo reconstructs, developed at the beginning of the century and should be framed within the broader cultural attention to the regional and the local emerging from the works of writers such as Luigi Verga, Matilde Serao, Mario Pratesi, and others, from influential periodicals like *La Voce* (The voice), and from a growing interest in ethnography and folklore.[58] Fascism supported regional culture to promote nationalism through local heritage. The *Guida Gastronomica d'Italia* (Gastronomic guide of Italy), published in 1931 by the Touring Club Italiano (Italian Touring Club) with the support of Fascist intellectual Ugo Ojetti, was the first serious attempt to systematically link food and place.[59] In her *Almanacco*, Bonfiglio Krassich offers her passionate support of regionalism:

> Non sorprenderà, quindi, se in questa Italia rinnovata dal Fascismo, la cucina viene considerata un'arte. Arte vera e arte bella che tende a dare nella vita sensazioni piacevoli, tali che dispongono l'animo al bene. Come la musica è l'arte dell'udito, la pittura e la scultura quella della vista, così l'arte gastronomica quella del gusto … Il folclore del nostro popolo … esso consiste soprattutto nella cucina le cui mete particolari variano da regione a regione. Ed è in questo appunto che consiste la nostra ricchezza.
>
> (It will not be surprising, then, if in our Italy renewed by Fascism, the cuisine is considered an art. True art, beautiful art, gives pleasurable sensations, such that it inclines human beings to goodwill. Just like music is the art of hearing, painting and sculpture are the art of sight, so gastronomic art is the art of taste … The cultural traditions of our people … consist, above all, of our cuisine which varies from region to region. And this is our real wealth.)[60]

Just as Randi was a supporter of the Fascist scientific approach to food, Morelli championed the national alimentary industry, and Foggia underscored the relevance of family unity, Bonfiglio Krassich emphasized regionalism and nationalism through gastronomy. Unlike Randi, Foggia cannot be considered a Fascist supporter because of her long-lasting commitment to the improvement of the lower classes' well-being. Equally, Bonfiglio Krassich's appreciation of gastronomy is not strictly Fascist. In her description of cuisine as an art, she invokes the senses, unknown to the Fascist characterization of women's role. It is true that what she defines as "pleasurable sensations" generated by the art of gastronomy are not to be attained for personal satisfaction but as the first step towards good behaviour. However, the evocation of the senses suggests alternative perspectives to the strict nationalistic food discourses of the time.

Bonfiglio Krassich and Fernanda Momigliano authored successful autarkic cookbooks for middle-class housewives, respectively *La cucina economica in tempo di sanzioni* (Economical cooking in times of sanctions, published 1936) and *Vivere bene in tempi difficili: Come le donne affrontano le crisi economiche* (Living well in difficult times: How women face economic crises, published 1933). As Jewish women, Bonfiglio Krassich and Momigliano soon saw their successful careers rapidly decline and went to live in hiding. But only two years before the enactment of Italy's antisemitic laws, in 1936, Momigliano could show her commitment to the integration of Jewish and Italian food. John Dickie reminds us that, in her 1936 *Mangiare all'italiana* (Italian-style eating), she introduced sixteen recipes labelled "in the Jewish style," with the suggestion that they could be appreciated by everyone, whatever their faith.[61]

Among the many cookbooks of the 1930s, a key role was played by Ada Boni's *Il talismano della felicità* (The talisman for happiness). Originally published in 1925 and republished several times during the 1930s, it is a very detailed and accurate cookbook inspired by criteria of "praticità [...] economia, pur conservando [...] la buona e sana cucina, fonte di benessere e di salute" (practicality ... economy, but still retaining the good and healthy cooking, origin of well-being and health).[62] *Il talismano della felicità* promoted the qualities of frugality, economy, and bodily health typical of the Fascist period. It is, however, a particular concept of frugality, with the female readership addressed in the opening pages imagined as capable of speaking foreign languages, playing tennis, and driving luxury cars. Her potential readers will also have to master cooking as an essential prerequisite for happiness in their future married life, leading Boni to conclude, "Quest'opera [...] è dunque veramente il talismano della felicità" (This book ... is then a real talisman for happiness).[63]

By 1937 *Il talismano della felicità* had reached its sixth edition, sold thousands of copies, and increasingly stressed its nationalistic values. The 1937 edition included an "Elogio della cucina italiana," not present in the 1931 edition. These additional pages explicitly advocated for the disengagement of Italian cuisine from French cuisine, starting with the names of dishes, which were to be presented exclusively in Italian. The ample selection of recipes from each region testifies to Boni's support of the Fascist promotion of regional entities as part of its unitarian and nationalistic goal.[64] As the preface explains using the first-person plural, only when the rich culinary tradition of the Italian regions is known by all, "avremo ... realizzato la vera cucina italiana, che ci emanciperà per sempre da ogni influenza straniera" (we will have [...] realized the real Italian cuisine, which will free us from any foreign influence).[65] Yet, despite its claimed support of Fascist policies, *Il talismano* included recipes for meat dishes, game, starters, pasta, risotto, desserts, sauces, and coffees, and the use of French words for sauces and dishes was also recurrent. Self-restraint and nationalistic language acquired a different meaning for Boni and the upper classes, to whom the book was addressed. Boni – founder of the women's magazine *Preziosa*, a well-known figure in the gastronomic culture of the time, and acquainted with the renowned French chef Auguste Escoffier – could project the image of an Italian cuisine able to compete at the international level. She represented the upper classes as cosmopolitan, familiar with French cuisine as well as with the novelties deriving from the colonial experience: Arabic coffee recipes and a detailed account of the history and the cooking technique of couscous were present in the 1937 post–Ethiopian war edition (but not in the 1931 edition).

The higher classes could also rely on a new food magazine, *La cucina italiana* (The Italian cuisine), which was first published in 1929 in Milan. Like *Il talismano*, *La cucina* supported Fascist alimentary policies but still expressed a cosmopolitan flair and an interest in foreign cuisine. Daniela Adorni and Stefano Magagnoli state that philanthropist Delia Notari and former Futurist Fanny Dini – one of the very few women to take part in the March on Rome – as collaborators and directors were pivotal in managing the periodical and in projecting the image of the new woman, not exclusively confined within the walls of her home.[66] *La cucina italiana* established several connections with the literary world: Massimo Bontempelli collaborated with them; Umberto Notari, founder and first director of *La cucina italiana*, was a writer himself and a close friend of Filippo Tommasi Marinetti.[67] Within the literary world, interactions between writers and cooking magazines were not unusual. Paola Masino, the poet Ada Negri, and Margherita Sarfatti collaborated with *La cucina italiana*.[68] Foggia and Negri exchanged a rich epistolary.

Futurist food manifestos, published also in *La cucina*, and Futurist food events represented another element of the variegated culinary panorama of the 1930s. The Futurist food campaign for an innovative and aesthetic eating culture had started two decades earlier. In 1913 an interview with the French chef Jules Maincave was published in Paris and came out the following year in Italian in *Gazzettino Azzurro* (The sky-blue gazette), with the title "Il Cuoco Futurista, ovvero Jules Maincave intervistato da André Charpentier" (The Futurist Cook, that is Jules Maincave, interviewed by André Charpentier).[69] The *Manifesto* by Maincave was then republished in *La cucina italiana* in 1930, but already in 1920 the poet Irba Futurista (alias of Irene Bazzi) published in *Roma Futurista* the manifesto *Culinaria Futurista* (Futurist cookery).[70] Marinetti, who had translated and re-adapted Maincave's *Manifesto* in 1927, published his *Manifesto della cucina futurista* in *La Gazzetta del Popolo* in 1930 and in *La cucina italiana* in 1931.[71] The volume *La cucina futurista* (*The Futurist Cookbook*) by Marinetti and Fillìa was published in 1932. This series of published manifestos represented only one facet of the Futurists' involvement in the renovation of Italian cuisine. Futurist dining events were being organized in several cities, and 1931 marked the opening of the Taverna Santopalato restaurant in Turin.[72] The Futurist culinary revolution encouraged the combination of unexpected flavours, disregarded the traditional menu structure and started dinners with desserts, and proposed a chauvinistic attitude. In their cookbooks, the female body was referred to as something to be eaten. Futurist cooking did not have the same impact on women's culture as other cookbooks analysed in this section, but it is worth noting that Futurist women also used recipes to make feminist claims. In *La cucina futurista*, the only recipe authored by a woman is Marisa Mori's breast-shaped cake recipe. As Jennifer Griffiths persuasively argues, with her ironic recipe of a breast-shaped cake, Mori displaces the Futurist's masculinist claims against a woman's body.[73]

In conclusion, women's domestic literature developed manifold interpretations of autarkic policies. Randi's scientific discourse complied closely with the nationalistic, expansionistic, and racist politics of the government. Her scientific tone conveyed a clear propagandistic message. Morelli's message was also propagandistic. In contrast, through her food columns Foggia supported family unity but also gave expression to her inclination as a health practitioner. Momigliano and Bonfiglio Krassich, with their references to Jewish cuisine and gastronomy as the art of "pleasurable sensations," hinted at a message that was dissonant with the dominant discourse. Boni, Dini, and Delia Notari supported Fascist policies by making sure that the privileges of upper classes and intellectuals were maintained in their publications. While domestic literature was one of the strategies to enact social change in support of Fascist ideology, for some of the women who took part in this propagandistic effort, it represented the possibility to express more personal interests. These women may appear as isolated figures, but the discourse on food pervaded the cultural environment, and not only because literary figures were interested in the food discourse of the time, as evidenced by *La cucina italiana*. Literature has provided a venue to make food imagery relevant in different ways. Romance fiction, the so-called "rosa," supported nationalistic alimentary culture; the successful novels by Liala narrated lunches and dinners full of typical Italian food.[74]

Critics have highlighted the disruptive force that the language of food has come to symbolize in the work of women writers of this period. Tristana Rorandelli has noted how the theme of food repulsion and anorexic behaviour that characterizes the protagonist of Paola Masino's *Nascita e morte della massaia* (*Birth and Death of the Housewife*, 2010) is a clear indication of resistance and opposition to Fascist ideals of womanhood and motherhood.[75] In her perceptive reading of the same novel, Lucia Re analysed the image of moulded bread, the protagonist's favourite and only food in the first part of her life, as a metaphor to attack Fascist ideas of nationalism, family, and procreation symbolized by bread and the Battle for Wheat propaganda.[76] In Re's reading, Masino's short story "Fame," which narrates a father's hunger-led killing of his children, engages in the same anti-Fascist critique.[77] While these discussions focus on hunger and the refusal to eat, in the following pages pleasure and desire for food, as well as an emphasis on the senses, will articulate a discourse of personal emotions able to dismantle nationalistic concepts of duty. As we will see, an additional model of femininity, more concerned with the intimate self, seems to find expression through literary food. The writings of Pina Ballario, a prize-winning popular writer and a supporter of the Fascist regime, and of Alba de Céspedes, an anti-Fascist intellectual whose novel became a bestseller during the *ventennio*, offer clear representations of how food-related imagery evoked the senses, brought about personal emotions, and displaced nationalism.

Pina Ballario: Self-Restraint and Food Pleasure

Ballario's support for the Fascist regime is explicit in her colonial novels and children's literature, genres which were encouraged by the government to promote Fascist ideals.[78] Her work was commended by the regime. In 1938 her children's novel on Gabriele D'Annunzio's Fiume venture, *I disperati della guardia*, was awarded the Premio Bologna and praised by Marinetti for its Italian spirit of adventure and heroism, which he defined as "assolutamente opposti al gangesterismo americano che purtroppo ha dominato per molto tempo letteratura e giornalismo dei ragazzi" (completely different from the American crime literature that unfortunately has dominated children's fiction and journalism).[79] Ballario also penned romance, historical biographies, and translations of children's books from French, English, and Russian. When her writing digressed from the confines of genre literature, she projected a model of femininity that departed from nationalistic pride and sacrifice. In her travel book *Come ho visto la Russia e altri paesi del mondo* (1936; How I viewed Russia and other countries in the world) and in her novel *Il figlio che mi hai dato* (1935; The child you gave me), a hybrid text set part in Somalia and part in Italy which cannot be defined as either a colonial or a romance novel, longing for emotional freedom and excruciating experiences of maternal love and jealousy emerge and intermingle with core Fascist positions.[80] Food-related images are the signifiers of this more intimate expression of femininity.

Come ho visto la Russia e altri paesi del mondo combines Ballario's impressions of her extensive travels throughout European and non-European countries: Russia, Denmark, Sweden, Germany, Hungary, Austria, Libya, Egypt, Greece, England, Norway, Finland, and Palestine. Women's travel writing was not uncommon in Italy and produced great works already from the previous century.[81] Fascist imperialism and the promotion of the model of the active *donna muliebre* made the option of travelling appealing to educated and middle-class women. Like other women writers and intellectuals, Ballario seized this opportunity.[82] The choice to travel while repeatedly proclaiming the benefits of Fascism is indicative of how well she adhered to the role of the dynamic, active new woman. Her travel book is interesting from a political perspective; it is dotted with comments on Italy under Mussolini's government that intertwine with her impressions of the places she visits.

Her writing style is palpably different from the erudite, well-documented, and well-argued Fascist writing of Augusta Perricone Violà, who published *Ricordi somali* in the same period. Ballario has a lighthearted, at times insolent, attitude in her description of the world that allows her to make comments discordant with the dominant discourse of the time. In a 1937 review in *Minerva*, Fortunato Rizzi praises Ballario's travel book, touching on that distinctive playful and carefree attitude. Yet his praise is expressed within an entirely male chauvinistic key that reproduces stereotypical Fascist values of femininity as domesticity and, effectively, as a force that must be contained:

> La Ballario [...] è un singolare caso di irrequietudine e mobilità [...] Una specie di Alfieri in gonnella.
>
> Penso che i lettori mi seguiranno volentieri nel ricercare in queste pagine agili e snelle i momenti e gli atteggiamenti squisitamente femminili di questa donna, che per aver girato mezzo mondo non ha dimenticato di essere una donna.
>
> (Ballario is a peculiar case of unrest and mobility [...] A kind of Alfieri in a skirt. I think that the readers will agree with me in finding in these easy-to-read pages the exquisitely feminine moments and attitudes of this woman, who after travelling half of the world has not forgotten to be a woman.)[83]

In his review, Rizzi underlines what he considers Ballario's feminine style. To this end, he takes into consideration metaphors and descriptions that relate to the world of the housewife (Russian society is seen as an air bubble on puff pastry, Leningrad as a princess at the kitchen sink wearing an evening dress), to that of fashionable women, and to that of the carefree woman interested in patisseries. He concludes his review by presenting Ballario as a typical woman of the 1930s: "Si dà delle grandi arie di moderna, delle pose di spregiudicata, ma in sostanza è rimasta sempre squisitamente donna e, sotto sotto, sì, anche un po' romantica" (She puts on airs of a modern woman, she has some unscrupulous attitudes, but she has always remained exquisitely woman and, in fact, yes, even a bit of a romantic).[84] What Rizzi has not emphasized is the political critique often intertwined with Ballario's light-hearted comments.

Characteristic of her observations of other countries is the nationalistic praise of Italy, which is invariably presented as superior to other countries. For example, England is described as out of touch with modernity, despite being defined as the cradle of modernity.[85] At the conclusion of her discussion of England, it is Italy that is portrayed as the true contemporary global power: England is "un mondo che non può camminare anche se crede di dare il tono a tutto il mondo. Chi può oggi tener dietro al passo marziale dell'Italia?" (a world unable to progress even if they believe they set the pace for the world. Who can keep the pace with valiant Italy today?).[86] "Passo marziale," indeed; the book was published at the peak of Italian expansionism. In the chapter on Denmark, reflections on Italy's powerful positions are again emphasized; she describes Italy as proudly blasé regarding other countries' perceptions, appreciations, or criticism. The commendation of the uniquely powerful position of Italy is again restated in Ballario's comparison of Paris with Rome, where the Italian capital is presented as the centre of global power, while Paris's power is circumscribed within the confines of its country: "Io cerco a Parigi l'espressione più vera della storia di Francia come a Roma io cerco quella del mondo" (In Paris I look for the true expression of the history of France, as in Rome I look for the history of the world).[87]

As we have seen, a concern for frugality and the healthy, rural, and virile way of living was part of Fascist ideology well before the autarkic policies. Tellingly, a recurrent criticism Ballario makes of most Northern European countries is that of their lengthy meals, which she finds perplexing, particularly in the time of sanctions and when compared to more frugal Italian eating habits.[88] Ballario describes in detail some rather extraordinary breakfasts, like the Finnish one:

> La mia bella deputatessa finlandese [...] ammucchia sul suo piatto salmone fresco, ossia crudo, e salmone affumicato, lardo di renna, formaggio olandese, prosciutto di Jork, fette di arrosto, insalata russa, budino di mele e quando ha consumato tutta quella ... società delle nazioni, torna a fare il bis girando intorno alla tavola rotonda.
>
> (My beautiful Finnish congresswoman stacks on her plate fresh salmon, that is raw salmon, and smoked salmon, reindeer lard, Dutch cheese, York ham, roast beef, Russian salad, apple cake and when she has eaten all that ... League of Nations, she comes back for seconds.)[89]

For Ballario, excessive food consumption is both unethical and damaging to the economy. It must be restrained in times of economic crisis, hence Germany of the 1930s is criticized for its big breakfasts.[90] The majority of European countries appear, in her judgment, incapable of self-restraint and therefore morally inferior to the more sober Italians. Commenting once again on the excessive breakfasts she experienced in Holland, she restates her sobriety, although with a minimum concession: "Ma a queste usanze noi non ci adattiamo e restiamo sobri anche in Olanda nonostante le mille lusinghe della gola, facendo eccezione per il latte che davvero è una delle glorie del paese." (But we don't get used to these habits and remain sober even in Holland despite thousands of food temptations. But we cannot resist milk, which really is one of the glories of the country.)[91] The use of the first-person plural in this depiction of personal self-restraint is a marker of collective identity. Ballario is representing herself as part of Fascist Italy engaged in autarkic policies and self-determination. And, in Fascist style, she reconnects the present Italian nation with the glorious Roman past:

> Se le altre nazioni dovessero sottoporsi ad un regime sanzionistico come noi nei momenti passati, non resisterebbero all'assedio. Forza incomparabile dei popoli sobri e sopratutto di noi discendenti legittimi per continuità di razza e di spirito di quelli latini della Repubblica che cenavano con un piatto di farro e di lenticchie anche se avevano raggiunto il consolato e le più alte cariche della magistratura.
>
> (If the other nations were obliged to suffer the economic sanctions we had to endure in the past, they would not survive. This is the unparalleled strength of sober populations and above all of Italians. For continuity of

race and spirit, we are the legitimate descendants of the Romans of the Republic, who would dine with a dish of spelt and lentils even if they had reached the consulship and the highest positions in the judiciary.)[92]

Given such a clear-cut representation of the moral superiority of Italians and Italy as an unstoppable world power, it is perplexing to find many greedy references to sweets, patisseries, and wine, which even Fortunato Rizzi had underlined in his review and explained as a sign of a carefree "feminine" attitude.

In the countries she criticizes for their lack of self-restraint, such as Sweden, Ballario is taken by the smell of vanilla and burned sugar, which evokes a memory of her childhood, and there she eats "certe paste mai mangiate altrove, farcite di fragole e panna" (certain cakes filled with strawberries and cream never eaten before).[93] In Germany she writes about an "invitante profumo di burro fritto e di frittelle di vaniglia" (an inviting smell of fried butter and vanilla pancakes).[94] In Oslo she appreciates the ethnographic museum in part for its open-air aspect, which affords rest in a snack bar offering "birra in ghiaccio, bibite gasate, gelati di panna e latte di renna appena munto" (cold beer, sparkling drinks, whipped ice creams and just-milked reindeer milk).[95] A loss of self-control is explicitly embraced thereafter, with reference to drinking and hashish:

> Preferirei il vino ... tanto più che dopo una discreta libazione posso permettermi il lusso di credermi chi voglio, anche un re ed ho visioni deliziose come dopo un tuffo nell'hascic [*sic*].
>
> (I would prefer wine ... because after some decent drinking, I can afford the luxury to pretend to be the person I want, even a king, and I have wonderful visions just like after trying hashish.)[96]

The Ballario who praised the lentil-consuming Romans bears little resemblance to the Ballario who mentions the effects of hashish and who, when in Paris, does not miss the opportunity to visit French patisseries. It appears that, as expressed by the individual viewpoint underlined in the previous quotation by the first-person singular ("posso permettermi," "ho visioni"), she has not absorbed the qualities of self-restraint and sobriety that she has identified as innate in Italians and herself as part of the collective. The insertion into the narration of her appreciation of excess and pleasure (expressed in the first-person singular) serves to mark her deviation from the norm. Food and eating are emotional experiences significant in shaping "individuals' subjectivity and their sense of distinction from others," Deborah Lupton reminds us.[97] In Ballario's case, an individual's subjectivity is created through reference to eating and pleasure, which conflicts with the dominant discourse of alimentary sobriety.

On the contrary, food is never an expression of personal enjoyment in Ballario's colonial novels. In *Fortuna sotto vento* (1931; Luck downwind), Ballario articulates her colonial views, which are the official views of the Fascist regime.[98] Colonialism will transform the African land and its economy in the name of Fascist modernity; it confirms the supremacy of the Italian civilization and race; it promotes adaptation to the new environment, rather than the imposition of assimilation, in accordance with a culture of colonialism aimed at differentiating Italy from other colonial powers. The need to adapt to the African environment while rejecting an old-fashioned form of colonialism that aimed at replicating the European way of living also unfolds through the description and discussion of food practices.

The inability of the novel's villain, Gian, to adapt to the colonial environment is ridiculed through his regular tea drinking, an upper-middle-class European custom that finds no space in the daily habits of the novel's heroine, Azizia. As a mixed-race young woman, an assimilated indigenous character who best expresses the Fascist ideals of the "civilizing mission" of Italian colonialism,[99] she perfectly exemplifies the adaptation to colonial life required by the Fascist colonizers through her matè drinking and her reproach of Gian's European habits. Yet cultural references to African food do not enter at all into the fabric of the novel, suggesting that adaptation did not equate with contamination of cultures.[100] Maté drinking can be considered a form of cultural appropriation for the benefits it projects upon the dominant Fascist culture. In bell hooks's analysis of racial difference, Western subjects, rather than the Other, are at the centre of the encounter of cultures and cultural appropriation; hence, ethnicity becomes a way to spice up white culture.[101] In Ballario's novel, references to African alimentary customs, such as maté drinking, are deployed to criticize a lack of adaptation to local customs and a nostalgic attachment to European customs, all characterized as unsuitable for the active, Fascist colonizer taking the colonies into modernity. Yet Azizia's maté drinking and her criticism of Gian's tea-drinking habits serve a type of colonialism which, while overtly encouraging adaptation, intends to assert the supremacy of the Italian culture and race. In *Fortuna sotto vento* and even more markedly in *La sposa bianca* (The white bride), conceived as a sequel to *Fortuna*, Ballario clearly outlines the separation between the races as one of the fundamental characteristics of African life. Food and drinks are not conveyors of personal enjoyment, as are desserts described in her travel book. Because maté drinking functions as a symbol of assimilation and supremacy rather than encounter and understanding of cultures, the appreciation of its taste – as a product of another country – is not relevant, and the same can be said of emotions. *Fortuna* is a romance novel that associates love with colonial protagonists, and indifference and hate with indigenous people, as Robin Pickering-Iazzi states.[102] In this sense emotions are what we expect to find in a colonial novel written for a white audience, just as their tastes in food reflect their supremacist relationship with the Other.

The heroine Azizia and her husband-to-be Vernerio, moral characters of the novel, are admired for their success in relating to the environment and the people around them. Theirs is a love story based on duty towards the land and Fascist ideals, not a relationship dictated simply by individual desires. On the contrary, a burst of personal emotions centred on the female protagonist are depicted in Ballario's later novel *Il figlio che mi hai dato* (The child you gave me). The transgression of dominant ideology becomes explicit as Ballario rejects Fascism's cardinal foundations of women's identity – motherhood and marriage – in the name of a concept of love that does not require compromise and social approval. The novel is interesting for its depiction of mixed-race breastfeeding. Through this experience imbued with pleasure, sadness, and jealousy, and through the use of food metaphors, Ballario rejects nationalistic duties, bourgeois rules, Italian civilization, and Fascist values in favour of personal pleasure, personal development, and the appreciation of African moral values.

Il figlio che mi hai dato narrates the story of Albiera, a young Italian woman who has moved to Somalia with her partner Guido and their newborn Bab. The move represents a new and happy venture for them, as they have left their former spouses to start a life together. The relocation, which is considered permanent by Albiera, is only temporary for Guido, who, after one year, starts to plan for their return to Italy. The second part of the book is set in Italy; Albiera now lives with Bab in Genoa while Guido has returned to his hometown and visits them occasionally. Their country of residence dictates how they experience their relationship. In Somalia, they live as a family, whereas in Italy their marital status and the return to a conventional way of life contribute to their separation. In Italy Guido re-establishes his relationship with his former partner, something Albiera discovers by chance. As is typical of Ballario's fiction, the plot is enriched by a range of minor characters and secondary events that build to the conclusion of Albiera returning to Somalia on her own, having left Bab with Guido.

The book's message revolves around the concept of spiritual, long-lasting love, conveyed and pursued by Albiera. In the name of love, relationships for Albiera must be free from compromise and obligation. For this reason, Albiera would never ask or oblige Guido to formalize their union. Throughout the book, Albiera's proud and generous idea of love is likened to the freedom and pride of African people: "Non vuole costringere Guido ad un legame che non ha nessun valore per la sua anima libera e signora [...] come le anime dei beduini padroni del cielo e della terra" (She does not want to obligate Guido to a relationship that has no value for her free and noble spirit [...] like the souls of the Bedouins in charge of the sky and the earth).[103] Her moral standards lead her to withdraw from the rarefied emptiness of her social class and feel attuned to African fighters.

Fascist gender politics receives a major rejection in this novel. A textual reference to Ada Boni's cookbook is among the elements that mark this revisitation. At the beginning of the first part of the novel, set in Somalia, one of Albiera's servants, Johannesù, persuades Albiera to see a Tigryan fortune teller and love potion maker. Johannesù's invitation reshapes the meaning of Boni's cookbook as she says to Albiera, "E allora vieni a chiedere il talismano della felicità" (come then and ask for the talisman of happiness).[104] If Boni's book was presented as a tool for a happy future married life for upper-class young women, here the reference acquires an ironic connotation, as domesticity and cooking skills are replaced by a search for emotional happiness. A second and telling scene for the development of Ballario's revised version of gender relationships occurs at the beginning of the story, when Albiera intervenes to mediate between Johannesù and her husband Taièb, at Johannesù's request. Taièb's promise not to leave his wife "fino alla morte come lo sposo la sposa bianca" (till death keep us apart, like the white groom with his bride) functions as an ironic remark.[105] In Albiera's tale, there is no undying love for *lo sposo* and *la sposa bianca* (the white groom and bride), since both she and her partner come from other marriages and their union will end after a few years. Moreover, the different ideological perception of the woman's role is constructed through a discourse of emotions around motherhood. Breast milk is the first human food; in this novel, the baby's pleasure when feeding and the pleasures of superfluous food, such as cakes, are brought together in a narration which aims to describe the physical pleasure of motherhood (versus its patriotic value) and thereby to exalt the importance of instincts over nationalistic duties.

To contextualize Ballario's depiction of mixed-race breastfeeding, already in 1933, Eritrea and Somalia had seen the implementation

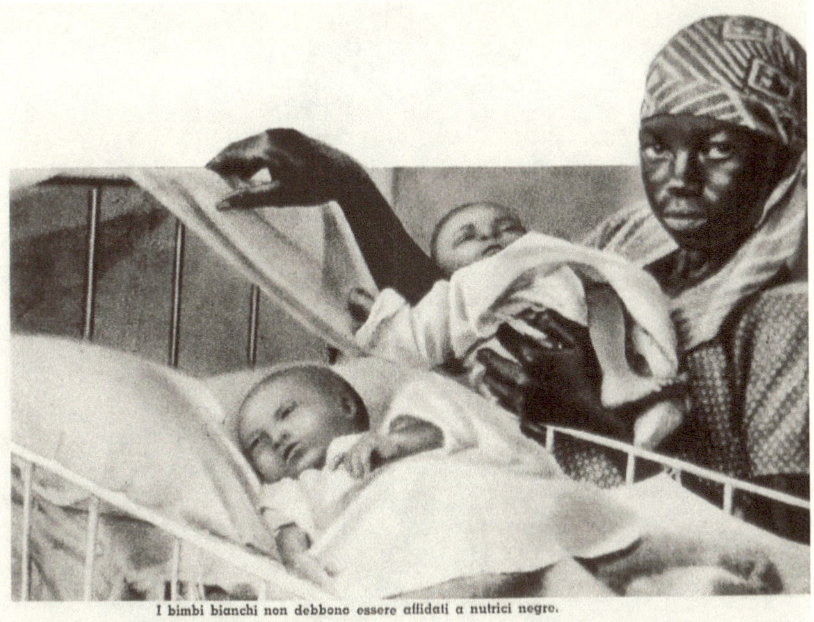

Figure 1.1 Picture of a Black wet nurse attending two white babies published in Giuseppe Lucidi's article "L'alimentazione del bambino in colonia." Biblioteca di Storia Moderna e Contemporanea, Rome.

of the first racial legislation establishing race as a criterion for the awarding of Italian citizenship.[106] If, as Barbara Sorgoni states, the number of mixed-race children continued to grow, it is evident that interracial sexual and social relationships continued even after the 1937 legislation that prohibited *madamato* (colonial concubinage) relationships with native women.[107] As Olindo De Napoli posits, the legislation aimed not to forbid interracial sexual relationships but to prevent affective relationships. It ensured that interracial sexual relationships took place in a context of subjugation and subordination.[108] In the Italian empire, mixed-race breastfeeding was regulated by racial laws. In 1939, *La difesa della razza*, the propaganda organ of racial policy published between 1938 and 1943, dedicated an article to the feeding of children in the colonies. Two warning pictures framed the article. One presented a Black woman with a white baby in her arms, with the caption "Un controsenso e un pericolo: balie negre per bambini bianchi" (a paradox and a danger: Black wet

Figure 1.2 Picture of a Black wet nurse holding a white baby published in Giuseppe Lucidi's article "L'alimentazione del bambino in colonia." Biblioteca di Storia Moderna e Contemporanea, Rome.

nurse for white children), while the other of a Black woman with two white babies carried the caption "I bimbi bianchi non devono essere affidati a nutrici negre" (white babies must not be nursed by Black wet nurses).[109]

The article justified the unsuitability of mixed-race breastfeeding on several grounds: a lack of hygiene, Black wet nurses' deficiency of maternal care, the risk of disease transmission, and finally the assertion that the milk of Black wet nurses was too fatty, hence difficult to digest. The article's author, Giuseppe Lucidi, summarized his argument:

> È risaputo infatti che i bianchi che hanno ricevuto l'allattamento da una nutrice negra (questa eventualità frequentemente si è verificata in America e raramente tra noi), hanno sofferto in seguito oltre che di malattie infettive, di malattie intestinali e nervose che li hanno resi dei tarati, dei minorati nel fisico e nello spirito.
>
> (It is well known that white people who were breastfed by a Black wet nurse – this has often happened in America but rarely in our country – suffered from infective diseases, intestinal diseases, and mental illnesses that have made them unhealthy, physically, and spiritually disabled.)[110]

In typical Fascist fashion, hygiene and nutrition have determinant values for a healthy body; breastfeeding, then, has racial and nationalistic connotations. On the contrary, in the case of Ballario's representation, mixed-raced breastfeeding is used to highlight personal emotional values.

Albiera cannot breastfeed and therefore employs wet nurses. She is torn by devastating feelings of jealousy and hatred at the sight of her Somali wet nurse Ningitù breastfeeding her baby, feelings that lead her to reduce Ningitù to animal status, characterizing her as a "milk animal," "goat," "buffalo," "mammal," and a potentially cannibalistic individual but civilized enough to prefer a roasted chicken to a raw baby. Nonetheless, when she looks at Ningitù "con invidia, con rabbia, con gelosia" (with envy, with hatred, with jealousy), Albiera acknowledges the powerful instinctual symbolism of the woman in the act of breastfeeding: "C'è in Ningitù, come in ogni donna che allatta, la potenza vivificatrice e solenne della terra. È un simbolo: la maternità." (In her, like in any breastfeeding woman, one can see the solemn and living power of the earth. She is a symbol: motherhood.)[111] In Ningitù's breastfeeding, Albiera sees the power of nature, an easy trope in colonial literature for the exotic conquered land, but the reference to every breastfeeding woman invites a shift of focus to the troubled onlooker's feelings. The scenes of Ningitù breastfeeding Bab, described by Albiera, are an expression of the pleasure desired by the onlooker:

> Quando ella [Ningitù] sprigiona il seno dal giubbetto, Bab più che farle festa entra in uno stato di frenesia, si protende verso di lei con strilli che rompono le orecchie, e quando si è impadronito della sua delizia poppa

> e brontola, succhia e minaccia roteando gli occhi sospettosi intorno per vedere se qualcuno gliela insidia, sino a che l'espressione di minaccia si muta in beatitudine, in estasi, in sogno.
>
> (When Ningitù takes her breast out of her camisole, Bab more than being happy enters in a state of excitement. He leans out towards her screaming so loud that it can almost break everyone's tympanums. When he has seized his delight, he sucks and whines, sucks and threatens, glancing around him to make sure that nobody wants to take it away from him. Then, finally, his threatening expression changes into a blissful, ecstatic, dreaming face.)[112]

Pleasure, possession, and blissful satisfaction are the feelings that separate Bab from Albiera. Bab's happiness when being breastfed is excruciating for Albiera. Feelings of being an incomplete and inadequate mother to Bab, despite her selfless love for him, are acute in relation to her incapacity to breastfeed. When in his mum's arms, Bab instinctually seeks the pleasure of breastfeeding; not finding that pleasure results in the opposite effect, pain and dissatisfaction ("spesso deluso perché la mamma non è zucchero"; often disappointed because his mum is not sugar), ending in screams and sobs.[113] In Albiera's imagination, Bab's perception of perfect happiness is represented by his exclusive relationship with Ningitù, and she fantasizes about him dreaming of a "Paradiso [...] nero, illuminato da una fontana di latte" (Black Paradise, enlightened by a milk fountain), a space of utter satisfaction.[114] This image of Bab's dream of Paradise is paralleled by another imagined Heaven, this time that of Ningitù. In one of her moments of envy, Albiera looks at the wet nurse, who has fallen asleep, and constructs what she imagines her perfect vision of happiness to be: a "Muslim Heaven" where all wet nurses sit around a table eating crème caramel.[115] If the Paradise of Bab's imagination is a reflection of a realistic situation, where the Black Paradise and the milk fountain can only be connected to his relationship to Ningitù, the dream Albiera projects onto the wet nurse is laden with symbols of her Western cultural upbringing but with a more personal take. Apart from the image of Paradise, reiterated here as a space of utter satisfaction, the metaphor of dessert consumption is once again utilized to signify pleasure. In her imagined fantasy of a Muslim Heaven, the Western-like desserts reflect what pleasure would be for the mother, Albiera. Bab himself is described as a delicacy and with reference to consumption: "Così biondo tra quelle braccia nere pare una ghiottoneria. Dà voglia di baci e di fame." (So blonde that in those Black arms, he looks like a delicacy. He inspires kisses and hunger.)[116] The emotional happiness provided by the image of the baby generates an almost cannibalistic desire; this is an expression of the mother's love and desire to make the beauty of her baby part of her own identity, while also alluding to the cannibalistic traits attributed to African people.

Unlike in *Fortuna sotto vento*, where alimentary imaginary supports the Fascist call for adaptation in the colonies, in *Il figlio che mi hai dato* literary food is connected to personal emotions. The act of breastfeeding is related not only to Bab's sensation of satisfaction and happiness but also to Albiera's perception of her own and Ningitù's bodies. Albiera's emotions determine her perception of Ningitù's body and hence her racist definition of the wet nurse as a non-human animal. In *The Cultural Politics of Emotion* and *The Promise of Happiness*, Sara Ahmed considers emotions as circulating in a social group and creating surfaces and boundaries, and she studies "how emotions circulate between bodies, examining how they 'stick' as well as move."[117] It is through this intensification of feeling that "bodies and world materialize and take shape, or that the effect of boundary, surface and fixity is produced."[118] Borrowing Ahmed's theorization, Bab's sensations when he is breastfed create jealousy in Albiera and make her conscious of both Bab's and Ningitù's bodies and – because of its difference – her own body. In this sense Albiera's maternal jealousy "sticks" (in Ahmed's terms) to their bodies. The images of pleasurable food, used to convey both Bab's sensations and Albiera's jealousy, define the maternal body and the mother-son dyad as the symbol of maternity, precisely what Albiera is lacking. Her personal experience of her own woman's body and of the emotions of maternity are given priority. Fascist ideals of domesticity and of motherhood as part of nationalistic empire-building could not be more remote from Albiera's vision of love and maternity.

Il figlio che mi hai dato develops moral tenets that depart from Fascist ideals. Not only has marriage, understood in terms of the undying love of *lo sposo* and *la sposa bianca*, shown its limitations but, crucially, Albiera actively refuses to think of marriage, concerned as she is with the spiritual and loving union of two individuals. Ultimately, she prefers to return to Africa, the land that better expresses her proud love, free of obligations. Senses and emotions are disruptive forces. As seen in the earlier quote of Giacomo Ottello, the "impulsi sensitivi" (sensual impulses) of women's fiction raised perplexity and disbelief, while emotional attachment in interracial sexual relationships was a core motivation of racial legislation implemented in the colonies. By emphasizing sensations, emotions, and personal fulfilment over and above the project of empire-building, *Il figlio che mi hai dato* elaborates an alternative and more intimate moral landscape.

Alba de Céspedes and the Well of the Senses

In 1938, when Ballario received the Premio Bologna for her children's fiction, Mondadori published *Nessuno torna indietro* (*There's No Turning Back*), the second novel by Alba de Céspedes. She had already published several short stories and a sports novel but had not yet acquired a vast readership. *Nessuno torna indietro* became a best seller republished in several editions, which the Fascist regime tried to stop. De Céspedes herself was questioned by police several times and exhorted to withdraw her book.[119] The circulation of the novel was, however, not affected by the imposition of the Fascist regime. In fact, Mondadori orchestrated an extensive publicity campaign that included ads on its women's magazines, publicity on national radio, and even postcards to collect readers' opinions to be used as endorsement.[120] The fortune of the publication must have played a part in drawing the censors' attention and, most importantly, de Céspedes, unlike Ballario, was considered suspicious by the Fascist police. In 1935, at the age of twenty-four, she had been imprisoned for six days for anti-Fascist points of view, an unclarified accusation probably related to a recorded phone conversation when she allegedly said France had paid Italy seven billion lire to fight in Abyssinia.[121] After her imprisonment she published *Io, suo padre: Romanzo sportivo* (I, his father: A sports novel), a novel of Fascist flavour, which now, with the knowledge we have of her lifelong anti-Fascist and progressive commitment, seems an improbable publication.[122] It shows, however, writers' ambiguity in trying to survive in the Fascist cultural panorama. Alba de Céspedes was loyal to anti-Fascist and progressive politics for the rest of her life. After September 1943, she would be one of the voices of Radio Bari, in liberated Italy, urging the Italian population to take an active part in the civil Resistance. In the post-war period, she was the founder and director of the prestigious, but short-lived, cultural and political journal *Mercurio*.

If all her later activities appear consistent with the description of her as an anti-Fascist intellectual, the plot of *Nessuno torna indietro* does not reveal any direct attack against the Fascist government. As critics have noted, the book displays the historical and cultural setting of the time, as well as models of femininity and beliefs that contrast with the dominant Fascist discourse.[123] Its anti-Fascist message lies, then, in the young women protagonists' way of living, their ambitions, and their desires. The story follows eight young women who share the boarding house of a convent in Rome, where they attend university. De Céspedes depicts a variety of women figures from different social contexts: the unwed mother Emanuela and the materialist Xenia – who gives up a new blooming love story to continue enjoying the wealthy life provided by her married lover – coexist with characters like the unfortunate and sick Milly and Anna, whose dreams of a married life are more traditional. When comparing the eight protagonists of the novel with the daring protagonists of Ballario's colonial novels, who led adventurous lives in an unfamiliar setting, some of de Céspedes's characters may appear more conventional. However, unlike Ballario's protagonists, the female figures of *Nessuno torna indietro* do not submit to the love of the male protagonist, nor are they dependent on it. They rather strive to follow their desires and inclinations, and hence their autonomy. Carole Gallucci states that de Céspedes, with her representations of women characters, tries to challenge models of femininity such as the Fascist new woman (of whom we have seen a good depiction in Perricone Violà's description of the Italian woman in the colonies).[124] Critics have interpreted de Céspedes's choice of the boarding house setting as explicitly connected to the historical context. De Grazia considers the young women's freedom within the constrictions of the house's rules and impositions as similar to the type of controlled freedom that women had during Fascism.[125] Pickering-Iazzi writes of "a city within the city – a women's city in Rome" to highlight the network of support existing among the young women within the limitations of the Grimaldi boarding house, which functions as a reminder of the Fascist regime's structures of discipline and hierarchical power.[126]

Despite the limitations imposed by the boarding house rules, the young women themselves are aware that living there gives them a level of independence – albeit limited – that makes them objects of envy for their peers who remained in their hometown and for men who cannot tolerate their acquired awareness of the world.[127] The setting has the power to accentuate the idea of young women whose destiny has not yet been framed, or, as one of them puts it, of their being on a bridge.[128] They are in what can be called, using postcolonial and postmodern urbanism theories, a "third space" of hybrid identities that establish new authorities and new meanings with their interactions. Literary food and an emphasis on the senses are key to highlighting the women's desire for freedom and eagerness to foster their intellect, as well as their enjoyment of communal life. Their talisman for happiness is made of pleasure for storytelling and enjoyment of the senses.

While their bland common meals function as a symbol of their boarding house experience, they are "ragazze che si nutrivano di libri" (girls who were nourished by books), eager to find nourishment in culture and their university life rather than in daily food.[129] At the beginning of the novel, their enthusiastic chatting about daily life is described as talking "con occhi ghiotti" (with greedy eyes).[130] As chit-chatting is associated with gluttony, so the image of the kitchen is evoked as the place of traditional storytelling. The young women desire their bedrooms, venue of their friendly chats, to become a kitchen, which is intended as an inviting place, suitable for listening to stories rather than cooking: "Se questa tua stanza fosse una grande cucina! ... Castagne sul fuoco e una vecchia serva che racconti" (If this room of yours was a big kitchen! ... Chestnuts on the fire and an elderly servant telling stories).[131] Words in the mouth of Vinca and Xenia transform in the gluttonous pleasure of eating. Vinca speaks in her native Spanish "come si mangia un dolce che piace" (as one eats a dessert they like), while Xenia "raccontava avidamente assaporando le parole con ghiottoneria" (would tell the story avidly tasting each word with greed).[132] On their return to the boarding house, the young women get together to chat about their dreams, munching the figs and drinking the wine they brought back from home. They become excited because of the wine and because they are talking about their future: "Riscaldate dal vino le ragazze parlavano eccitate, facevano progetti per il futuro, narravano degli interessi comuni" (Warmed up by wine, the girls spoke with excitement, made projects for their future, spoke of their common interests).[133] Spoken and written words and storytelling, rather than healthy and frugal eating, are their nutrients. Augusta, who never leaves her room, busy as she is with writing unsuccessful fiction, and Silvia, who has an inclination for academic life, patently express their love for study and writing.

While the women's interests within the space of the boarding house focus on words, their presence in Rome and their interaction with the outside world are underscored by an emphasis on the senses. Pickering-Iazzi has demonstrated how the recurrent wandering of the young women within the city can be interpreted as transgressive of hierarchical power.[134] Emanuela is the character who is most often depicted while walking in the city with pleasure and attracting attention; hence she is a destabilizing presence in the Fascist gender order. Together with the wandering through the city, outside the confines of the Grimaldi boarding house, the exaltation of the senses becomes a form of assertion of the young women's autonomy. The women avidly absorb the world around them through their senses. For example, on Sunday morning, to relax from her study, Anna would go to the market and buy roasted chestnuts. In a synaesthetic image, smell, taste, touch, and sight combine in her thinking about herself during her wandering in the city while munching chestnuts on the parapet of the Tiber River: "Anna sgranocchiava le castagne mangiandone l'odore piuttosto, godendo di quel caldo tra le mani, guardava il fiume andare pacifico alla sua meta, e pensava a sé." (Anna was munching chestnuts or rather eating their smell. Enjoying that warmth in her hands, she was looking at the river proceeding calmly towards its destination and was thinking of herself.)[135] Sensing and thinking blend in this description highlighting Anna's full immersion in the perception of the world and herself. The characters of Emanuela and Xenia further amplify the significance of the senses.

Emanuela's first date with Andrea takes place in a small restaurant, just after the funeral of their mate, Milly. Despite that sad event, Emanuela's attention is entirely focused on sensing the environment. Everything from the smell of the napkins to the inviting lunch contributes to her happiness:

> Emanuela assentiva contenta e guardava in giro: quattro pareti bianche, due boccali di maiolica a fiori su una mensola, ma era veramente piacevole, anche i tovaglioli spiegandoli mandavano un grato odore.
>
> Andrea sceglieva sulla lista delle vivande perplesso ...
> Risotto?
> Risotto.
> E dopo filetto di tacchino?
> Benissimo.
> Il vino bianco, fresco
>
> (Emanuela nodded, happy, and looked around: white walls, two flower-decorated majolica jugs on a shelf, but it was truly pleasant, even the napkins smelled nice when they unfolded them.
>
> Andrea was choosing from the menu perplexed ...
> Risotto?
> Risotto.
> And turkey fillets as a second course?
> That will be excellent.
> White wine, chilled.[136]

Soon after, thinking back on her lunch, Emanuela considers changes in her life: sending her daughter to a boarding school in Switzerland and beginning a new life with Andrea. The description of the materialist Xenia, at critical moments, is apt to underscore autonomy, independence, and pleasure. Xenia imagines Silvia blaming her for becoming the mistress of a married man. Literary food and a reference to reading and pleasure define her reply:

> "Perché fai questo Xenia?" Xenia, immaginando tale domanda, si accostava meglio sul divano, metteva in bocca un dolce, apriva un libro e rispondeva ad alta voce: "Perché lo faccio? O bella, perché mi fa comodo, perché mi piace."
>
> ("Why are you doing this, Xenia?" Imagining this question, Xenia would sit more comfortably on the sofa, would put a cake in her mouth, open a book and would answer aloud: "Why am I doing this? Oh, baby, because it is convenient for me, because I like it.")[137]

De Céspedes uses literary food also to accentuate the young women's distance from the traditional roles of duty and female self-restraint. Emanuela's mothering experiences and Augusta's and Valentina's narration of their tea with a former Grimaldi lodger exemplify this point. Emanuela has a daughter from a former boyfriend who suddenly died before the baby was born. She has chosen to live at the Grimaldi boarding house because of its vicinity to her daughter's college. Her suitability as a mother – and indeed the actual reality of being a mother, at times not even perceived as a concrete fact – is a constant worry for Emanuela. The depth of her perceived ineptitude is illustrated in the scene of her daughter's disappointment for not receiving sweets during her mother's visits. All mothers bring sweets to their children, says her daughter. It is a moment of crisis for Emanuela, who shows through her life journey the complexity of mothering. She is herself "divorata" (devoured) by anxiety when blaming herself for her daughter's disappointment: "Avrei dovuto portare le caramelle, si diceva, certo tutto è dipeso dalle caramelle" (I should have brought her sweets, she was saying to herself, surely all was caused by the sweets).[138] On a different occasion that equally refers to expected behaviours, Augusta and Valentina articulate their uneasiness with the acquired snobbish manners of a former Grimaldi mate who, just married, invited them for tea. Bonded by the experience of eating bland cabbage soups at their boarding house, they perceive the classy tea served by a maid as the measure of their distance and eat disproportionally.[139] On the contrary, a more expected performance of femininity is that of Dora, Professor Belluzzi's wife, who exudes seductiveness and refinement through her perfume, her makeup, and the daily ritual of serving her husband a cup of tea.[140]

As we have seen in the criticism of women writers of the 1930s, emotions and the senses were viewed as inappropriate for women. In *Nessuno torna indietro*, de Céspedes represents women appreciating the intellect as well as the senses, which are regularly emphasized.[141] Emanuela perceives the pleasure of everything around her when she walks around the city and when she lunches at a restaurant. She reiterates the pleasure of sexual intimacy with her partner Stefano, which she describes as wonderful, joyful, and peaceful.[142] The stories of Ballario's and de Céspedes's many protagonists all illustrate that in women's literature of the time, the search for an emotional dimension counteracted the power of state-imposed emotions that the Fascist regime enacted in its policies over women. The exhortation to save on food preparation, as well as the duty to find the talisman for marital happiness in suitable upper-middle-class cooking, was part of a constant and pervasive rhetoric aimed at making normative the emotions around family and personal relationships. Women's magazines, cookbooks, and women's literature were conjured up to create normative emotions, through what can be defined, according to the historian of emotions William Reddy, as an "emotional regime," an exercise of power on feelings and desires. Both Ballario and de Céspedes put into practice a mobilization of the emotions, of a contrary direction to what so widely dominated the Fascist rhetoric. They articulated, albeit starting from different political views, an emotional community, using Barbara Rosenwein's terminology, as they share common modes of emotional expression. In their writing, women characters are often distant from the sacrality and nationalistic duties of the Fascist models of femininity. Ballario's exuberant and greedy persona in search of patisserie, the sad and proud Albiera, the sensual Emanuela, and the excited chatting of the girls at the Grimaldi boarding house all highlight, through the senses, aspects of women's subjectivities discordant with dominant models of femininity. Food-related images – literary food – allow the construction of those perceptions.

If Fascism aimed to shape Italians' private and public lives in line with its pervading nationalism, women writers provided alternative paths which gave value to the specific structures the regime was trying to control: food, senses, and emotions. Years later, in 1948, de Céspedes referred again to the importance of women's emotions. In the last issue of her journal *Mercurio*, she published Natalia Ginzburg's invited contribution on women's condition. Ginzburg's piece was followed by de Céspedes's reply, written in epistolary form. As Valeria Babini aptly observes, at that historical conjunction, the published exchange between the two women writers aimed to discuss the political question of women's freedom in democratic Italy.[143] Women had obtained the vote, but for de Céspedes the 1948 historic elections implied a transatlantic shift that, as she would explicitly state years later, would lead to a false sense of freedom based on consumeristic ideals.[144] In this exchange, Ginzburg commented that women's life was hindered by the suffering of centuries of subjugation and by their inner self, often shaped and constrained by the responsibilities of motherhood. Ginzburg calls this difficulty a feeling of "falling in a well." De Céspedes replied that women's perception of "falling in a well," hence their emotional life, their anxieties and fears, enriches their knowledge of themselves and the world:

> Ma – al contrario di te – io credo che questi pozzi siano la nostra forza. Poiché ogni volta che cadiamo nel pozzo noi scendiamo alle più profonde radici del nostro essere umano, e nel riaffiorare portiamo in noi esperienze tali che ci permettono di comprendere tutto quello che gli uomini – i quali non cadono mai nel pozzo – non comprenderanno mai. È questo il difetto degli uomini, a parer mio: quello di non abbandonarsi mai totalmente, mai lasciarsi cadere nel pozzo. Sicché a volte io penso con affettuosa compassione che essi non abbiano pozzi in cui cadere e quindi non possano mai venire a contatto immediato con la debolezza, i sogni, le malinconie, le aspirazioni, e insomma tutti quei sentimenti che formano e migliorano l'animo umano e che – sebbene inconsapevolmente e per un succedersi di ignorati tranelli – pesano anche sulla vita dell'uomo più conforme al modello virile.
>
> (But unlike you, I think that these wells are our force. Every time we fall into the well, we go down to the deepest roots of our being, and in emerging again we take experiences that allow us to understand what men – who never fall into the well – will never understand. This is the defect of men, in my view, that of never freeing themselves and never letting themselves fall into the well. Then sometimes I think, with kind compassion, that they do not have wells in which to fall, hence they cannot ever come in close contact with weakness, dreams, nostalgia, aspirations, that is with all those feelings that form and better the human character and that – albeit unconsciously and accidentally – are relevant even to the man most compliant with the virile model.)[145]

The importance of being fragile and in anguish and the ability to understand their emotional journeys are claimed by de Céspedes as an essential element of women's freedom, something to retain and be conscious of. The virile Fascist woman and the exemplary woman of Fascist education have all vanished. As we will see in the next chapter, in the crucial time of World War II, the representation of women's agency and freedom would often find forms of expression in the senses and food imagery.

Chapter Two

World War II, Food, and Women's Bodies

For decades a gender analysis of World War II has been absent from historiography. Apart from a few works published in the mid-1970s, more systematic reading of the role of women during the war did not begin until the 1990s, with works on prostitution and violence against women being published only in the last decade.[1] World War II is a period of historical changes for women's sense of agency and visibility and for anxiety about the new models of femininity that women's activities were generating. In this chapter, I show that the same women's organizations that supported and encouraged women to participate in food protests mediated women's role by emphasizing their morality and their dutiful and sacrificial role within the family. These representations persisted in the press available to women, be it domestic literature for the middle class or women's magazines published during the war in liberated Naples and Rome.

While women enthusiastically took part in the war, either in the Resistance or in Fascist groups, their bodies were obscured in the memory of the war. The knowledge of war rapes and hunger-led prostitution further complicated the disembodied war memory. In the reading of food scenes in the memoirs by Cesarina Bracco and Giovanna Zangrandi here analysed, I consider the action of tasting and eating as a performance. By creating these performances in their memoirs, the authors give new emphasis to the body, redeeming it from the site of anxiety where it had been relegated. The joy of active life in the Resistance and the enjoyment of an acquired sense of personal autonomy and independence are the emotions that such scenes reveal, capturing the embodied sense of self that the partisan war secured for women. On the other hand, Ada Prospero Gobetti's memoir is more reticent in expressing personal emotions, which remain, like the food scenes, more centred on the family and the nation. The three books represent the experiences of women of different social classes and had dissimilar circulation. Zangrandi's diary is currently readily available in Italian and known among scholars of the period, whereas Bracco's book was published in 1976 by the local Institute for the History of Resistance in the province of Vercelli and has not had visibility at a national level. Gobetti's *Diario partigiano* (*Partisan Diary*) currently remains the best known in Italian and English. Before the analysis of these texts and of the media representing women's active involvement in the war, I will outline how the discourse of food impacted women at the outbreak of the war.

Women at the Outbreak of World War II

The interlocking ideas of modernity and tradition – characteristic of the Fascist period and its representation of women – continued to feed bourgeois culture at this time. Cookery books published in the first years of the 1940s addressed middle-class women conscious of their role as wives and mothers, as well as modern younger women who had not fully embraced those responsibilities. Amalia Moretti Foggia, who had acquired prominence in the 1930s for her medical and cooking advice, continued to play a key role in the everyday cooking practice of bourgeois families. The titles of her cookery books summarize well the difficulties faced by the middle class: *Ricette di Petronilla per tempi eccezionali* (1941; Petronilla's recipes for exceptional times), *200 suggerimenti per … questi tempi* (1943; 200 suggestions for … these times), *Desinaretti per … questi tempi* (1944; Suppers for … these times). Her writing provides an insight into the interplay of modernity and tradition. It also confirms both the persisting desire of the middle class to maintain appearances and the restatement of the caring role of women.

Using a setting reminiscent of Boccaccio's *Decameron*, her *Ricette di Petronilla per tempi eccezionali* narrates women's inclinations and their family relationships. Ten women including Petronilla herself regularly meet up, in the afternoon, at each other's houses to talk about the "eterno tema" (everlasting theme) which – apart from world events – concerns every woman, that is, how to cook with what is available, spending little while maintaining a suitable nutrition level.[2] The ten women all have different attitudes to cooking. Adriana stands out for her creativity, Gemma is an expert in Friulan cuisine, Giulia shares scientific information acquired from her husband, and Giovanna plainly admits using tinned sauces and tinned fish to save on the rationed fat and to not spend too much time in the kitchen. In turn, different aspects of their lives are highlighted, from their knowledge of local cuisines to the need to satisfy the difficult tastes of their gourmet husbands, from the decision to cultivate vegetables in their gardens following the government's advice to the pleasure of self-indulgence when discussing desserts with gusto. Despite the range of situations and preferences, the book reinforces the traditional role of women as food and happiness providers. It concludes that, for the love of their family, women can solve all household problems and satisfy "non solo l'appetito, ma persino la gola dei figlioli e del marito" (not only appetite but even her children's and husband's gluttony).[3]

The image of the ten women in fashionable clothes and hats at the opening of the book would soon look like a picture of a very distant past, as the end of 1941 marks a deterioration in living conditions at the national level. Underfeeding begins to be a national problem in the winter of 1941–2, becomes a general problem in 1943, and reaches a very serious level in the years 1944 and 1945.[4] Rationing started in Italy with law 557 of 6 May 1940, which established the norms for use of the rationing card, presented in the national press as a necessity to accelerate the progress of the war.[5] Coffee was among the first items to be rationed, following a logic that prioritized luxury and expensive food. Bread was rationed in October 1941, a late decision and part of Mussolini's strategy not to generate alarm among the population but which had serious consequences for its availability at a time when wheat production was decreasing. As Massimo Legnani argued, bringing together the very limited data available for the period, in 1942 the majority of the population began to resort to the black market as a regular source of supply rather than a supplementary one.[6] The statistical data collated between 1942 and 1943 by Pier Paolo Luzzato Fegiz, Professor of Statistics at the University of Trieste, illustrates a substantial decrease in the percentage of people living below the survival standard. Legnani relates these statistics to the data of average food consumption made available by the Istituto nazionale di statistica (National Institute for Statistics) for that period, showing a drop from 2,631 calories per person in 1940 to 2,123 calories in 1943 and down to 1,800 calories in the last two years of the war.[7] He concludes that, given that the rationing system did not aim to cover food consumption in its entirety, the improvements in the survival standard are to be attributed to a more consistent and regular use of the black market. Petronilla gives us a sense of how extensive and accepted the illegal food market was when, in *Desinaretti*, she admits that the illegal market, albeit expensive, is the only way to obtain all that one needs.[8]

More products were being rationed year after year following a regional scheme.[9] The inefficiency of the rationing system, however, became soon evident, as the number of crimes involving the breaking of rationing regulations demonstrates. Antonio Lovallo reports that between 1940 and 1948, 34.5 per cent of the verdicts of the Bologna courts were related to crimes against food rationing and 17.3 per cent of them to the illegal trade in rationed food.[10] The same situation was common in the south of Italy. In June 1942 the Fascist weekly newspaper *L'Adriatico* gives news of several verdicts issued by the Court of Pescara in the Abruzzi region. Punishment was not light: a woman in Pescara was sentenced to one year in prison and a 5,000 lire fine for "diverting from the normal market" 2,800 kilograms of wheat flour; a man from the same area was sentenced to three months in prison and a 4,000 lire fine for "diverting from the normal market" 14 kilograms of fat and 3 kilograms of butter.[11] The crime they were accused of was contributing less food than requested to the mandatory Fascist food deposits called *ammassi*. Farmers were obliged to allocate a large part of their production, retaining a part for their own needs, but no clear system was devised to keep control of the quantity produced and the quantity given over. This made it possible to retain larger quantities than needed to then sell them on the more remunerative black market.

The cooking advice given to women in newspapers, magazines, and recipe books offers a glimpse of the deteriorating living conditions. In November 1940, *La donna fascista*, the magazine of the women's organization of the Fascist National Party, published an article titled "Benvenuta Autarchia" (Welcome autarky) advising housewives to use the residual fat obtained by the cooking of meat as a pasta sauce.[12] This first plea to save cooking fat scaled up to more drastic restrictions when, in April 1942, the advice was to first cook meat for only a few minutes to take out the residual fat – to be used for other recipes – and then complete its cooking with a spoonful of water.[13] Petronilla in *200 suggerimenti per … questi tempi* suggests filling up the milk bottle with water in order not to waste the smallest residue of milk and using that liquid to cook vegetables.[14]

However, although the suggestions of recipe books of the time reflect the historical data about rationing and criminal punishment, the psychological representation of the bourgeois woman remains that of the "angel of the house." In *Ricette di Petronilla*, the woman's role in the house and her devotion to her husband were still crucial characteristics to aspire to:

> Si ha infatti un bel predicare l'emancipazione, nonché l'istruzione superiore femminile, ma la sacrosanta verità sarà sempre questa: che noi, donne, per essere felici, dobbiamo *sentirci* molto amate dai nostri mariti, e per *sentirci* dai mariti molto amate ed apprezzate, più della filosofia, della

> letteratura, della politica e della … emancipazione, sempre ci è valso – e sempre anche vi varrà – il saper preparare una buona e soprattutto *varia*, mensa famigliare.
>
> (It is all very well preaching about emancipation and higher education for women, but the real truth is this: to be happy we need to *feel* loved by our husbands, and to *feel* loved and appreciated by our husbands, more than philosophy, literature, politics and … emancipation, being able to prepare a good and *varied* family menu will always be valuable to us, as it has always been.)[15]

It is a remarkable passage to read in 1943, when women had already been vocal in social protests and political activities. On 23 August 1942, in the village of Monteleone in the Apulia region, women protested against the police's confiscation of a small amount of corn they intended to grind for their own use. In the spring of 1943, women workers were involved in many factory strikes in the north of Italy, which were evidence to the Fascist authorities of popular disaffection with the government and its leader. The strikes were spontaneous and generated by the exasperation with the dire living conditions.[16] They mark the beginning of women's wide involvement in anti-Fascist activities. It is difficult to list all the activities that made women dynamic protagonists of the Resistance and that changed the way they were identified. They were physically present in squares, mountains, factories, city streets, and the countryside. Women's bodies acquired new importance in everyday life, outside the nationalistic maternal functions. However, women demonstrated their political awareness and agency not only in the Resistance fight.

The decision of Fascist women to join the Salò Republic is also part of the larger women's involvement in the war. In the spring of 1944, thousands of Fascist women joined the newly formed Servizio Ausiliario Femminile (SAF), a women's army in support of the Fascist troops. As Cecilia Nuboli reconstructs, young women volunteered for the Fascist SAF to replace the soldiers who had defected after the armistice.[17] Others joined the Fascist armed bands that killed civilians and tortured partisans or worked as collaborators of the Nazi-Fascist government. All of them expressed the desire to be protagonists of history and, as a woman of the time put it, some of them communicated their anger against the inactivity of men of their generation.[18] The search for food, food protests, and strikes were not a concern for these women who, through their association with the Nazi-Fascist forces, would have had easier access to food supplies.Although their eagerness to be protagonists is eye-opening for understanding the changed visibility and agency of women in the war, the food discourse, with all its implications for women, is more strictly connected with civilian life and the partisan Resistance.

Women's Bodies as a Site of Contention and Anxiety: Food Protests

Several of the women involved in the Resistance described their experience as life-changing and enriching. Marisa Ombra, when narrating her partisan experience, writes of the discovery that "la vita era, poteva essere qualcosa che si svolgeva su orizzonti molto più vasti di quelli fino allora conosciuti" (life was, could be something that would unfold on wider horizons than the ones experienced so far).[19] Ida D'Este, who took part in the partisan Resistance in Veneto, using a taste metaphor, describes that period of her life as an adventurous, unique experience: "La vita ha un'altra luce: un pizzico di rischio e di aria carbonara dà un sapore nuovo di giovinezza che non troverò più" (Life has another light: a pinch of risk and revolutionary atmosphere gives a new taste of youth that I will never find again).[20] Historian Addis Saba, in her analysis of women's Resistance activities, interprets the Resistance as the moment of rupture with a tradition of passivity, a period when women became citizens for the first time as they acted en masse for the good of a rediscovered sense of homeland.[21] While the experience of the Resistance brought a new outlook on life to a large demographic of women, their visibility in the public domain of the home front created anxiety. On the one hand, women's experience of the war can be defined as an embodied one, where their bodies were no longer the procreating tool needed by the imperialist power but subjects actively and voluntarily taking part in the shaping of history and claiming their legitimacy as citizens. On the other hand, it is the very visibility of women's bodies that gave rise to concerns over their roles in society.

In the first years of World War II, Petronilla was reasserting the image of women who, although in tune with modernity, were crystallized in an economy of emotions that kept them attached to their homes and family. In truth, the streets, the black market, the countryside, the mountains, and the public spaces of the cities were criss-crossed by women. The constant search for food kept the impoverished middle class and the lower classes in constant movement outside their homes. The network of women who supported the Resistance worked within this extensive web, in largely female cityscapes. The women who delivered arms, information, and food and took part in the armed Resistance, sharing prolonged periods with male partisans, were easy targets for accusations of lack of morality. Not only the most traditional sections of society but the partisans themselves questioned women's sense of morality for the experiences that had taken them outside the conventional female sphere. This became evident when in the liberation celebrations, in 1945, women partisans were often asked not to take part in the celebratory marches or, if allowed, they were required to wear a nurse's armband to disguise their participation as one in the more traditional framework of female care.[22] The concern over integrity was exacerbated and made more pervasive by the knowledge of rapes committed against women throughout the war by the Nazi-Fascist and the Allied armies. Although these stories remained largely untold for decades, local authorities were aware of them. Denunciations of violence in the liberated south of Italy were reported but ignored by the Allied command, which decided to turn its back on the atrocious violence against women perpetrated by the Moroccan Goumiers, troops of the French Expeditionary Forces, part of the Allied armies.[23] As Cinzia Venturoli reconstructs, in the post-war period, psychological and social reasons strengthened the silence on the violence suffered by women.[24] When addressed, wartime violence against women was explained in racist terms, attributing the responsibility to Black soldiers, as both the Allied Military Government and the Italian police explained the rapes in the Tombolo area.[25]

Lack of food and starvation triggered the large sex market that dominated the areas around the Allied camp of Tombolo, near Livorno. Interpretations of the events around the Tombolo sex market had repercussions on the symbolism of women's bodies and on their civil rights. A total of eight thousand women are calculated to have been part of the sex market in that area in the period 1944–7 when the American GIs left.[26] The pinewood of Tombolo had been chosen by the Allies as a large provision storage and camping site for the use of the 92nd Division, the only American unit formed solely of Black soldiers. As Chiara Fantozzi argues, the story of the degraded area of Tombolo sparked moralistic judgments from critics of all political areas. The Communist media presented it as the negative outcome of American occupation, while the newspapers of opposite political views criticized the moral standards of the left-wing parties, given that the Livorno area had a left-wing political tradition.[27] The figure of the wartime prostitute became the scapegoat for the violated sense of honour of the national community and the symbol of the foreign occupation.[28] The Tombolo prostitutes were condemned by society at large as anti-Italian. It was within this moralistic discourse of the prostitute as corrupted and anti-nationalistic that the exclusion of clandestine prostitutes from the 1946 universal suffrage took shape.[29]

The discourse on women's morality was therefore fuelled by many elements at the time when women's activities against the Nazi-Fascists were numerous and widespread. Among these activities, food protests attracted a large participation of women. Hence, they created similar concerns and a complex narrative. Many of the women's food protests were spontaneous, as in the aforementioned case of Monteleone in Apulia, and many others were planned by the Gruppi di difesa della donna e per l'assistenza ai combattenti della libertà (GDD), the first women's mass organization against Nazi-Fascism. The GDD was formed in the autumn of 1943 under the influence of the anti-Fascist parties and in particular the Communist Party.[30] The constitutional document of the group stated their refusal to send food to stockpiles and their commitment to delivering provisions for partisans as part of their action plan. Crucially, it made explicit the link between the diversion of produce from the Nazi-Fascists and the liberation of the country: "Difendere il nostro pane vuol dire aiutare a cacciare i Tedeschi" (Defending our bread means to help oust the Germans).[31] Encouraging women of different political groups as well as non-politicized women to take part in the anti-Fascist fight was a primary task of the GDD. The GDD promoted a diversification of women's subgroups structured according to work categories, which were made known in local papers: the tasks of the subgroups constituted by housewives were specifically to protest about rations and disseminate anti-Fascist sentiments when queueing for rationed food.[32] The specific task of the women farmers' group was to divert produce destined for Nazi-Fascist food stockpiles.[33]

Their clandestine press was pivotal for the achievement of their objectives. Papers were circulated among women, distributed in factories and other places of aggregation. As the GDD was organized into local groups, several local GDD papers were published in occupied territory. *La donna*, *La difesa della lavoratrice*, *Donne in lotta*, and local issues of *Noi donne* were all presented as the press organs of the GDD. They provided information about the anti-Fascist fight and instigated women to organize strikes and protests and to widen the membership basis. Leaflets were also used to the same effect. A leaflet of the Modena group, for example, praised local women who, on the symbolic date of 8 March, had stolen a large quantity of meat destined for the Nazis from a food company, and exhorted them to organize further protests for food and clothes.[34] But how was the GDD's call to action presented to women at a time when their bodies were a site of contention, when hunger-led prostitution, rapes, and violence complicated the image of the female body inherited from Fascism? *Noi donne* represents well how food stories were subjected to a rhetoric that on the one hand exalted women's actions and their visibility and on the other tried to obscure bodies behind a moral image of femininity.

In occupied Northern Italy, the GDD started publishing clandestine local copies of *Noi donne,* which, in June 1944, was also published in liberated Naples and later in Rome as an official publication.[35] Hence, in the last part of the war, local underground issues circulated in the occupied territory while the official paper was published in liberated Italy. Aiming to engage women in a constant daily battle against Nazi-Fascism, *Noi donne* provided information about women's work in the Resistance and advice about daily tasks. Women's emancipation through participation, at various levels, in the fight for the liberation of the country was at the heart of the magazine. To this end, the official issues presented biographies of heroic deeds undertaken by women, reports on women fighting in other countries, with particular attention to Soviet women, war-themed short stories on heroic mothers and women, and articles on women workers' rights and the right to vote.

The official and the clandestine issues were substantially different. The clandestine issues were double-sided cyclostyles designed to allow easy copying and distribution. The exhortation to the fight against Nazi-Fascism was not only explicit but aggressive: the lines "morte ai tedeschi e ai traditori fascisti" (death to the Germans and to the Fascist traitors) were regularly reported in the masthead. Fascists and Nazis were labelled "carogna" (swine), "affamatori del popolo" (people starvers), "tiranni" (tyrants), and "belve" (beasts). Reports on food protests and calls to divert food produce from the Nazi-Fascist stockpiles were recurrent on the pages of the clandestine *Noi donne.*

In a clandestine issue published in Emilia Romagna in May 1944, an article signed "una donna Cattolica" (a Catholic woman) encouraged women to sabotage the Nazi-Fascist food storages and send provisions to the partisans in the mountains.[36] An article signed "Una Contadina" (a peasant woman), in a July 1944 issue published in Tuscany, called on women to not take food to Nazi-Fascist stockpiles but rather to hide and distribute it among the population or destroy it.[37] The same issue also urged women to follow the example of the women of Peretola, who stormed the wood storage of the Todt factory and robbed it of wood to use for cooking and heating in their homes. In the days when Florence was almost without bread and expecting the incursion of the Nazis during their withdrawal towards the north, women were encouraged to be united in the fight to demonstrate "ai tedeschi e ai fascisti traditori di cosa sono capaci le donne toscane" (to Germans and the Fascist traitors what Tuscan women are capable of).[38] A June issue in Emilia Romagna reported the news of a protest of 300 women and 150 men to obtain an increase in rationed food. The women confronted the *maresciallo dei carabinieri* (police marshal) and improvised a sit-in during which, the article underlines, men brought food to the protesting women. The successful outcome of the protest led to the distribution of 200 grams of cured meat per person.[39] A Veneto issue of May 1944 reports about women's protests held in Schio and Torrebelvicino against the skimming of milk, done to produce butter for the German troops. The protest concluded with the distribution of the rationed butter, as well as the promise of regular distribution of all other provisions, while the attempted repression of the protest resulted in the retreat of the Fascist soldiers.[40] In the same issue, the women of Castelnuovo were praised for obtaining the distribution of cooking fat, and a report of a women's protest in Alpetto triggered by the order to bring eggs to the food stockpiles concluded with the news of policemen being hit by the women.[41] In a Milan issue, women were praised for their increasing participation in the fight for "il pane e la libertà" (bread and freedom).[42] In an article from a November 1944 issue published in Liguria, the accidental killing of animals by Allied bombing was seen positively because it prevented the meat from ending up on Nazis' plates.[43] In a 1945 special issue dedicated to the celebration of International Women's Day, published in the still-occupied Reggio Emilia, two articles reported a series of successful women's protests that obtained the distribution of meat, salt, eggs, and fat. The article concludes with a call to fight against the Nazi-Fascists:

> Ciò dimostra in modo esplicito che è soltanto con la lotta energica di tutte, che si ottiene quello di cui abbiamo bisogno. Un'altra volta occorre andare dove vi sono i depositi di viveri e prenderseli perché è roba nostra, è roba prodotta col sudore di tutta la popolazione italiana.
>
> I nazi-fascisti conducono una politica di affamamento, essi continuamente gozzovigliano, si ubriacano e mangiano mentre noi e i nostri bambini si muore di fame.
>
> Ai nostri bimbi manca lo zucchero che è il loro alimento base
>
> Le donne devono a tutti i costi salvare i loro bimbi da prematura morte …
>
> Combattiamo donne! Con tutte le nostre armi contro gli affamatori e assassini del nostro popolo.

> (This shows that it is only by all of us fighting energetically that we can obtain what we need. We must go again to the food storages and take the food because it is ours, it is food produced by the work of the entire Italian population.

The Nazi-Fascists are practising hunger politics: they feast, get drunk, and eat while our children are starving.

Our children do not have sugar which is their basic food

Women must, at all costs, save their children from premature death …

Let's fight, Women! With all our arms against the starvers and murderers of our people.)[44]

There was some communication between the official magazine and the women writing in the occupied parts of the country. This is proved, for example, by an article in the September 1944 issue of the official magazine that reports the news available in a *Noi donne* issue they received from occupied Italy.[45] However, the approach to the representation of women in the official and the clandestine issues was different. The official issues too focused on women's political and social demands and their active participation in the war against Nazi-Fascism, and the topic of food was also used to narrate the war against Nazi-Fascism.[46] The magazine reported on food protests, but the image of women in their articles was less aggressive and rebellious and associated more with moral and maternal qualities. This is apparent in an article on the April 1944 food protests which took place in Rome and led to the killing of Caterina Martinelli. The protest is presented as an outburst of suppressed indignation: "Un gruppo di donne … lasciò che esplodesse l'ira già tanto repressa, e gridò, per la via Candia, la sua indignazione" (a group of women let their long-repressed anger explode, and along Candia Street shouted their indignation).[47] In the space of a few days, several protests erupted. Martinelli was shot dead during one of these violently repressed protests. The title of the article on her death, "Una madre italiana: Caterina Martinelli" (An Italian mother: Caterina Martinelli), is indicative of the type of narrative chosen by *Noi donne*. It opens with Caterina's words: "Io non volevo che un po' di pane per i miei bambini, non potevo sentirli piangere tutti e sei insieme" (I just wanted a bit of bread for my children. I could not bear to hear them crying, all six of them together).[48] Caterina's maternal role and her sense of responsibility towards her children frame her as an innocent victim. It is a clear attempt to mediate women's active participation and depict women's actions in food protests within non-transgressive parameters. In this sense, Martinelli's story is legitimated through her familial role, following a pattern not uncommon in the Resistance.[49] The following month, with no overtones, the magazine reported a protest in non-liberated Bologna describing the successful distribution of 200 grams of salami per person obtained by the women. In the same article, the additional news of thirty-five similar protests in the province of Bologna was detailed without any comments.[50]

In liberated Italy, food protests were still vital to women's political activism. *Noi donne* reports on a protest at the city council organized by women of the UDI (Unione donne italiane), the newly constituted local group in Macerata in 1944. The women distributed among the population food provisions withheld by Fascist individuals. Their action, the article underlines, is dictated by a sense of political justice and organizational skills: "L'ordine perfetto che regnò durante la manifestazione e successivamente ha dimostrato che non si è trattato di 'saccheggio' di una popolazione affamata ma dell'azione organizzata delle donne che vogliono intervenire per far cessare gli abusi e le irregolarità" (The perfect order during and after the protest demonstrated that it was not a case of "plunder" undertaken by a starving population, but an organized action of women who want to intervene to put an end to abuses and irregularities).[51] The outcome of their protest, the article continued, was decisive for the UDI, which was later involved in the local nomination of the *prefetto* (prefect) and proposed two women as councillors. The author concluded that the women of Macerata "vedono affermarsi la loro autorità" (see their authority acknowledged).[52]

The narrative of the protest in Macerata corroborates the political target of the right to citizenship that *Noi donne* had been promoting throughout. The emphasis on the well-organized action and the perfect order of a demonstration dictated by ideals of equity and justice carefully obliterates any references to women's transgression and violence. *Noi donne* acknowledged and supported women's armed struggle, as an article on Gruppi d'azione patriottica (GAP) women illustrates.[53] Women's food protests, however, had a different narrative value. They were able to generate a much larger participation than the restricted group of the GAP women, who could be considered exceptional women. The narrative around food protests would contribute to shaping the representation of common women at the home front at a moment when anxiety over their bodies was widespread and when women's claim to legitimacy, and their acquisition of political subjectivity, was more concrete than ever. Reading the articles in the official and clandestine issues of *Noi donne* reveals that already before the end of the war women's agency, so clearly manifested during the conflict, was being redefined into more traditional roles.

What Kind of Memory for Women's Resistance?

In the memories of the Resistance written by women over the decades, the victimization epitomized in Caterina Martinelli's story very rarely emerges. The emotional topic of food, which dominated people's lives, is recurrent in World War II memoirs and, as we will see, provides a means to convey the complexity of emotions that women's active presence generated, from anxiety to joy, and defiance of power structures. It provides a key to narrating the memory of the vast participation of ordinary women in the fight against Nazi-Fascism. It is generally acknowledged that 70,000 women were GDD members and 35,000 were fighting partisans, but historians have calculated that up to two million women took part in the Resistance.[54] Despite a level of involvement that must have made women visible to everyone, their work remained hidden from historiography, at least in the first post-war decades.

The memory of women's participation was kept alive only by associations such as the UDI, and a full analysis of their work in the liberation war was neglected.[55] In the post-war years, the memory of the Resistance was very much focused on the armed struggle, hence a type of memory that excluded the many women's interventions in various aspects of social life. Consequently, the large mass of women who provided support to partisans, the women who organized strikes and food protests, were not given credit for their activities. Only nineteen women received the gold medal for military service. In the 1970s the seminal books *La Resistenza taciuta* by Anna Maria Bruzzone and Rachele Farina and *Compagne* by Bianca Guidetti Serra initiated a revaluation of women's Resistance.[56] Other factors contributed to this reassessment: a change in the political climate around the commemoration of the Resistance as a whole, the development of feminist studies, and the research into oral history that was to follow.[57] A further development has taken place since the end of the 1980s thanks to the work by Jacques Semelin.[58] He demonstrated that ordinary people, all around Europe, engaged in a wide range of activities to protect individuals at risk or sabotage the Nazi-Fascist plans. This meant that the focus of research was shifting from an analysis of a traditional concept of power, war, and heroes that privileged the armed Resistance to an understanding of the war that could include the countless activities undertaken by women at all levels of society. Yet this approach once again weakened the discussion on women's participation.

Addis Saba argued that women's involvement had a specificity that the new research on civil and unarmed Resistance did not manage to make visible.[59] Anna Bravo and Anna Maria Bruzzone in *In guerra senza armi* developed a similar criticism of the idea of civil Resistance, arguing that the "armed/civil" dichotomy was being applied to something that effectively could not be split into two.[60] Later, Bravo returned to the need to reassess the concept of civil Resistance, underlining that the tendency to consider it as exclusively female has led Italian historians to circumscribe the phenomenon into "another enclave." It has, then, stagnated the discussion of women's participation.[61] Instead of considering the civil Resistance as the unarmed branch of the Resistance, or as a disorganized and non-political group, Bravo looks at it as "a network of relationships ... and an ensemble of behaviour" that is as a wide and unaccountable series of activities.[62] As she summarizes, the paradox of civil Resistance is to use practices that are associative and open to women within a structure that is traditional and male. Bravo argues that instead of connoting women's participation by the marginal function that the dimension of care acquires within a patriarchal framework, women's Resistance requires study of the female subject outside structures into which she could disappear, that is, the family and the anti-Nazi/anti-Fascist organizations.[63] This shift would allow a radical rethinking of the subject "woman" in the memory of the Resistance.

In Bravo's assessment, the multitude of voices arising from the many memoirs now available and the oral interviews she undertook is a rich source to understand women's work in this period. She finds that women's memoirs offer a combination of lived experience, desires, and hopes, while never projecting their authors as victims. These testimonies teach us that "la realtà deborda dai linguaggi disponibili per raccontarla, che le idee non nascono per germinazione da altre idee, ma nella loro tensione con il vissuto corporeo, affettivo, mentale" (reality overflows from the languages available to its narration, and ideas are not born from other ideas but are created in the tension with the bodily, affective, and mental lived experience).[64] In my reading of women partisans' memoirs, stories and images of food construct embodied memories that express desires, hopes, the joy of participation, and defiance of authority, and therefore they illuminate a lived experience that narrates material aspects of the war but also sheds light on the women's sense of independent self.

Wartime food narratives have represented a vital outlet of resilience for men and women across the world. Cara de Silva's volume on the women at the concentration camp of Terezin and Anne Georget's documentary *Imaginary Feasts* show how, even in the gloomiest of situations during World War II, the thinking through images of food and the memory of food and taste have played a role in the expressions of the subject's emotions. Reconstructing the stories of war prisoners who, with the most unlikely resources, put together recipe books dictated by their own memories, de Silva and Georget illustrate the crucial relevance of food memories for the psychological survival of prisoners of war.[65] In those cases, the reconstruction of the recipes offers the prisoners respite by reconnecting them to a past identity that, through a personal memory of family meals and a cultural memory of local and national dishes, restores in them the sense of self stripped of them by concentration camps and war prisons. In the memoirs by Cesarina Bracco, Giovanna Zangrandi, and Ada Prospero Gobetti analysed here, the memories of communal eating or typical dishes only occasionally emerge as moments of reconnection to a past life. Rather it is the women's reimagining of taste and, through it, their bodies and emotions that appears crucial.

Theorists interested in phenomenology have highlighted the interconnection between the senses and cognition and therefore the special function of the body within this process. As David Le Breton summarizes, we live our lives through our bodies even though we are often unaware of it; "our being in the world is embodied," which means that body and mind intertwine in the elaboration of experience and that thought is not a product only of the mind.[66] For Le Breton sensory experience is what goes unnoticed and translates into perception, which is the origin of meaning. Sensory perceptions "coincide with a unique individual's way of organizing categories of thought based on what he or she has learned from peers, travel, acquaintances, or interests, or from his or her particular skills as a cook, a painter, a perfume maker, a weaver, etc."[67] Emmanuel Levinas's phenomenological interpretation of the subject adds to this concept. For him, the subject is defined by sensibility, the body's ability to respond to needs and to enjoy the world or be fatigued by it. Levinas proposes an affective body that is absorbed into the enjoyment of life and of its needs, which is prior to the definition of itself as a cognitive and agent subject.[68] As philosophers Kathleen Lennon and Anthony Wilde explain, in Levinas "sensible affectivity articulates the primary contours of subjectivity."[69] The self is in the first instance absorbed in the satisfaction of its needs, and therefore focused on itself. Giovanna Colombetti takes this discourse further, explaining how the experience of the world depends on one's bodily self-awareness, or as she puts it, it is through a certain experience of one's body "that we experience the world as affecting us in one way or the other."[70] As we have seen, Perullo argues that experience of the self through taste is an awakening event and a way for the subject to acquire knowledge about herself. In the reading of women's memoirs that follows, memories of taste reveal an affective body that not only reacts to states like hunger and food scarcity but expresses self-awareness. This focus allows a study that considers the women partisans' stories both as part of a choral narrative of the Resistance and as an expression of a new autonomous self. The corporeal memory emerging in the books by Cesarina Bracco and Giovanna Zangrandi enables us to understand the women partisans' distinctive experience of the war, their agency, and their sense of autonomy, illuminating their expression of legitimacy in ways that are distinct from their idea of family and, at times, also from the concept of partisan hierarchy.

Cesarina Bracco's *La staffetta garibaldina* and Giovanna Zangrandi's *I giorni veri*

Risk-taking, naivety, the memory of Nazi-Fascist massacres, violence, light-heartedness, and exhaustion are all ingredients of Cesarina Bracco's narration of her Resistance life. Bracco was active in Piedmont as part of the Garibaldi Brigades, affiliated with the Communist Party. She was a member of the "Fratelli Bandiera" (Bandiera Brothers) contingent, and later of the 2nd "Biella" Brigade and the 75th "Giuseppe Boggiani Alpino" Brigade. In the post-war period, she was awarded the title of "partigiana combattente" (fighting partisan). Bracco contributed to the construction of the memory of the Resistance right from the first years after the war. Initially, she provided short, handwritten accounts of her partisan work, which were collected in the local Institute for the Study of the Resistance and are reproduced here.[71]

The three handwritten pages briefly describe the steps of her work as a partisan. She testifies to having been a member of the Resistance since its beginning in September 1943 and describes it as a personal decision: "Mi misi in contatto con i responsabili delle formazioni" (I got in touch with the partisans in charge of the brigades). Her first tasks were keeping contacts between the towns and the partisan brigades, carrying arms, and taking new recruits to the partisan refuges in the hills. In autumn 1944, because her name was by that time known to the Nazi-Fascist groups, she started spending longer periods in the mountains with the brigades. In this short account Bracco mentions being arrested twice and describes a Nazi-Fascist attack at Castel Masino and the attack that took place in Zimone, where she and her friends witnessed the killing of a partisan while they were hiding partisan materials. These episodes would be narrated in detail in her later memoir, *La staffetta garibaldina*, published in 1976.

La staffetta garibaldina is divided into nineteen stories, each focused on a particular event of Cesarina Bracco's life as a partisan and covering the period from 21 December 1943 to 15 April 1945. Her writing is filled with emotions – joy and fear – as well as humour in narrating both awkward and dramatic events, adventurous expeditions, and ingenious tricks to avoid Nazi-Fascist controls. Bracco came from a working-class family and worked in the local textile factories from

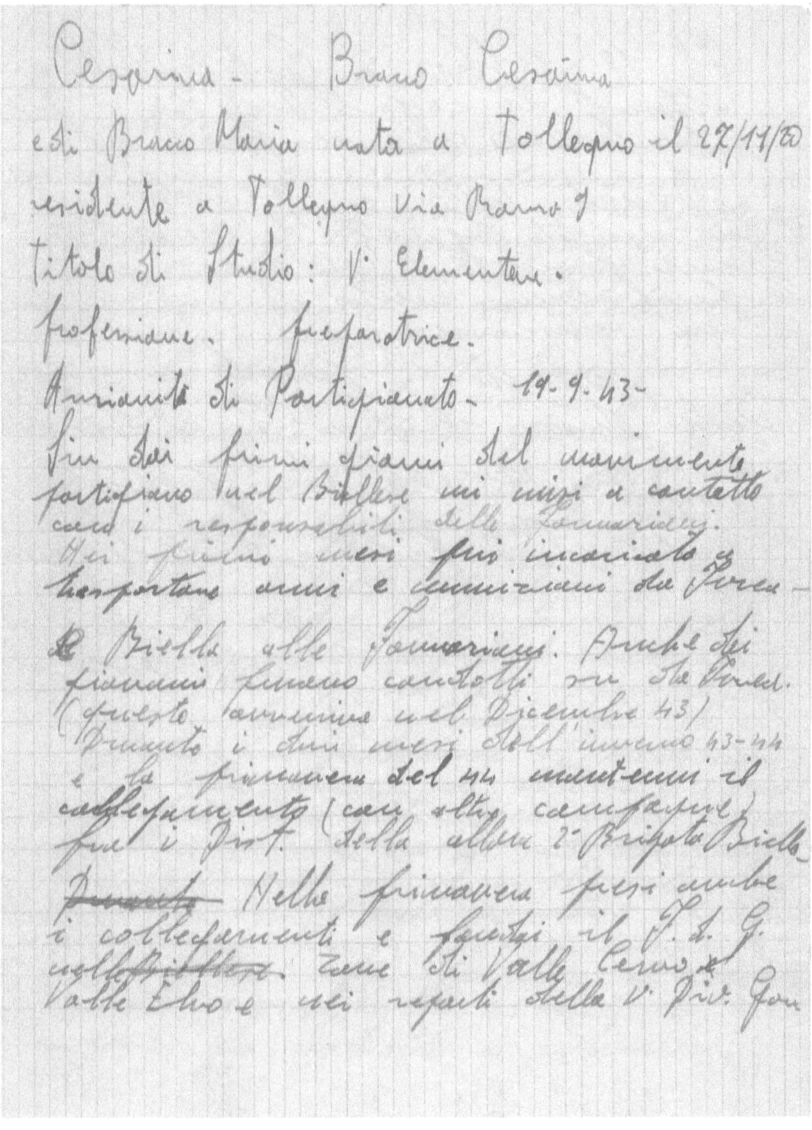

Cesarina - Bracco Cesarina
di Bracco Maria nata a Tollegno il 27/11/20
residente a Tollegno via Ramo 7
titolo di Studio: V Elementare.
professione. preparatrice.
Anzianità di Partigianato - 14-9-43-
Fin dai primi giorni del movimento
partigiano nel Biellese mi misi a contatto
coi i responsabili delle formazioni.
Nei primi mesi fui incaricata a
trasportare armi e munizioni da Biella
Biella alle formazioni. Anche dei
giornali furono condotti su da Biella.
(questo avvenne nel Dicembre 43)
Durante i due mesi dell'inverno 43-44
e la primavera del 44 mantenni il
collegamento (con altre compagne)
fra i Dist. della allora 2ª Brigata Biella
Nella primavera presi anche
i collegamenti e feci il S. d. G.
nelle zone di Valle Cervo e
Valle Elvo e nei reparti della V Div. Gar.

Figure 2.1 Page 1 of the autobiographical notes by Cesarina Bracco. Archivio dell'Istituto per la storia della Resistenza e della società contemporanea nel Biellese, nel Vercellese e in Valsesia.

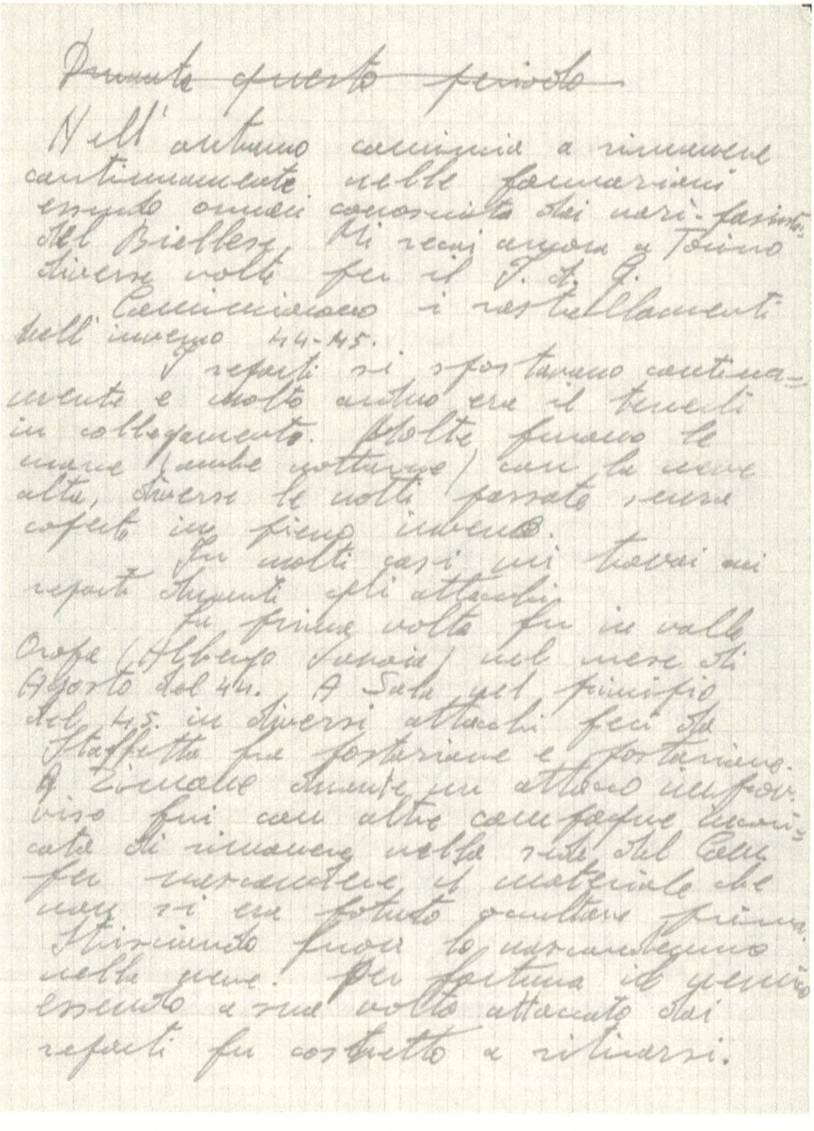

~~Durante questo periodo~~

Nell'autunno cominciai a rimanere continuamente nelle formazioni essendo ormai conosciuta dai vari fascisti del Biellese. Mi recai ancora a Torino diverse volte per il F. d. G.

Cominciarono i rastrellamenti dell'inverno 44-45.

I reparti si spostavano continuamente e molto arduo era il tenerli in collegamento. Molte furono le marce (anche notturne) con la neve alta, diverse le notti passate senza coperte in fienili umidi.

In molti casi mi trovai coi reparti durante gli attacchi.

La prima volta fu in valle Oropa (Albergo Savoia) nel mese di Agosto del 44. A Sala nel principio del 45 in diversi attacchi feci da staffetta fra postazione e postazione. A Zumaglia durante un attacco improvviso fui con altre compagne incaricata di rimanere nella sede del Comando per nascondere il materiale che non si era potuto portare prima. Strisciando fuori lo nascondemmo nella neve. Per fortuna il nemico essendo a sua volta attaccato dai reparti fu costretto a ritirarsi.

Figure 2.2 Page 2 of the autobiographical notes by Cesarina Bracco. Archivio dell'Istituto per la storia della Resistenza e della società contemporanea nel Biellese, nel Vercellese e in Valsesia.

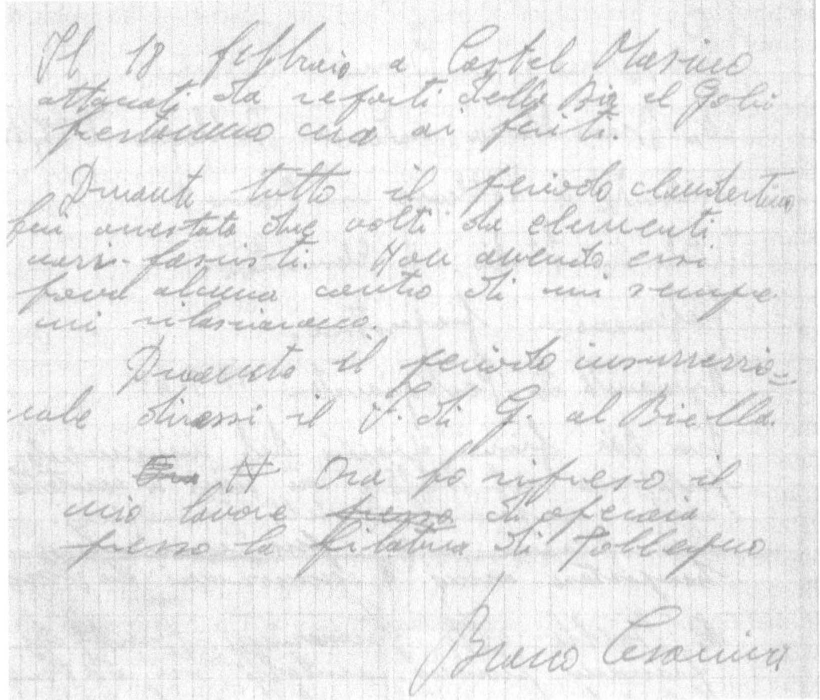
Il 18 febbraio a Castel Marino attaccati da reparti della Brig. il Gobi prestammo cura ai feriti.

Durante tutto il periodo clandestino fui arrestata due volte da elementi nazi-fascisti. Non avendo [illegible] prove alcuna contro di mi sempre mi rilasciavano.

Durante il periodo insurrezionale diressi il F. di G. al Biella.

~~Ero~~ H Ora ho ripreso il mio lavoro ~~presso~~ di operaia presso la filatura di Tollegno

Bracco Cesarina

Figure 2.3 Page 3 of the autobiographical notes by Cesarina Bracco. Archivio dell'Istituto per la storia della Resistenza e della società contemporanea nel Biellese, nel Vercellese e in Valsesia.

the age of thirteen. A shared sense of participation in the Resistance rather than heroic representation is a key element of her memoir and intertwines with her appreciation of the solidarity of the local people, especially of the lower classes. Her friends Neva, Nella, and Tina (young women partisans themselves) make regular appearances in Bracco's narration. She is keen to share with them the credit for successful and demanding partisan activities. Often in her writing, references to food underline the communal partisan experience and the local people's solidarity, as if to represent the support of an extended family and define their fight against Nazi-Fascism as ethical. Food memories are also central to the delineation of the young Bracco's agency.

In the chapter titled "La battaglia di Zimone," Cesarina and Neva, in possession of important documents of the 75th Brigade, expose themselves to the danger of being caught by Fascists in an isolated empty house and, in shock, witness the violent killing of a partisan. Fear and distress are eased by the support of a local woman who, once they escape from the house, offers them refuge: a warm camomile tea slowly dissipates the cold and anxiety that had gripped them.[72] When the two women manage to rejoin their brigade, it is for them a return to the affection of a family. The partisans are moved at seeing them safe, showing that, Bracco concludes, the partisan brigades "erano qualche cosa di più di un esercito" (were something more than an army).[73] Similarly, in the chapter "Dal castello alla stalla," the humanity and support of a farmer, who offers Cesarina, Nella, and Neva food and a straw bed in a stable, are contrasted with the inhospitable manners of a butler met in a castle at the centre of a partisan action. The generous simplicity of the lower classes is for Bracco nourishing, a symbol of human warmth and care.[74] In her memoir, their engagement in the anti-Fascist fight is framed within a narrative of morality, as the account of the first Fascist retaliation Bracco witnessed also testifies. The series of events that led to the retaliation had at its origin the strike in the textile factories of Bracco's hometown on 21 December 1943. It was one of the many strikes of that period which had women as protagonists. On this occasion too, women were striking for increased food rations and salaries. The partisans' intervention to protect the workers on strike resulted in an armed fight, with the death and injury of two members of the Nazi-Fascist group. The Fascist retaliation on the town of Tollegno was immediate and ferocious, leaving several civilians and two children shot dead in the streets. The young Bracco, who had just joined the Resistance, at that point felt her choice was indeed moral and obligated: "Di fronte a tutto questo capii che la scelta che avevo fatta, quella di lottare, era giusta e obbligatoria" (Facing all this, I understood that the choice I had made, that is to fight, was right and an obligation).[75]

Together with the representation of moral support and solidarity that food scenes help to delineate, and which is not unusual to find in partisans' accounts, Bracco's book makes use of a more personal aspect of food memory. In these circumstances, the attention is not on the ethical value of the Resistance choice but on a personal sense of elation. On several occasions, in Bracco's account and (as we will see) in Zangrandi's memoir, stories about food and taste give attention to a joyful and, at times, selfish appreciation of food. These food scenes can be considered like performances where by focusing on what would be ordinary actions in a normal situation, the authors focus on the body as a form of expression of emotions. The idea that emotions are expressed not only by speech but also by the actions of the body, as well as ceremonies and rituals, has been sustained by critics like Michel Feher, Monique Scheer, and Margrit Pernau and Imke Rajamani, who in different ways focused on how gestures and bodily actions manifest and reinforce emotions.[76] The food scenes we will examine create the memory of a lived experience, and through it the memory of the emotions experienced that shed light on the protagonists' agency. They offer a glimpse into the enthusiastic memory of the Resistance that Bravo saw as distinctive of many women's memoirs.

On one occasion, at the house of an informer, Cesarina saw a basket of white bread, a very rare delicacy at the time. Captivated by that spectacle, a "tesoro" (treasure) to her eyes, she started salivating. She was offered the bread with sausages and found the taste so irresistible that she, like her friend Nella, thought themselves capable of giving up anything to have it.[77] They were given two loaves, which, with all good intentions, they decided to take to the partisans' base. But Cesarina and her friend ended up eating it all:

> Ma cammin facendo i nostri propositi cominciarono a vacillare. Diciamo l'un l'altra: "Certo non possiamo mica accontentare tutti, abbiamo solo due pagnotte." "Sarebbe un torto darlo a due soli."
>
> (But while walking, our intentions became shaky. We said to each other: "For sure we cannot satisfy everyone, we have only two loaves." "It would be unfair to give them only to two people.")[78]

Theirs is not a justification but only a feeble pretence to give free rein to their greed. Their belated sense of guilt was finally resolved when they were told that the other partisans, on that day, had been able to eat not only bread but also chocolate. Chocolate is the subject of another story that, in Bracco's style, shows the parallel narratives of difficult militant commitments and a light-hearted attitude. Having transported two heavy bags of ammunition up to a partisans' refuge in the mountains, Cesarina and her friend were offered the unexpected treat of a bowl of hot chocolate, which they had not tasted for a long time. They emptied the first bowl and, "come i bambini piccoli" (like kids), they stretched their necks, "fissando la pentola ancora colma con goloso desiderio" (staring at the still full saucepan with greedy desire).[79] After the second bowl, the girls would have liked more. It was not possible, yet for their journey back they were given a small packet of pieces of chocolate. Again, their greediness led them to eat it to the point of developing a stomach ache.[80] On another occasion, during a long walk, Cesarina, Nella, Neva, and Liliana stopped at a restaurant. There they spent all the money they had, not only on a pasta dish and salami but also on good wine that would cheer them up and make them feel "tutte allegre" (all joyful).[81] The meal brought back their energy and their zest for their work, and they went back to their mission "ridendo e scherzando" (laughing and joking).[82]

The light-heartedness of the food scenes focusing on Bracco and her friends' personal enjoyment narrates the enthusiasm of the young women's participation in the Resistance. By including these episodes in her memoir, Bracco voices the young women's excitement for partisan life through scenes that highlight the bodily action of taste and the memory of the senses. Sensory perceptions give emphasis to the body, as Le Breton explains.[83] Colombetti widens the discussion to affectivity. In her phenomenological analysis, Colombetti maintains that the body's experience of the world is not only sensorial but affective and depends on bodily self-awareness, "such as the possibilities of action that are available to one's own body."[84] For Colombetti it is possible to incorporate objects into the bodily affective experience of the world. She uses the example of a pianist who expresses emotions in their piano playing. At that point, she asserts, the piano becomes the tool through which affectivity is expressed.[85] In a similar way, the food in the analysed scenes in Bracco's memoir relate to the protagonist's affective experience of the world that is incorporated into bodily awareness. The memory of the food-related episodes expresses how the affective experience of the world (the active participation in the Resistance) has impacted the young women, making them protagonists who claim legitimacy as embodied subjects. In Giovanna Zangrandi's memoir, emotions and the senses intertwine to give voice to a subject able to acknowledge the importance of the body and of her independent self. In both Bracco's and Zangrandi's books, the protagonist woman partisan is distinct from the self-abnegated maternal woman partisan. Their stories about food are key to perceiving, using Bravo's words, their own "vissuto corporeo, affettivo, mentale" (bodily, affective, mental lived experience).[86]

Originally from the province of Bologna, Giovanna Zangrandi, whose real name is Alma Bevilacqua, moved to Cortina d'Ampezzo in the Dolomites in 1935. The reason for the move was a teaching position, but her passion for the mountains was no secret. Unlike Bracco, who became a factory worker at thirteen and was an anti-Fascist from then on, the middle-class Zangrandi graduated from Bologna University and in 1935 became a member of the Fascist National Party.[87] In 1939 she was made female sports officer of the Fasci Femminili in Cortina d'Ampezzo.[88] Penelope Morris, examining Zangrandi's journalist writing for the Fascist press, uncovers that she was never fully supportive of the regime.[89] The ambivalence of middle-class women like Ballario (analysed in chapter 1) and Zangrandi reveals the lure of Fascism for women of their social class. The participation in competitive sport, in Zangrandi's case, and the possibility of travelling for cultural and journalistic purposes, in Ballario's case, responded to their desired activism by offering them the prospect of a false sense of freedom. Like Bracco, Zangrandi, in 1943, joined the Garibaldi Brigades. She joined the Calvi Brigade in Cortina, yet her experience in South Tyrol, on the border with Austria, was very different from Bracco's. In this area, annexed to Italy after World War I, the population largely welcomed the Nazi occupation, as they considered Germany a natural ally and their country of belonging. The Italian minority of the area was called, using Zangrandi's words, "Italiani immigrati" (Italian immigrants) and "una *razza* inferiore" (an inferior *race*).[90] Moreover, the Italian community was highly fragmented, divided into regional groups that often used regional cuisine to define their identity.[91] In this context, it is not surprising that Zangrandi's first chapter – a preface to the period of the armed Resistance, dated autumn 1942 – reverberates with social and psychological loneliness and suffering caused by the political situation. The words she uses to describe her house and herself speak of her isolation:

> ... in questa mia casa costruita per sbaglio in un mio primitivo, infantile entusiasmo per la conca stupenda, stregata. Ed ora capisco che mi ci sono ridotta come in un maso pusterese alto sulla valle e solo: le mie patate, le mie verdure conservate, una conigliera e un pollaio fecondi, scambi di merce, *il mio* stomaco, *io*.
>
> (... in this house built by mistake in my first primitive, childish enthusiasm for the wonderful, bewitched valley. And now I understand that in it I ended up becoming something like an isolated farm at high altitude in the Pusteria Valley, my potatoes, my pickled vegetables, a rabbit hutch and a productive henhouse, food exchanges, *my* stomach, *I*.)[92]

Her home is described as isolated – although it was close to the railway station – and filled with nothing else but a list of goods able to guarantee her physical sustenance. Accordingly, she is just a stomach, a metonym for a human being preoccupied with her daily survival.

In the same chapter, in her discussion with her tenant, an Italian about to leave for the Russian front, she talks about her anti-Fascist feelings, her former enrolment in the Fascist university student organization, and the war. In the first occurrence of the intertwined description of taste and emotions found in her book, their cup of tea, with no sugar, is described as "amaro con amaro" (bitter taste with a bitter taste) to stress the painful mood of their conversation.[93] They reflect on their loneliness and isolation in that area of Italy as a minority Italian group. Zangrandi also poses a fundamental reflection on nature and society. While originally attracted by the beauty of the place and by her long-lasting passion for the mountains, she must now face the cold social dimension in her town, exacerbated by the war. In the reflective mood of the opening pages, Zangrandi reports the words her mother used to say to her: "Ti accorgerai un giorno che non c'è solo la natura ... Ti accorgerai che c'è la gente e non possiamo farne a meno" (You will realize one day that there isn't only nature ... You will realize that there are people, and we cannot do without them).[94] Her participation in the Resistance and, as a consequence, her experience of new social relations and a new perception of her self will signify a transformation of her outlook on the outside world. Food images and food narratives are means through which Zangrandi discloses her perception of society and of her own emotions.

Pain, grief, and anger shape Zangrandi's partisan choice. A month after the armistice, the social dynamics in Cadore had polarized: the local people distanced themselves from the Italians and organized separate religious masses and schooling.[95] Due to this split, the regional differences that had connoted and divided Italians in the area dissolved because, Zangrandi writes, "il dolore non ha regioni" (grief does not have regions).[96] Grief and hatred become everyday elements in Zangrandi's Resistance life, but not necessarily as negative emotions. As she remarks using a food metaphor, "L'odio ... impasterà il dolore e sarà forza" (Hatred will ... knead grief and become strength).[97] The kneading metaphor is only one of several explicit connections between Zangrandi's wartime experience and the domain of food. Elsewhere, meaningful and peaceful social relationships evoke the taste of sweetness:

> Per sciogliere la rabbia ho dato una bevuta di latte, Dio, com'è buono e dolce il latte; quando mai, quando mai più avremo una terra senza odii dove ci sia da bere latte per grandi e piccoli, dove non si senta dire come lassù da noi: "Non dargliene, che le crepi il bambino, *no* a quel ranocchio di *razza* italiana."

> (To melt down my anger, I sipped some milk. My Goodness! How good and sweet milk is! When will we have again a land without hatred! When will we have a land where there is enough milk for grown-ups and children, where people won't say as they do up here: "Don't give it to her, may her baby die! *Not* to that toad of Italian *race*.")[98]

The sweetness of milk is life-saving; it soothes racist hatred and anger. Likewise, when she finds refuge at a friend's place, the sweetness of food blends with the sweetness of their conversation. Their exchange is nourishing for the hope it communicates: "Vuole che mi peli e mangi un po' delle sue patate e sono tanto morbide e tiepide, dolcemente si sciolgono in bocca, anche le nostre parole di speranza si sciolgono lente, calde" (She wants me to peel and eat some of her potatoes; and they are so soft and warm, they slowly melt in my mouth, also our words of hope melt slowly and warmly).[99]

For Zangrandi the Resistance fight is nestled in the kitchens ("annidata nelle cucine").[100] It is in this common space that partisans find respite, plan activities, and meet other partisans. It is indeed the place where food and words become significant and the place that gives visibility to the positive emotions of the partisans' sociality. In the kitchens, differences are eased, overcoming the regional subdivisions among Italians: "Con meraviglia ci troviamo ad amarci noi diversi" (With astonishment we find ourselves loving each other in our differences).[101] Being Italian, such a contested identity in that part of Northern Italy, finds a resolution in the kitchens, as she summarizes at the end of the book: "Nelle cucine … mi sento in Italia, italiana" (In the kitchens … I feel in Italy, Italian).[102]

As Marina Zancan argues, the war in Zangrandi's pages is a period of transformation, both of the self and of places.[103] Zangrandi's use of food-related metaphors confirms this point:

> Certe volte mi succede di osservare questa gente, soprattutto i mezzadri, come se io fossi affamata di qualcosa, si può essere affamati di *gente*? Per sentirsi ancora gente, una di loro e non la selvatica della Marmarole.
>
> (Sometimes I happen to observe these people, the farmers above all, as if I were hungry for something. Can we be hungry for *people*? I want to feel still like a human being, one of them and not the uncouth woman of the Marmarole.)[104]

In this passage, Zangrandi contrasts her hunger for social relationships with the animal-like status of her life in the Marmarole mountains between November 1944 and February 1945. At that time, following General Harold Alexander's puzzling order to stop the partisan war during the winter, she lived in hiding in the mountains, suffering hunger and cold. Reconstructing that period, she describes herself in harmony with the flock of sheep she is watching at Forcella Piccola in the former Galassi refuge, in fact eating as they do: "Pasturiamo io e il gregge nella mirtillaia" (We feed ourselves, the flock of sheep and I, in our pasture of blueberry bushes).[105] In the passage above, then, Zangrandi highlights her personal transformation by leaving behind her animal-like status and opening to new social relationships. In fact, in Zangrandi's book, the partisan war is a place of experience, as Zancan aptly puts it.[106] With her hunger for social relationships, Zangrandi seems to return to and revise her mother's warning in the prologue. At the beginning, she represents herself as a stomach, that is as a person at a survival stage; but at the end of her memoir, the reconstruction of her past partisan life has led her to see herself as a sociable human being, nourished by the humanity she finds in partisan kitchens.

From those social relationships developed in kitchens derives the nucleus of her idea of the Italian nation: a national identity based on a moral choice. Zangrandi offers plenty of evidence of a widespread, civilian, voluntary system supporting the Resistance, often through food sharing and food donations. As in many stories of the Resistance, Zangrandi highlights the generosity of people who decide to share with her the very little they have with dignity and affection.[107] But in addition, she delivers a nuanced class perspective. She dissects the gestures, the silent glances, and the unspoken words laden with suspicion of some bourgeois women who judge her choice to live in the mountains with male partisans, labelling her an unmarried woman of dubious morality.[108] Zangrandi confirms the ostracism suffered by women who took part in the armed Resistance. Unlike Bracco's representation, Zangrandi's book shows that women partisans were ostracized even within sympathizing sections of society.

While food metaphors structure the sense of Zangrandi's war experience, depicting a transformation from individual isolation to sociality as the basis of the concept of nation and from anger to a more reconciled idea of human relationships, the descriptions of taste reveal the protagonist's newly acquired self-awareness. Daydreaming of tasty meals is not unusual in wartime narratives. Primo Levi's narration of the obsessive food-dreaming and daydreaming of his Auschwitz inmates in *Se questo è un uomo* is a prime example of this. In *I giorni veri*, food daydreaming is occasionally a source of respite from the suffering of the present: the thought of the white bread she can taste once the war is over or dreaming of the aroma of coffee in her mother's house are thoughts that connect Zangrandi to her past and future.[109] More intriguing is the function attributed to taste in her actual experience of the war.

In April 1945, together with a friend, she gave refuge to prisoners who had escaped from concentration camps and had just arrived in the area. At the same time, the commanders of her Calvi Brigade and other partisans needed hospitality in the same house. The situation became more complicated when a Nazi group also appeared at the door demanding to stay overnight. Together with her friend, the owner of the house, Zangrandi managed to accommodate the Nazis in the kitchen while keeping the partisans hidden on the first floor and the prisoners in the barn. In the morning, at the moment of the Nazis' departure, after offering barley coffee to the Nazis and mixed coffee to the escaped prisoners, she and her friend Angela indulge in a well-deserved cup of real coffee:

> Ce l'hanno portato ieri sera, dalle razioni di lancio, dice Angela: "Svelta, ce ne beviamo due tazze, ce lo meritiamo, Cristo, prima che scendano capi e tirapiedi ... " Ci siamo trovate a berlo sedute, impettite, berlo adagio tenendo la tazzina con religione, a sorsi esperti in modo che vada per il palato e il naso: caffè vero. Dopo tanto. Poi Angela comanda: "E adesso, Anna, vai a svegliare quelle pelandre dei comandanti, tutto libero."
>
> (They delivered it to us last night, it is from the rations launched by the Allied aircraft, Angela says: "Hurry up, let's have two cups, we deserve it, for God's sake, before the commanders and the others come down ... " We drank it sitting down, upright, slowly, keeping hold of the cup devotedly, sipping with expertise so that the coffee would go through the palate and the nose: real coffee. After such a long time. Then Angela said: "And now, Anna, go and wake up those sleepyheads of the commanders, all clear.")[110]

The language of coffees – barley, mixed, and real – is revelatory of the two women's priorities, with the Nazis at the bottom of the ladder and themselves as privilege-holders. The pace of the narration slows down, zooming in on their tasting action. Only after the enjoyment of this real treat are they ready to get in touch with their partisan commander. Defiance of danger (with regard to the Nazis) and dismissal of maternal and caring stereotypes (in relation to the hidden prisoners) and of hierarchical structures (as with the partisan commanders) characterize Zangrandi's emphasis on taste. Zangrandi celebrates her independent self through references to taste. The memory of that cup of coffee illuminates the sense of personal freedom and achievement that the Resistance signified for women partisans. Zangrandi shows how the memory of taste symbolizes much more about her own experience of war.

Food memory in Zangrandi's and Bracco's books underlines the transformative function that the Resistance had on the women who actively took part in it. The memory of taste proves significant as a description of nourishment and respite but also acts as a metaphor to express a discovered independence. In the World War II context, when women's bodies were widely visible either as active protagonists or as victims, the memory of taste is a symbol of affective bodies that, as Levinas puts it, through the senses highlights the first elements of subjectivity.[111] The recurrence of food scenes in the two memoirs calls attention to the protagonists' bodies as metaphors for personal emotions. The elation of the young Bracco's participation in the Resistance and Zangrandi's courage and defiance towards the danger posed by the Nazi troops, as well as towards the partisan male hierarchy, depict the emotions of independent selves. It is an embodied sense of independence that both partisans desired to leave as a testimony of their experience of the war. A different perception of women's bodies, of women's attitudes around food and domesticity, and therefore a different perception of subjectivity is expressed in Ada Gobetti's *Diario partigiano*.

Ada Prospero Gobetti's *Diario partigiano*

An intellectual, a translator, one of the founders of the Partito d'Azione, writer of children's fiction, co-founder of the GDD, and deputy mayor of Turin in the post-war period, Ada Gobetti does not represent the average woman taking part in the Resistance. Her *Diario partigiano*, published in 1956, stands out among memorialist texts for her descriptions of the overall organization of the Piedmontese Resistance, for her political analysis of the partisan groups, including the dynamics of the newly organized women's groups, and for her insight from her managerial role in the Comitato di Liberazione Nazionale (CLN). Her involvement in the partisan war was intense. She took orders to the commanders of local brigades; in her house in Meana, in the Susa Valley, she worked with leaders of other parties to establish the local branch of the Partito d'Azione; she promoted and organized the women's group of Giustizia and libertà as independent from the GDD. Yet *Diario partigiano* is far from being a merely political account. Italo Calvino, in the introduction to the first edition, highlighted how the book was very much a narration by a fighter as well as an attentive mother. In fact, in presenting the author Ada, Calvino focused on her identity as a woman, underlining her family relationships and duties. He explained her anti-Fascist experience in the pre-war period as influenced by being the widow of anti-Fascist intellectual Piero Gobetti rather than as Ada's personal political choice. In his description of Ada's Resistance, her strength and vitality as a fighter are entwined with her laborious and pragmatic skills as a mother.[112] This type of interpretation, where political analysis and action blend with the emotions of the mother, created some difficulties in the book's reception at the time of its publication. A book review in the journal *Il Politico* opened by stating that "l'autrice è prima di tutto una madre" (the author is first of all a mother) but concluded by affirming that the book should not be considered "soltanto come il diario di una madre" (only as a diary of a mother).[113] More balanced is the review of the historian Piero Pieri, who, in the French journal *Revue d'historie de la Deuxième Guerre Mondiale*, praised Gobetti's deep humanity and empathy evident in her descriptions of dire events.[114] Underlining these qualities, Pieri synthesizes those political and personal characteristics many have noted in the book. In his introduction to the 1996 edition, Goffredo Fofi stressed Gobetti's ability to render the Resistance years through the combined narration of political, military, and familial events, suggesting that "forse quelle [cose] che nella narrazione piaceranno di più ... sono quelle familiari" (perhaps what will be more appreciated ... will be the family stories).[115] In her book on women partisans, Caroline Moorehead, discussing the activities of Ada Gobetti and her friends Bianca Guidetti Serra, Silvia Pons, and Frida Malan, on several occasions underscores Gobetti's anxiety for her son.[116] In the introduction to her 2014 translation of *Diario partigiano*, the first in English, Jomarie Alano too emphasizes Gobetti's role as a mother. For Alano, the maternal perspective is a means through which Gobetti can communicate the values of the Resistance to a wide spectrum of the female population, regardless of their political or religious beliefs.[117] The food-related stories often confirm Gobetti's maternal role. They also echo the atmosphere of Petronilla's recipe book, where women were encouraged to cook without the required basic ingredients, frequently the only option for Ada Gobetti too. However, her upper-middle-class taste for fine treats and comfort emerges as part of her reconstruction of the wartime experience. The memory and experience of food in *Diario partigiano* differ, then, from the occurrences examined in Bracco's and Zangrandi's accounts, and the representation of the woman subject's lived experience of the war seems to be dissimilar too, as we will see.

Despite the reference to a diaristic form in the title, the narration of *Diario partigiano* has a strong memorialist base. The book is the elaboration of notes taken, day after day, from 10 September 1943, the day of the Nazi occupation of Turin, until 25 April 1945. For security reasons, Gobetti wrote in a cryptic English that would have been impossible to understand if the material had fallen into the wrong hands. With Benedetto Croce's encouragement, two years after the liberation Gobetti started writing the book, which was published years later. *Diario partigiano* is therefore a memorialist account that, in a complex process of memory reconstruction, includes, as Serena Pezzini demonstrates, an interplay of voices supported by the use of different tenses to stress the present of the post-war time, the before of the pre-Resistance years, and the memory of the beginning of the Resistance from the standpoint of its end.[118] In Pezzini's reading, this combination of voices highlights the different attitudes towards the Resistance experienced by Gobetti: from a sense of renovation to the illusion of a complex, democratic change and finally to the perception of the disillusionment that would follow at the end of the war, when the hopes of a democratic revolution seemed largely unmet.[119] Her notes are not the only source in the reconstruction of events. Moments of great distress, like her son's participation in a dangerous partisan action, went unmarked in her notebook, but the sense of anguish associated with those events etched them in her memory:

> Trovo a questo punto, nelle mie note, una lacuna. L'angoscia di quei giorni fu così grande che non ebbi la forza di buttar giù neanche i soliti appunti. Ma la stessa angoscia incise ogni particolare nella mia memoria, nei miei nervi. Per cui m'è possibile oggi, a oltre quarant'anni di distanza, ripensando a quei giorni, rivisitarli ora per ora.
>
> (I find at this point a gap in my notes. My anguish of those days was so intense that I did not have the strength to jot down even the usual notes. But it was that same anguish that carved every detail in my memory, in my nerves. Therefore, today, after more than forty years, I can think back to those days and live them again hour by hour.)[120]

It is thanks to the impalpable power of emotions that, at the moment of writing, she is able to experience those days again.

The Resistance years were for Ada Gobetti a period of significant personal changes and revaluation of lifelong beliefs. She reassessed the relevance of her intellectual work, no longer the essence of her life commitment but a superfluous and even insignificant task. The dire and strenuous wartime conditions revolved around the primary daily necessities even for the skilled intellectual Gobetti, as she herself acknowledges:

> Ieri il frutto del mio lavoro intellettuale mi pareva importante e prezioso; oggi le cose che contano son quelle che servono ai bisogni fondamentali della vita, a riparar dal freddo, a salvar dalla fame.
>
> (Yesterday my intellectual work seemed to me important and precious; today what counts are the things required for the fundamental needs of life, to shelter from cold, to save from hunger.)[121]

In her reconstruction of her Resistance years, group organization, political discussion, and gestures of solidarity are often associated with the sense of aggregation given by the dinner table.

Her Turin house, via Antonio Fabro 6, becomes an organizational centre for the Partito d'Azione and the Resistance. Many partisans drop in, either for meetings or to bring information materials, or to discuss other political matters, including the planning of a cross-party women's group that would become the GDD. In the home setting, Gobetti never acts as the home carer or housewife; in fact she employs domestic help, but she is aware of the importance of communal eating as a moment of solidarity and aggregation: "Una sosta intorno a una tavola – anche poveramente imbandita – serve a placare gli animi, e a rinsaldare le amicizie" (A break around a table, even if poorly set, is useful to calm down the spirits and make friendships stronger).[122] The dinner with a group of people visiting her is an "agape fraterna" (brotherly convivium); when in a partisan hide in the woods, on a bitter and snowy day, home-made tagliatelle fill the refuge with "festoso fervore" (party energy); her cake-making is a symbol of solidarity and affection. In Petronilla's style, she defines her cake, without eggs and sugar, as more "nutritious" than "tasty," hence still performing the function of bringing serenity to the family.

The memory of pleasurable eating, even as a respite from the stressful wartime conditions, is rarely mentioned in *Diario partigiano*. When it appears in the narrative, it is briefly cited: "Pranzammo (da quanto tempo non si mangiava un risotto così succulento, condito con grasso di pecora!)" (We had lunch – it was a long time since we'd eaten such a succulent risotto, and with mutton fat!).[123] More recurrent is a sense of nostalgia for her past middle-class life. This emerges particularly on the occasion of her visit to Susa. Here Ada meets a colleague to discuss future partisan initiatives in the comfortable room of Don Rescalli, a painter-priest who soon provides tea and biscuits for the two. Relief from the fatigue she had encountered and guilty feelings and nostalgia for the beautiful things once common in her life are the emotions that materialize through her tea drinking:

> Godetti con un senso di sollievo – pur accusandomene come d'una debolezza – della sosta in quell'ambiente comodo e accogliente, dei bei mobili antichi, delle tazze di vecchia porcellana, dei cucchiaini d'argento con cui mi veniva offerto il tè. E mi dicevo intanto: Dio mio! Com'è confortevole tutto questo! Eppure ho sempre creduto di non tenerci affatto. Possibile che i miei istinti siano tanto borghesi?

(I enjoyed with relief – even though I perceived it as a weakness – the break in that comfortable and welcoming environment, the beautiful antique furniture, the old bone china cups, and the silver spoons I was offered for my tea. And I was saying to myself: Good Lord! How comfortable all this is! And yet I always thought I did not care at all about this comfort. Is it possible that my instincts are so bourgeois?)[124]

Nostalgia for what was once a comfortable daily life seizes her again during the arduous walk from Grenoble to Turin through the snowy Alps. She travelled to Grenoble together with her son Piero, her second husband, Ettore Marchesini, and four other partisans to liaise with the Allied troops and the French Resistance. A desperate thirst makes her think back to a typical Italian bar, with clinking crystal glasses, a sparkling espresso machine, and fresh soda water.[125] The harsh reality they were facing, on the contrary, meant they could only drink Nescafé mixed with snow. A pang of "nostalgia disperata" (desperate nostalgia) for what she defines as familiar things of a normal life gives us a glimpse of her bourgeois taste, which would have been difficult even to imagine in the memoirs by Zangrandi and Bracco.[126]

In a book that, despite the detailed narration and the intermingling of political and family events, tends to hide the pleasure and relief that taste can bring in moments of penury and difficulty, the occasion of Ada's arrival in their first warm environment after departing from Grenoble is noticeable. They find refuge at the house of the sister of the Corallo brothers, who were part of their group. The soup on the stove leads Ada to inhale "la fragranza con troppa delizia" (the smell with too much delight) in what seemed a "rapimento estatico" (ecstatic rapture); no food ever seemed to her "more gustoso" (tastier).[127] This description of smell and taste after the strenuous walk through the mountains is anticipated by her being recognized immediately by the homeowner as Paolo's mother. Unlike in Bracco's and Zangrandi's books, where taste evokes independence, defiance, and pride, in Gobetti's *Diario,* the comfort of food and taste is associated either with her identity as a mother or with nostalgia for middle-class ease. Her home cooking is minimal but shaped by maternal care. Her duck meat cooked to welcome her son returning from a partisan mission is memorable. It is real caring and family food, starting from the word "loca," as he used to call it as a child, which is what she writes in a note to tell him that duck meat is ready for him.[128]

Even though *Diario partigiano* stands out as a remarkable account of a woman who led an exceptional life before, during, and after the war, Ada Gobetti's narrative is underscored by traditional tones. The senses, an essential part of wartime life, especially in connection with deprivation and hunger, appear controlled and kept at bay by her identity as a mother and a bourgeois woman. The disruptive force that is coupled with the senses and that we have seen surface distinctively in Bracco and Zangrandi gives way to a measured and maternal representation of engagement with food. It is not so much the body of Ada Gobetti that is involved in the war, despite the strenuous efforts she endured, but her mind. Despite the many occasions when Ada finds herself in a group of male partisans, or on her own asking for food from people she does not know, her role as Paolo's mother protects her from the suspicious and spiteful glances that Zangrandi sustained. Her sense of nostalgia, associated with a past of comfort, reveals the desire to preserve elements of her bourgeois past.

In *Diario partigiano*, Gobetti outlines her plan to create a women's group of Giustizia e libertà that would be autonomous and independent from the Gruppi di Difesa della Donna, which was dominated by Communist women. In expressing her convictions regarding the need not to subsume women's political groups under the GDD umbrella, Gobetti reflects on the meaning that politics has for her and expresses her reluctance concerning substantial changes: "Che cosa era per me allora la politica se non fedeltà, nostalgia sentimentale e aspirazione morale, umanitaria e indistinta?" (What was politics for me, if not loyalty, sentimental nostalgia, and moral, humanitarian, universal aspiration?)[129] Her vision of politics reflects a desire to be part of a system. This memoir reconstructs the actions of a woman leader supported by accepted social norms. Capable of intellectual achievement, political initiatives, and management – an exceptional woman in many respects – she projects a female image linked to accepted roles. In Bracco's and Zangrandi's books, meaningful episodes of taste experience become bodily metaphors and intensifiers in the reconstruction of the empowerment that the partisan war brought for the two women. The memory of those moments is embedded with political power, that of women who desire to give visibility to their own embodied self and their lived experience. In her introduction to the translation *Partisan Diary*, Alano underlines how little Gobetti tells us about her personal feelings apart from her preoccupations and joy regarding the well-being of her son.[130] The priorities of Gobetti's narrative are the dynamics of the Resistance within her family and within anti-Fascist organizations. Bracco's and Zangrandi's memoirs, on the contrary, allow the study of the subject that Bravo advocated for a new form of memory of women's Resistance, one that looks at the woman subject outside the structures into which she could disappear, the family and political organizations.

Chapter Three

The Politicization of the Everyday

Sono tornata molte volte sui sentimenti che si mescolarono confusamente: grande gioia, certo, era finita la guerra. Ma anche un presagio di nostalgia per quel che stava finendo, quasi una tristezza per la normalizzazione che ci attendeva, per i desideri più tranquilli e senza tensioni alte che avrebbero ordinato la nostra vita. Che non sarebbe stata mai più straordinaria. Finiva, per noi ragazze, la trasgressione.

(Often, I thought back to the confusing mix of emotions: great joy, certainly, the war had ended, but also, an omen, a nostalgia for what was ending. Almost a sadness about the normalization that was awaiting us, about the quieter and carefree desires that would regulate our life. No longer an extraordinary life. For us girls, the age of transgression was ending.)

– Marisa Ombra, *La bella politica*

Marisa Ombra's words capture the conflicting emotions experienced in 1945 by women like her who had actively taken part in the anti-Fascist Resistance. Despite the newly acquired right to vote, for most women the post-war years were far from the daring activism so vividly portrayed in women's World War II memoirs. In fact, the post-war political and public debates, including the discussion about the Constitution, never accounted for the transformative effect the war had had on the affective lives of Italians. No consideration was given to how the experience of new relationships or living in isolation, in prison, or in the mountains had changed men's and women's perceptions of the family during the war.[1] On the contrary, the normalization of the private sphere became a determining factor in the politics of both Communist and Catholic parties. As Fiammetta Balestracci argues, the Partito Comunista Italiano (PCI) was not able to register the change in moral values that had taken place during the war and that were promoted by its women's organization, UDI, and the Women's Section of the party, from the mid-1950s in explicit contrast with the PCI's leading group.[2] Meanwhile, the Centro italiano femminile (CIF), the organization bringing together the women of the Christian Democratic Party and the Catholic associations, promoted domesticity and motherhood as the foundation of women's life.[3] As we will see in this chapter, the disillusionment of women who had taken part in the Resistance was, as a consequence of the post-war normalization, echoed by a general sense of disquiet in a larger proportion of middle-class women. Thanks to the opening of new job possibilities and emancipationist legislation, the economic situation showed the first signs of improvements that would further develop in the following decades. Yet the perceived increase in freedom and the difficulty of embracing new models of femininity sparked anxiety and discontent among women. The emotional uneasiness experienced by women in the post-war years and in the 1950s was only the preamble to the revaluation of the inner self that was to become central in the 1970s. The expression of emotions was a key tool in feminist practices to rethink politics and the female subject woman in the 1960s and 1970s. It is through the voicing of their emotions that feminists tried to influence and modify the space around them and to subvert the methods and structures of power. Emotional communities of women become political communities at this time when the personal became political. In the reconstruction of this period, literary food not only gives expression to personal emotions but is manipulated to convey the subversion of political structures at the heart of feminism. My reading of Dacia Maraini's *Il treno per Helsinki* (*The Train*) and *Mangiami pure* (*Devour Me Too*) demonstrates the echoes of feminist anti-systemic theoretical tenets that present the revaluation of the corporeal as an alternative political dimension. Through the analysis of Clara Sereni's *Casalinghitudine* (*Keeping House*) and the "relational cooking" of the Libreria delle donne di Milano (Women's Bookshop in Milan), we will see how in more recent decades the feminist kitchen intertwines with the practice of care. First, I outline how women's uneasiness grew in the 1950s.

From Transgression to Disquiet

Despite the concern about the general sense of normalization of women's roles expressed by Marisa Ombra, women pursued and gradually obtained emancipatory policies. Two significant pieces of legislation were promulgated in that decade: the 1950 law protecting women's jobs during maternity leave and the 1960 legislation on equal pay. Both were evidence of the concern around issues of women's employment. Political discussions on women's sexuality received a more hostile reception. Outdated moralistic attitudes towards women's sexuality were widespread both in Parliament and in the judiciary, as exemplified by the legislation on women's adultery. As Guido Crainz ironically observes, in 1961 the Constitutional Court defended its decision in favour of criminalizing women's adultery (and not men's), stating that it did not conflict with the principle of equal rights because it was simply a case of "a different situation to which a different legislation has been applied."[4] Further evidence of Parliament's anxiety around issues of sexuality is provided by the bill regarding the closure of state brothels, promoted by Tina Merlin. Finally approved in 1958, the Merlin law and the discussion surrounding it shed light not only on the issue of the legitimacy of state-governed prostitution but also on the double standards of prenuptial sexuality, where the virginity of the bride was in a sense supported by the legal brothels, which assured "experience" for the husbands-to-be.[5] The political environment of the period certainly did not elicit but rather repressed the transgressive feelings that Ombra, and many others like her, found so precious in her Resistance days. Family and domesticity were the lenses through which women's roles were increasingly reframed.

At social and economic levels, economists and historians refer to the 1950s as a period of intense dynamism, but its effects on women were as contradictory as they were on their role in the political arena. At the European level, the period between 1950 and 1973 has been labelled the Golden Age of European economic growth, or the Miracle Years. In the case of Italy, the economic boom is historically considered to begin in 1958, the year of significant growth. Historians of consumption have shown that it would take until well into the 1960s and the 1970s for the effects of that economic growth to be experienced in the country at large.[6] The everyday started acquiring a new value for women given that the new economic affluence and technological innovations were transforming the construction of the home environment.

Household appliances were promoted and made accessible through television and magazine advertising, as well as home and food magazines. Modernity and efficiency of housework were central in the new perception of the house, but a persistently low education level and the ever-present media portrayal of housewives and mothers in weekly magazines and women's publications created a dominant cultural discourse promoting traditional roles and modern environment.[7] Moreover, in the north and south of the country, modern appliances were not always experienced as a step towards a different lifestyle. A survey reported in a 1966 article of *Il Corriere della sera* found that in Southern and Central Italy the prime factor in the decision to buy household appliances was the confirmation of social prestige through their possession rather than their utilization. Women in the south still prioritized traditional housework over the faster technology-enhanced methods. In the north, on the other hand, refrigerators, washing machines, and dishwashers were by now an unnoticed part of the home and perceived as a way of giving women a more balanced life.[8] A process of material and cultural homogenization had begun thanks to access to modern appliances.[9] Throughout all these changes, however, the work of housewives was modified only in form, not in substance. Ready-made foods, supermarkets, and domestic appliances did not alter the fact that cooking and household management were a woman's duty. Images of impeccable houses, publicized in magazines and advertising, increased the pressure on household chores. The advertising developed by Italian and American manufacturers of key appliances, such as the refrigerator, was crucial to transmit the model of the American housewife and her modern and perfect kitchen.[10]

In terms of food consumption, we are looking at a period that, as Scarpellini aptly puts it, is the watershed in the twentieth-century trend, clearly marking a before and after, of past and new consumption habits.[11] At the beginning of the 1950s Italy was a country where food choice was not an option for many, where the reconstruction had started but the full economic development of the country was not within easy reach. In 1951 Parliament commissioned an independent investigation, the *Inchiesta parlamentare sulla miseria* (Parliamentary inquiry on deep poverty), to establish the level of poverty in the country and study opportunities for social improvement. The research focused on situations of extreme need, below the poverty level, labelled as "miseria" (deep poverty). It resulted in the bleak picture of six million people living below the poverty level. Recorded daily expenditures evidenced that while a lower-middle-class family had access to an average of 520 grams of meat, a family below the poverty level could consume only 120 grams of meat per day; the consumption of sugar in a family below the poverty level was 50 per cent lower than a middle-class family, while fruit was non-existent in the shopping baskets of the poor.[12] The investigation portrayed a country divided into a more industrialized north and a south where families were obliged to spend 62 per cent of their income to cover the cost of food, which would rarely include meat and sugar.[13]

In this lopsided national panorama, economic expansion started with the introduction of new foods. The confectionery industry was the most innovative and successful, with an increase in production that reached 12 per cent per year.[14] Crackers and industrial ice cream were introduced in 1951, while biscuits and cakes became the leading force of the industry.[15] The meat industry was transformed by the demand for the easy-to-cook veal steak, almost a symbol of the dynamism of the newly born society of the economic boom. New packaging techniques for cold meats were also introduced in this period. In 1958, Citterio distributed the first vacuum-packed cold meats, an innovation that fitted with the new ways of shopping made available to Italians: the first supermarket and the first food department of the Standa general store opened in Milan, the former in 1957 and the latter in 1958. The desire for consumption of the many new products was promoted and nurtured by the novel form of advertising provided by *Carosello*, the successful RAI show which started in 1957.

An iconic cookbook, *Il Cucchiaio d'Argento* (The Silver Spoon), still in print today, came out at this time. Originally published in 1950, it had five editions during the first decade, testifying to its popularity. Like *Il talismano della felicità*, it provided a comprehensive collection of regional recipes. *Il Cucchiaio* was authored by two multitalented women: journalist Vera Rossi Lodomez and engineer Franca Matricardi. Both were involved with the fashion industry media. Vera Rossi Lodomez regularly wrote for women's fashion magazines like *Annabella* and *Novità* and had a well-known recipe column, "Annabella in cucina" (Annabel in the kitchen), which she authored as Vera, the name that made her a recognized writer of domestic fiction. Following the success of her column, in 1955 her recipes were collected in a cookbook of the same title, equally popular. In 1953 she compiled a cookbook sponsored by the gas company Agipgas, which in the spirit of the time was titled *Far presto* (Hurry). Franca Matricardi was an athlete, one of the first female engineers in the history of the country, a partisan, and an editor of the magazine *Domus* and the Rizzoli publishing house. She did not author domestic literature apart from the collaboration with Rossi Lodomez but was clearly an expert in the dynamics of the publishing market.

The success of *Il Cucchiaio d'Argento* shows that while the consumption of meat and sugar and the processed foods deriving from them increased exponentially, traditional recipes and regional cuisine were maintained and expanded beyond local borders. They were transported into the homes of more than one and a half million internal immigrants who had moved from the south to the industrial cities of the north. As Scarpellini highlights, for this reason, ready-made meals never replaced fresh food or traditional cuisine. Rather, a "culinary dualism" emerged as dominant.[16] Behaviours changed, especially among the younger generation; in turn, they also influenced the older generations and their families.[17] Yet women were in a difficult position in the changing society. Historians have evidenced the contradictions between the transformations in daily living and the models of femininity still imposed on women in this decade.[18] Women were exhausted by double workloads, in and outside the home. They were blamed by the most conservative section of society for the changes in the younger generation. At the same time, new positions in contact with the public, such as those of hostesses and beauticians, were making them more visible.[19] Alba de Céspedes, in her novel *Quaderno proibito* (*Forbidden Notebook*), penned an enlightening and perceptive outlook on the progressive shift of sensibilities that women were experiencing in the 1950s. Her representation is helpful to understand how behind the modern transformation, a sense of disquiet was becoming apparent. This was to be a determinant for the feminist directions of the following decade.

Quaderno proibito was published first in instalments between 23 December 1950 and 9 June 1951 in the illustrated magazine *La settimana Incom illustrata* (The illustrated Incom weekly), and then it came out as a book in 1952. The novel is structured as the private diary of a woman, Valeria, who jots down her own thoughts and feelings as she notes her daily life. It is presented as a story that any woman could have written. It thus clearly depicts the society of the time. Valeria, rooted in her family values, suddenly finds herself buying an exercise book which she uses as a diary, kept private and secret from her family. Through Valeria, we see both the past, traditional, and old-fashioned world typical of the pre-war period and the changing world of the 1950s. The relationship with her daughter is significant to understand the shift between the two worlds.

Consumerism and material goods are central features of the difference between the worlds of mother and daughter. Valeria wants to invite Mirella's friends for tea; Mirella answers that now people have cocktails instead. Mirella is keen on nail varnish and fashion; Valeria is always conscious of the cost of products. They differ in their taste as much as they do in their perceptions of themselves and their roles. Mirella's values are centred on her own self; her desires and dreams are not linked to her role as daughter or future wife and mother. She has a relationship with a married man and does not think of marriage as a prospect or possibility in her life. She represents a new generation of women at the beginning of the post-war sociopolitical transformation. However, it is the character of the mother, Valeria, that better represents the 1950s as a period of changing values. She is indeed the carrier of values that belonged to the pre-war world, but in her sudden and impulsive need to pour out on paper her emotions and thoughts, she demonstrates that she has reached a turning point. She starts finding a voice above and beyond the predetermined role she has always performed in her family. In de Céspedes's intentions, Valeria represents the women she had come to know through the letters she received after the success of her novel *Dalla parte di lei* (*Her Side of the Story*). Hence, Valeria is not completely a fictional character but one who reflects the traits of the real female readership de Céspedes had inspired with her novel.[20] As Elisa Gambaro argues, the chosen format for the first publication, in instalments for a popular magazine of the time, works in synergy with the diaristic format of the novel to accentuate a correspondence between the protagonist and the readers, as the dates given in the diary precede by one or two weeks the publication dates of each instalment.[21] In fact, during the 1950s the "agony columns" of several illustrated magazines – a novelty of the time – were the venue where women writers and journalists established a dialogue with their general public of women on personal problems. In chapters 1 and 2, we analysed how columns on cooking and medical advice had made Foggia's pen popular among middle-class Italian families. At this time, the function of women's advice columns changed. The agony letters were focused not on practical problems of families' health and well-being but on women's issues and their sentimental life. They are indeed evidence that women's emotional lives had become of crucial importance to them. De Céspedes herself wrote an agony column titled "Dalla parte di lei" for the magazine *Epoca* from 1952 to 1959. The title evoked her 1949 novel, which, with the protagonist's killing of her husband, a former partisan, expressed women's disappointment with their post-war situation. The column often provided advice on marriage problems and expanded to discuss love as a broader moral problem.[22] As Penelope Morris indicates, reporting a letter from de Céspedes to Arnoldo Mondadori, her approach to the discussion of love and its problems, both in her columns and in her fiction, has always been one that links the topic to "the morality and customs of our time."[23] In fact, letters to the editor and agony columns become, in the words of historian Amalia Signorelli, a "social observatory" to study the malaise women were experiencing at the time.[24] Signorelli writes of a male "tacit pact," transversal to political parties and social classes, that promoted norms and legislation on family, sexuality, and reproduction aimed at creating unity in the country based on a restored traditional role of women.[25] Women had obtained the vote, but husbands had the right of decision-making in family matters, including children's education, and, until 1963, even had the right to check their wives' correspondence.[26] Adultery had different penal consequences for men and women; jobs like the judiciary remained inaccessible to women. In addition, as Fiamma Lussana has established, during the economic boom, one million women lost their jobs, and from the end of the 1950s, women became the main consumers of tranquillizers.[27] Their isolation as a social category was also determined by the lack of memory of women's active role during the war, which, as analysed in chapter 2, started being rediscovered only from the 1970s.

In *Quaderno*, Valeria can feel the spark of a new personal emotional dimension and a desire to value her own individual self over her family role. She falls in love with Guido, her wealthy boss, and he reciprocates. However, when she has to make the decision to leave for a short vacation with him (or indeed to leave for good with him, as he suggests), the superstructure of moral values and duties that has framed all her life does not allow her to make that resolution. She remains subsumed in her rooted values, although she can understand how unhappy her married life is and how her own self has disappeared behind her role of mother and wife. Valeria has internalized the constrictions society and legislation have imposed on her private life, as she conveys through the image of an internal prison when she explains to Guido the impossibility of their relationship: "Sbarre che non possiamo abbattere perché non sono fuori di noi, ma in noi stessi" (Prison bars that we cannot demolish because they are not external to us but are within ourselves).[28] Although she is aware of experiencing love for the first time in her life, her idea of love can be justified only within the family; otherwise it is a source of guilt ("Per me l'amore, se non è giustificato dalla famiglia, è una colpa"; For me love, if it is not justified by family, is guilt).[29] Like the girls of the Grimaldi boarding house, Valeria is aware that what she is experiencing at an emotional level is different from what is expected of her. She is, in de Céspedes's intentions, a representation of an ordinary middle-class woman of this period. She exemplifies the change in women's perceptions of their private life and their still evident inability to act on it. The younger generations, on the other hand, value disobedience. It is up to Valeria herself to ascertain what fundamental difference this implies:

> Non avevo che da affidarmi, ubbidire. A pensarci bene mi sembra che questa sia la causa dell'inquietudine di Mirella: la possibilità di non ubbidire. È ciò che ha cambiato tutto, tra padri e figli, e anche tra uomo e donna.
>
> (I did not have to choose anything else apart from trusting the others and obeying. Thinking about it, I believe this is the cause of Mirella's disquiet: the possibility of not obeying. This has changed everything, between fathers and children, and men and women.)[30]

Disobedience and the need to give public articulation to the emotions that Valeria could speak only to herself characterized feminism, the cultural shift marked by 1968, and the decades to come.

Feminism, Emotions, and Power

Economists see the early 1970s as the end of a period of prosperity. The beginning of the oil crisis in 1973 is thought of as the turning point of the growth period. From the social view, on the other hand, the end of the 1960s and the 1970s mark the beginning of a period of change, perhaps more gradual but which lasted for decades. Geoff Eley identifies in the protests and upheaval that developed in Europe between 1967 and 1974 the crucial time of passage between the post-war reconstruction period based on anti-Fascist and democratic common goals and the neo-liberalist decades that followed.[31] Unfortunately, the narrative around the 1968 protests has often neglected gender issues and devalued women's achievements in the post-war period.[32]

Anna Bravo observes how most of the "storiografia maschile" (male historians) have generally drawn a line of cause and effect between 1968 and feminism, wrongly deriving the feminist movements of the 1970s from the student revolt.[33] She makes a distinction between the subversive anti-systemic revolution of the Beat generation that became visible in Italy in the late 1950s and the more structured student revolution that started in the mid-1960s and aimed at regenerating the system and at preserving its fundamental power structures, rather than subverting them. The rejection of ideologies, hence an anti-systemic approach, was a clear point of contact between the Beat generation and feminist thought.[34] Lussana too underlines the distance between the student movement and the radical thinking of the neo-feminist groups that refused all political ideologies and preceded in time the student revolt.[35]

From the mid-1960s emancipationist policies, pursued in Parliament by women like Nilde Iotti and Adriana Seroni, and often also supported by the neo-feminist groups, were implemented. In 1963 women were finally admitted to all professions, including the career of magistrate. In the same year, job dismissal on the grounds of marriage was outlawed. In 1971 two more laws in favour of working women were promulgated: the protection of working conditions of mothers at work and the implementation of municipal kindergartens. In 1969 women's adultery was decriminalized – until then it could have led to up to two years in prison. In 1965 the divorce law started its thorny parliamentary debate, leading to its promulgation in 1970 and to its final majority approval in the 1974 referendum.[36] In 1975 the new Family Law established parents' shared responsibility in decisions over their children, putting an end to the husband's exclusive authority and introducing equality between husband and wife. During this same period, the women's movement came together as a mass political practice that, while fighting for some of the emancipatory legislation achieved in that period, transformed in a more pervasive way the consciousness and the desires of thousands of women. It laid the basis for a revolution destined to last decades.

Italian feminism of the 1970s was a phenomenon of several voices, in particular between the late 1960s and the mid-1970s. Although Carla Lonzi had already started her theorization of anti-authoritarianism in 1965, it was between 1969 and 1971 that a large number of feminist groups were born. They followed different feminist approaches, which makes the narrative about Italian feminism of the 1970s difficult to summarize. Consciousness-raising was a practice followed all over Italy by many groups that came into being in small towns and in cities. Consciousness-raising was concerned with an investigation of the inner self, inspired by American feminism, whose themes circulated widely among Italian feminists. For example, *Donna è bello*, a collection of writings on American feminism, was published in 1972 in Milan by the Gruppo Anabasi, which also practised the consciousness-raising approach.[37] This focus was very common but certainly not the only feminist approach of Italian women. Women close to the Radical Party formed the Movimento di liberazione della donna, which was particularly active around the issue of abortion. The lesbian groups Fuori! Donna and Coordinamento lesbiche italiane also formed in this period. Non-governmental self-help clinics autonomously managed by women – which offered advice on contraception, mental health, and abortion – carried out important work in making women aware of their bodies.[38] Neo-feminist radical groups like Rivolta femminile, starting from an anti-systemic stand, implemented a theorization that, in the name of a search for an authentic self, led to new concepts of politics and society. Intrinsic to the approach of neo-feminist groups was their autonomy and independence from political parties, although this did not prevent them from joining forces with political parties in specific battles, such as the divorce law and its abrogative referendums. In this sense, they were different from feminist groups in other countries.[39] Women associated with the extra-parliamentary parties constituted groups characterized by specific political goals. This was the case for Lotta femminista, founded by Mariarosa Dalla Costa, previously a member of Potere Operaio.[40]

Lotta femminista's main proposal focused on a political restructuring of the concept of labour. Present in several cities in the north and south of the country, it was particularly active in the Veneto and Emilia Romagna regions. It was originally founded in 1971 and called Lotta femminile, a name which was later modified. In 1972 Dalla Costa and other women of the group founded the International Feminist Collective with the purpose of launching their project at the international level. They collaborated with the American feminist activist Selma Jones, founder of the International Wages for Housewives campaign, and shared views with British, French, and American groups focusing on domestic work. Dalla Costa and Jones published *The Power of Women and the Subversion of the Community*. They organized conferences on the topic of domestic work in Rome, London, and France, and political materials in English and French were translated into Italian.[41] Instead of giving importance to work outside the home as a form of emancipation, Lotta femminista saw it as a form of exploitation created by the consumerist society that would simply oblige women to work both outside and inside the house. Based on Marxian premises of class exploitation, Lotta femminista took a radical anti-systemic stand by redefining the concept of class. They claimed that capitalism is principally based on the free and unpaid housework of women who procreate the workforce and allow them to take part in paid work. For Lotta femminista, the real, meaningful class struggle is between paid and unpaid workers. They therefore proposed a salary for men and women doing domestic work, which they regarded as the most universal and historic form of unpaid work.[42] This approach, they argued, would also widen the active political participation of women.[43] In their discussions, they associated the unfair treatment of those working low-paid jobs and of untenured women professors with the unfairness of unpaid domestic work. In their view, this strategy would encourage all women – as all are involved in domestic work – to take part in the fight for a *salario garantito* (minimum wage) for everyone working outside and inside the home.

The common ground of these various feminist approaches was the reconceptualization of power and an emphasis on all the aspects of women's lives that had been devalued in society. As Carmen Leccardi summarizes, feminism debated the foundations of the social order by redefining the meaning of the everyday as both a starting and arrival point in the transformation of power relationships.[44] While Lotta femminista reconceptualized the idea of labour, discussions on sexuality found their way into lesbian groups and consciousness-raising groups, and women's bodies were given new priority in self-help clinics. All these approaches converged at the importance of the private sphere, the personal, and the body. Like feminist groups all around the world, Italian feminists were making the slogan "the personal is political" their own political project that would turn the private and personal sphere into a "site of resistance," as Megan Boler puts it. Boler credits the practice of consciousness-raising as being the first articulation of the feminist politics of emotions that was collectively pursued.[45] Emotions acquired a different meaning, as they became both a tool for personal self-understanding and the foundation for the reconceptualization of power. In that bold vision to construct a society on a new basis and reshape the concept of power, we find echoes of the theorization of the philosophy of food by Heldke and Curtin, seen in my introduction. They write of the possibility "to reground [philosophy ...] in the matters of everyday life" and to look at the "marginalized aspects of life."[46] As we will see in Dacia Maraini's works, literature, through literary food, offers a crystallization of the reconceptualization of power and emotions. But first, what is the function of emotions in feminist politics?

Already in 1965 Carla Lonzi advocated the rejection of any political systems on the grounds that they are made by men for men. The manifesto of the Demau group, founded by her in 1966, sets women's autonomy as the necessary step towards the constitution of a new society. The Demau group, as Bracke underlines, anticipated and influenced the feminist debate of the 1970s in its emphasis on the search for an authentic self, sexual difference, and autonomy from party politics.[47] For neo-feminist groups the search for a truer, authentic self involved both the work on women's emotions that would allow them to become autonomous subjects and the construction of a new political system distinct from the authoritarian political structure. The establishment of new ways of doing politics and the expression of emotions were interconnected. Primo Moroni – founder of the historic bookshop Calusca, the first bookshop in Milan to make available writings of the feminist movement – and Ida Farè portray this in a conversation discussing the culture of the period. They recount that the common dynamics of women's intervention in political discussions were characterized by a woman taking the floor and declaring: "*Io mi sento male*" ("I feel unwell").[48] That expression of uneasiness represented both discomfort with a system regarded as detached from women's subjectivity and the voicing of the need to change the structure of the political debate to make the personal, affectivity, and emotions a core part of it. Using William Reddy's terminology, women's expression of malaise at that time can be defined as "emotives" – not an ordinary utterance but one that is self-explorative, because it leads the subject to think of connected aspects of their expression of emotion. Moreover, emotives "are themselves instruments for directly changing, building, hiding, intensifying emotions."[49] And therefore they influence the surrounding world. Women's expression of uneasiness was a manifestation of the effect of patriarchal power structures as much as the stimulus for its subversion.

At the beginning of the 1970s, anger against patriarchy brought women together and was a dominant emotion in consciousness-raising groups. This feminist separatist practice focused on the sharing of women's personal experiences in women-only groups, where autonomy from the male sphere and the relations among women were intended as strategies to resolve negative emotions. In similar ways to what happened in the American groups, analysed by Jasper, the transformation and resolution of anger into accepted and rational emotions was their primary goal.[50] It was, at the same time, also its limit. By focusing only on women's issues and women's relationship with patriarchy, the consciousness-raising groups predominantly discussed the aggressive relationship of men towards women and vice versa. Among the many feminist groups practising consciousness-raising from 1968 to the second half of the 1970s, the feminist groups in Milan were the most interested in developing further theoretical approaches based on the practice of relationships among women (*relazione tra donne*). It was here that a new practice was adopted to try to resolve the impasse of the consciousness-raising groups. The problem of women's unresolved emotions, in particular in relation to themselves, their mothers, and other women, motivated the psychoanalytic approach of the *gruppi dell'inconscio* (groups of the unconscious practice). Highly influenced by the French feminist group Psychanalise et Politique (Psych et po), the *pratica dell'inconscio* (practice of the unconscious) gave relevance to women's own sense of anger, as opposed to anger towards men. Even more than in the consciousness-raising groups, the expression of emotions appeared as a new and disruptive force. Women counteracted the culturally imposed management of emotions that Hochschild defined "feeling rules," that is, the shaping and control of emotional behaviour according to prescribed societal rules.[51] The same concept of women's emotional work was developed by a group working on the family at the Faculty of Political Science at the University of Milan, who coined the expression "labour of relationships" to indicate women's work to interpret, coordinate, and satisfy the emotional needs of each member of the family.[52]

The *pratica dell'inconscio* was a political choice arising from the realization that the body and sexuality are vital in the fight towards women's liberation.[53] For Italian feminists, patriarchal culture transformed institutions such as family and school into places where women, deprived of everything, would be aggressive towards other women in order to dispossess them of what they have.[54] In this light, what was felt as missing in relationships among women, and what psychoanalysis could help to achieve, was a different idea of a woman's body. A woman's contribution at a workshop during the 1975 feminist conference at Pinarella di Cervia perfectly framed the need for a revaluation of the body and affective life:

> Tutto ciò che riguarda il corpo e quindi la vita affettiva in tutti i suoi aspetti, le fantasie che ci portiamo dentro, le costrizioni a ripetere certi atteggiamenti, è stato negato e separato da tutto il resto. La politica, e la cultura sono cresciute e crescono tutt'ora su una negazione di fondo che è la negazione del corpo della donna e, a partire dal corpo, dalla sessualità, la negazione di tutti i possibili livelli di esistenza delle donne.
>
> (Everything concerning the body, and therefore the affective life in all its aspects, the fantasies that we carry with us, the constriction to repeat certain behaviours, all this has been denied and separated from all the rest. Politics and culture are born and keep on growing because of a fundamental denial, which is the cancellation of women's bodies. Starting from the body and from sexuality, this leads to the cancellation of all possible levels of women's existence.)[55]

The revaluation of the body is, then, seen as a form of political practice that aims at subverting the traditional patriarchal power relations. In this framework, food imaginaries become a tool to imagine new possibilities. Literary food gives access to a more personal dimension of the self, as we have seen in the previous chapters, but also, in literary works related to this period, it proposes food as a metonym of the body to suggest an alternative, anti-systemic approach. The work of Dacia Maraini illustrates this take on literary food particularly well. The same need for the subversion of political power structures is observable in the food discourses circulating at the time. These included alternative eating habits and a new interest in the environment that developed in two different directions: the critique of mass food production and the revaluation of local and regional cuisine. First, we will analyse how Maraini politicized food to create alternative gender structures.

Dacia Maraini and the Politicization of Food

Maraini acknowledged the importance of food-related imagination in her writing, explaining it as a memory of the starvation endured as a child in a concentration camp in Japan, where she was imprisoned with her family during World War II.[56] Later she returned to the role of this imagination for her creative process:

> Il cibo promette qualcosa che attira i nostri sensi e che non è solo puro nutrimento, ma attraverso l'incanto degli odori, dei sapori, dei colori, promette una metamorfosi magica.
>
> (Food promises something that attracts our senses and that is not only nutrition but, through the allure of smell, taste, and colours, promises a magical metamorphosis.)[57]

The senses are for Maraini "il mio strumento di conoscenza storicamente più vicino" (the means of knowledge historically closest to me). It is a gender-specific closeness, as she defines it, that highlights the importance she attributes to women's experience and to corporeality.[58] The body is for her not only "prigione" (a prison), that is a site of objectification, but something more that becomes also "un mezzo di conoscenza" (a means of knowledge).[59] In her interview with Severino Cesari, she demonstrates what she means by pointing to her successful novel *La lunga vita di Marianna Ucrìa*. Here, she says, she was influenced by David Hume, who indeed considered the senses a means of knowledge. Likewise, she is attracted by the mystics, who through body practice – starvation or breathing – exalt their body's sensibilities to feel closer to God.[60] Recreating the experience of the senses in her characters is, then, central to her work.

The analysis of food imagery in the 1978 collection of poems *Mangiami pure* (*Devour Me Too*) and in the 1984 novel *Il treno per Helsinki* (*The Train*) illustrates how Maraini narrated the power relations and the emotions that animated feminist groups, and it sheds light on the evolution of the concept of love. Food imagery allows her to emphasize the corporeal dimension and therefore to counteract the construction of the disembodied self. In her writing, she exemplifies the anti-systemic approach that we have seen as a characteristic of feminist groups. Food becomes a means to narrate the "authenticity of the gesture of protest," using Rivolta femminile's words, that is, to protest against all systems that led to the subjugation of women by rethinking the means of politics.[61] As Deane Curtin argues, considering the concept of food seriously means rejecting the dualistic thought of mind/body, self/other, and reason/emotion that has characterized Western culture.[62] Thinking of food philosophically means looking at the subject outside pre-established categories. It implies valuing the body in the construction of a subject no longer considered as the rational disembodied self of Western tradition.

The sophisticated and sustained use of food imagery in Maraini's writing analysed here gives voice to the same concerns of feminist groups of the 1970s examined in the first part of this chapter, and it allows us to revisit the inadequacy of the system-regenerating approach offered by the 1968 cultural liberation.

Mangiami pure captures the dynamics of feminist groups, from the anger and aggressiveness towards men to the rethinking of the woman subject through relationships among women. As Patrizia Guida synthesizes, it marks for Maraini the passage to the recovery of the importance of the mother figure and, at a political level, the move from the denouncement of women's oppression to "solidarietà tra donne come unica arma per sfaldare la cultura fallocentrica" (solidarity among women as the only weapon to disintegrate phallocentric culture).[63] The poem that opens the collection, "Va bene, mangiami pure," stages a conflictual relationship with a partner "amante nemico" (lover enemy), distant from the poetic subject's emotions and psychology. The dissimilarity between the two is framed by images of an unpleasant and stifling everyday life spent together, which contrasts with the poetic subject's joyful participation in women's protests. A series of food-related images narrates a poisonous everyday ("è velenoso il fungo che mi dai ogni mattina"; the mushroom that you give me every morning is poisonous), and daily drinks are transformed into noxious products for the partner ("il caffelatte che sa di cloro"; a latte that tastes of chlorine; "il vino diventerà aceto nella tua bocca gelosa"; wine is going to turn into vinegar in your jealous mouth).[64] Women's physical fights with the police during street protests are evoked with some sense of joy ("i denti allegri"; joyful teeth) and as a rejection of domestic chores ("non posso più sbucciare patate"; I can no longer peel potatoes). At the end of the poem, the violent clash with the police is represented through the women's frugal eating ("mangiamo pane e salsiccia"; we eat bread and sausages) in a conscious rejection of domesticity at a moment when they can only expect to be hit by the police.

Most striking is the cannibalistic invocation of the collection title (*Devour Me Too*) that becomes a trope in the opening poem, while cannibalistic and eating images return in other poems of the collection. Her interest in cannibalistic love seems rooted in the culture of the time. In a 1979 interview for the magazine *Fermenti*, she refers to the work of the philosopher Giulio Cogni, who in the 1960s had written on this matter, and explains that the aim of mysticism, as well as poetry, is total unification with another being. The idea of cannibalistic love can be seen in this respect as the elimination of a position that sees the other as opposed to us.[65] If the hope of reaching union is the meaning of the cannibalistic trope of her 1978 poetry collection, however, the contrasting relationship with the partner that dominates the second part of the volume, its anger and aggressiveness, suggests that the elimination of the position "del dirimpetto" (the facing position) is dictated by the awareness of its impossibility. The approval and exhortation of the female subject in the first and last verses of the poem ("Va bene, mangiami pure / ingoiami pure ti dico grazie addio"; Go on, eat me up / swallow me I thank you goodbye) can be interpreted as the impossibility of eliminating oppositions in a relationship presented as conflictual throughout the poem.

The relationships among women evoked in *Mangiami pure* are also conflictual, and as hostile and aggressive as were the relationships experienced in the consciousness-raising groups. In "Non mi dire che le donne sono buone" (Don't tell me that women are good), the convivial image of women eating together in a field turns into aggressiveness.[66] They start biting each other's necks, an image that suggests the impossibility of finding a union. In the poems of this collection, the relationship between women, however, is always recomposed in images of collaboration and solidarity. Just like in Italian feminist theorization, the relationship among women, and in particular the mother-daughter relationship, becomes central for the creation of political meaning that counteracts patriarchal structures. Both in the consciousness-raising groups and the *gruppi dell'inconscio*, the *relazione tra donne* – the relationships among women – create women's empowerment that redirects the emotions fixed on the male world and projects new meanings. In an article titled "Mater mortifera," the Demau group rephrased these objectives, highlighting the fundamental role of the relationship among women:

> Del femminismo si vede la protesta contro il maschio-padrone e non si vede il resto, che è l'essere nostro di donne insieme, la possibile liberazione del nostro corpo già iniziata, di emozioni bloccate o fissate univocamente sul mondo maschile, lotta per dare un linguaggio a questa gioia desiderante (delle donne).
>
> (Of feminism people see the protest against the authoritarian man and not the rest: our being together among women, the already begun liberation of our body, the freeing of our emotions which were blocked or aimed only at the male world, the fight to give a language to these women's desiring joy.)[67]

Maraini's poem "Demetra ritrovata" echoes these interests of Italian feminism. From the feminist groups of the 1970s to the theorization of the symbolic of the Mother in the 1990s, the relationship between mother and daughter was considered within Italian feminism the prime relationship for the revaluation of the subject woman. In "Demetra ritrovata," a reunion between mother and daughter is played out through food images. Mother and daughter are separated by the values of a consumerist society in which the daughter was trapped:

dove corri con la gola profumata	where are you running to with your perfumed throat
ad ingozzarti di bignè alla crema	to stuff yourself with profiteroles
bevendo infernali aperativi colore	drinking hellish aperitifs the colour
del sangue con le dita piene di anelli?	of blood with your ringed fingers?[68]

On the contrary, the re-found mother-daughter union is evoked through the image of natural fruit that symbolizes their heart and gender identity ("quel nocciolo di pesca che è il cuore di donna"; that peach kernel that is a woman's heart). The mother-daughter union re-establishes authenticity and discards consumerist values. It is the language of food that allows the narration of conflictual relationships and new possibilities. Food-related images, in this poem and in the rest of the collection, perform the balancing act of representing a medium of communication outside patriarchal language, albeit using language. In the 1978 *Fermenti* interview, Maraini mentions that for a woman writer, it is important to use "their" language (intended as male patriarchal language) to communicate women's culture ("usare la loro lingua per dire cose che fanno parte della nostra più arcaica tradizione culturale femminile"; use their language to say what is part of our most archaic women's cultural tradition).[69] Her manipulation of food-related language points in this direction.

In *Il treno per Helsinki* too, emotions and the relationship with the other are revisited from the woman's perspective thanks to literary food. The novel narrates, as a long flashback, the events around a group of friends in the late 1960s and their participation in the international youth festival in Helsinki. The friends' sentimental life is at the heart of the book's memory journey. Theirs is a series of unreciprocated love stories reminiscent of Shakespeare's *Midsummer Night's Dream*: "Nico è innamorato di Dida che è innamorata di Cesare che ama non riamato Ada che a sua volta ama Dida" (Nico is in love with Dida who is in love with Cesare who unrequitedly loves Ada who loves Dida).[70] The plot also reflects the story of the theatre piece that the protagonist and narrating voice, Armida, is writing. She follows a similar ill-fated sentimental trajectory as she falls in love with the elusive Miele, lives the painful experience of a miscarriage, goes through the crisis and end of her marriage, and has an unhappy love story with Miele characterized by jealousy on her side and his continuous absences. The novel is a critical revisitation of the emotions and ideals that animated the 1968 movement and their implications for the woman subject. Tommasina Gabriele, Carol Lazzaro-Weis, Grazia Sumeli Weinberg, and Alba Amoia all agree in reading the novel as a representation of the defeat of the 1968 anti-authoritarian discourses and as criticism of the underlying patriarchal structures evident in heterosexual relationships of young people of the time.[71]

As the novel is rich in descriptions of the complex web of emotions and feelings, so is it abundant in literary food. Gabriele highlights how the novel's memory theme is aptly conveyed by the comparison with soup in the opening page: "Il passato ha la consistenza di una minestra ... dalla gola alle viscere ... verso il marasma delle emozioni" (The past has the consistency of a soup ... from the throat to the guts ... towards the chaos of emotions).[72] In Maraini's suggestive image, Gabriele identifies the character's interiorization of past, present, and future: a fusion of time "that is inside the 1980s (and 1960s) protagonist" and the metaphorical visceral journey into the past that also marks the emergence of a new self.[73] Through her revisitation, Armida can finally articulate her detachment from the fascination of the patriarchal structure she was still subjected to in 1968, in spite of her conviction of being part of a movement constructing a new, free, more democratic world. Maraini creates Armida's journey as the unpacking of "il marasma di emozioni" (the chaos of emotions) of her past and as a feminist reading of the 1968 movement. In this process, at the beginning of the 1980s, Maraini shows rooted feminist tenets.

Maraini's novel makes visible Anna Bravo's distinction between anti-systemic and system-regenerating protests. As examined earlier, Bravo underlines the rejection of ideologies and of competition as typical characteristics of the Beat and feminist movements. The group of friends in *Il treno* protest the Vietnam War, engage with European discussions of peace and equality, and believe in open liaisons. Their life project seems devoted to a rethinking of all structures of society, from their sentimental life to politics. In this sense, their protest appears to be anti-systemic. Yet they also show a fascination for those schemes that they were trying to destroy. The character of Miele, despite his ideals of peace and equality and his political commitment, replicates traditional power dynamics in his position as leader, as well as trite libertinism in his love relationships. He embodies the downsides of a system-regenerating perspective, in Bravo's analysis a characteristic of the student movement. His elusiveness in his relationship with Armida, despite his reiterated commitment, provokes her emotional suffering. At the end of the novel, Armida's memory journey leads her to detach from her fascination with

Miele. In this way, Maraini captures the feminist movement's disillusionment with some of the ideals of the 1968 movement that, as she shows in Miele, replicated patriarchal schemes. The novel also makes apparent the re-vindication expressed by the Demau group in the 1974 article "Mater mortifera," that is that the primary focus of their practice was the liberation of emotions fixated on the male world and the search for a language able to express such explosive desire.[74] Food-related imagination dominates the writing in this novel, as if to underline a form of communication that departs from traditional power structures and re-evaluates the everyday and the corporeal, expressing the sense of liberation stated in the Demau article. This stylistic choice subverts the system-regenerating story of Miele and the 1968 student movement and adopts an anti-systemic language that evokes the corporeal.

The unusual name of the male character Miele, "honey" in Italian, is an evident occurrence of food-related language. The narrator herself acknowledges the oddity of the name, but the reasons for the sweetness evoked by it soon become clear: he represents the mellifluous substance in which Armida remains trapped, like an insect in honey. In fact, the narrator describes her involvement with the mysterious Miele as being caught like "una mosca nel latte" (a fly in milk).[75] A birthday cake becomes a means for Armida to understand Miele's character. On Paolo's birthday Miele brings as a present a sophisticated cake, which Armida perceives as a form of communication:

> Aspetto che [la torta] mi dica qualcosa di più su di lui. Ma la glassata bianca nasconde l'interno del dolce. E quelle violette sono così brillanti così finte non dicono la verità.
>
> (I wait for [the cake] to tell me something more about him. But the white icing hides the inside of the cake. And those violets are so vibrant because they are fake and don't tell the truth.)[76]

By looking at the cake Armida sees the characteristics that, at the end of the novel, will clearly appear as Miele's dominant qualities: a misleading appearance with the capacity to fascinate. Miele's authentic self is hidden like the inside of the cake by the white icing; his intellectual and social skills are charming tools, like the brightly coloured decorative cake violets.

Miele, with his interest in a political career and his ego-centred attitude, represents what the ideology of the time was trying to subvert: a search for power and rationality. He lives in a world of certainties ("vive in un mondo di certezze").[77] He represents, in Lacanian terms, the place of the Father, the place of rationality and knowledge. In the novel, Ada, in conversation with Armida, perfectly defines him as the son of patriarchy: "Miele che lo voglia o no fa parte di un mondo che ci ha rese prigioniere Armida il mondo dei Padri l'affascinante grandioso mondo di cui tutte siamo innamorate" (Miele, whether he wants it or not, belongs to the world that made us prisoners, Armida, the world of the Fathers, the alluring grandiose world with which we are all in love).[78] Armida will have to slip through to the position of the adoring woman in love before being able to detach from her fascination with Miele.

Contrary to the belief in open relationships publicly professed by Armida and her friends, during the whole period of her relationship with Miele, she suffers from attacks of jealousy and in fact desires a monogamous relationship with him. When the first burst of jealousy seizes her, it is again through a food-related image that Maraini expresses Armida's feelings. Jealousy is conveyed as an old-fashioned lady turning up unexpectedly for dinner: "Ma la signora è già entrata nell'ingresso. Si è seduta si è tolta il cappello e si prepara al suo primo abbondante pasto notturno." (But the lady has already entered the hall. She has sat down and taken off her hat and is getting ready for her first abundant night meal.)[79] As an unhappy woman in love, Armida is torn by emotions. When Miele is absent, she lets herself be submerged by the uncertainty and anxiety of her long wait for his phone calls. These uneasy periods of waiting are a "deliziosa pena" (delicious pain) that nourishes her ("che la nutre").[80]

The trope of cannibalistic love seen in *Mangiami pure* is echoed in *Il treno* to describe happy moments between Armida and Miele: "La delizia di mangiare e di essere mangiati predatore e preda l'uno dell'altro accaniti nel riempirsi la bocca dei pezzi più desiderati" (The pleasure of eating and being eaten, predator and prey of each other persistently filling their mouths with the biggest morsels).[81] Also Dida's obsessive love for Cesare is portrayed in terms of ingestion and indeed indigestion: "È lui che ho mangiato. E non riesco a digerirlo. Mi contrae le viscere mi strozza la gola." (It's him that I have eaten and I cannot digest him. He contracts my bowels and strangles my throat.)[82] The resolution of oppositions in the dream of uniting love given by the cannibalistic trope is short-lived in Armida and has negative effects on Dida.

In *Il treno*, food metaphors are a political tool that responds to the lack of gender equality dominating the 1968 movement. Maraini shows that love, jealousy, anxiety, and anger can be expressed and understood only through a language that evokes the embodied and disempowered feminine. The embodied and disempowered feminine is the site of emotions, Lupton summarizes, assessing the similar characteristics of food and emotions:

> Emotions, like food and eating, are commonly regarded as the preserve of the embodied self rather than the disembodied, philosophizing mind. Like food and eating practices, the emotions are traditionally linked with the feminine, the disempowered and the marginalized. The term "emotions" is associated with disorder, with being non-systematic.[83]

In *Il treno*, the embodied dimension that both food and emotions encapsulate regarding the woman narrator forms an "anti-systemic" language – using Bravo's categories – that counteracts the power structures hidden behind the "system-regenerating" attitude of Miele, that is, male leadership, rationality, and trite love relationship schemes.

In many respects, Armida's journey to self-awareness echoes the trajectory of the women's movement from the end of the 1960s to the beginning of the 1980s. At the end of the novel, Armida is detached from politics, which is still successfully practised by Miele. As we have seen, feminist groups in the early 1970s moved the discussion beyond the notion of emancipation and looked for answers outside the arena of established political parties. The representation of this detachment from politics is the key to the sophisticated use of food metaphors and alimentary imagination in the novel. They project a feminist revisitation of gender dynamics through a women's point of view that strives for an alternative political dimension, a subversion of traditional power structures.

The Food Scene

The fight against authoritarianism and the search for a more authentic self have substantial and variegated ramifications in the late 1960s and in the 1970s. Joachim Häberlen and Mark Keck-Szajbel synthesized all the drives towards change, characteristic of the late 1960s and 1970s, as a drive towards a truer self.[84] A rethinking of eating habits, also in tune with a search for authenticity, appeared as a necessary route for a world-changing way of living. The rejection of post-war industrialization and its damaging consequences appeared at this point as a must for a concrete change in living habits. In America, the 1962 publication of Rachel Carson's *Silent Spring* sparked debates on the effects of pesticides on food and health, while the successful *Diet for a Small Planet* by Frances Moore Lappé, published in 1971, argued for the first time for the social and environmental importance of vegetarianism.[85]

Macrobiotic diets and Hare Krishna food were popular among people who had interests in Asian philosophies and religions. Parallel to these new approaches to food was the development of health food shops. As Catherine Carstairs has demonstrated with her study on Canadian health stores, these enterprises modulated their response to food issues by focusing on the individual's health and expanding information on vitamins, supplements, and new types of food, rather than on collective and social responsibility and political issues.[86] Health concerns also drove the campaign for the "Mediterranean diet" in the United Kingdom, which in that period, Diego Zancani argues, ended up promoting Italian cuisine as an example of a healthy diet.[87]

In 1971 Alice Waters opened in Berkeley her restaurant Chez Panisse, which was to become internationally known for its use of organic and locally grown produce. In 1970s America, vegetarian cookbooks with a political angle were gaining visibility, and some had a women-centred and feminist agenda. *Laurel's Kitchen* (1976) by Laurel Robertson, Carol Flinders, and Bronwen Godfrey was to become a seminal vegetarian cookbook which made health-consciousness concerns and respect for nature explicit.[88] The Bloodroot Collective, which established its restaurant in 1977 in Connecticut, published the influential *Political Palate: A Feminist Vegetarian Cookbook*, enriched with a bibliography that includes feminist theories and poetry.[89] For Thanksgiving, for example, it proposes "womb-like squashes to honour Mother Earth," rather than gathering "around a carcass like the imperialist Pilgrims."[90] A different form of countercultural fight was inspired by vegetarian cookbooks like Mollie Katzen's *Moosewood Cookbook* and Anna Thomas's *The Vegetarian Epicure* that posited the pleasure of the senses as the basis of their vegetarianism and opposition to Western society.[91] In the meantime, Edward Espe Brown, with his early 1970s *Tassajara Bread Book* and *Tassajara Cooking* and his later work, gave wide exposure to the Zen Buddhist philosophy of a life in harmony with nature and humanity through vegetarian cooking.[92] In short, the period of the 1960s and 1970s in the United States, Canada, and the UK was characterized by new dynamics in food-eating habits that reflected the belief and the ideals of countercultures and that in the following decades were to become global mainstream discourse. The results, however, are debatable. In his *Appetite for Change: How the Counterculture Took on the Food Industry* (2007), Warren Belasco concludes that the radical change envisioned by the countercultures has not taken place, even though organic food products are available everywhere. The capitalistic interests that they were trying to destroy remain fundamentally untouched.[93]

In similar ways, in Italy in the 1960s and 1970s, the political demands for society's renovation generated changes in cooking and eating habits. Feminist communities took initiatives as well, and at the end of the 1970s cooking was used as a method to rethink values and redefine the subject woman, as we will see. Like in America and Canada, also in Italy, the fascination for Asian philosophies promoting a life in harmony with nature and personal happiness was gaining a foothold. Macrobiotic shops and restaurants opened at the beginning of the 1970s, like the Centro Macrobiotico Milanese (Milanese Macrobiotic Centre) – which is still in business. The restaurant business landscape consisted mainly of traditional restaurants; however, in a time of fear of adulterations and concerns about the effects of processed food and chemicals on well-being, macrobiotic cuisine found its niche of supporters. Women contributed to the codification of macrobiotic cooking. Mariarosa Sclauzero, in her *La cucina macrobiotica in Italia*, presented the principles of a macrobiotic diet in terms of its ability to facilitate life in harmony with nature and adapted it to the Italian environment by choosing local ingredients.[94] The perception of macrobiotic food was, however, commonly aligned with the "green revolution," the preoccupation with the environment shared by many at the time, as is evident from a review of Sclauzero's book titled "Ecologia in cucina" (Ecology in the kitchen).[95] Similar to a macrobiotic diet is the whole food diet promoted by Liliana Buonfino in *La cucina integrale*.[96] Based on the health benefits of natural food, it was originally inspired by the need to find a solution to her son's ill health. The growing number of *erboristerie* (herbalist shops) that opened throughout the country is testimony to a new interest in the power of medicinal herbs. Simultaneously, the preoccupation around food adulteration loomed large in mass media and found a venue of political discussion in magazines such as *Quaderni di controinformazione alimentare*, which began publication in 1976.

Concomitant with the interest in new eating habits, much media coverage was being devoted to the revaluation of regional culinary traditions. These two apparently opposite trends were, in fact, often generated by the same fear of the risks of ecological damage and food adulteration. In 1974 Luigi Veronelli and Luigi Carnacina published the four-volume cookbook *La cucina rustica regionale* (Rustic regional cuisine), which, as the title suggests, focused on simple, traditional regional cuisine. Already in 1966, Veronelli had started his valorization of local knowledge and traditions through his book with the Proustian title *Alla ricerca dei cibi perduti* (In search of lost food). Over the years, he made simple country cuisine the leitmotif of his publications and popular TV shows. In 1976 Veronelli explained his TV success, attributing the revaluation of cuisine to the impact of the green revolution and people's interest in reconnecting to the Italian peasant traditions.[97] The cultural aspects of cuisine had already gained a renewed interest in 1970. A new edition of Pellegrino Artusi's *La scienza in cucina* was published that year, but it was a more prestigious edition this time. It opened with an introduction by food historian Piero Camporesi and came out with the leading publishing house Einaudi.

A woman, a food writer, and an expert in food media had already made a major contribution to the revitalization of regional culinary traditions. In 1967 Ada Gosetti della Salda published *Le ricette regionali italiane,* still in print today after seventeen editions.[98] With a colossal number of 2,174 recipes, Gosetti della Salda created an unparalleled testimony to the cultural food history of Italian regions. After two years of research that led her to travel throughout the country four times, she produced the most detailed account of local cuisine, even reporting variations in recipes of adjacent towns. When her book was published, she was already a name in the Italian gastronomic world. With her sisters Fernanda and Mina, she had successfully directed *La cucina italiana* for thirty years, having bought the magazine from Umberto Notari at the end of the war. Gosetti della Salda wrote about regional and traditional food at a time when food innovation had modified Italian foodways. Cookbooks such as Erina Gavotti's *Menù per un anno* attempted to mediate between the advantages of mass-produced food in busy contemporary everyday life and attention to seasonal food. Her easy recipes took into account the fact that for many women cooking was, at that time, an additional job.[99] Vera, author of the popular *Annabella in cucina* and co-author of *Il Cucchiaio d'Argento,* returned to her readers with a cookbook that acknowledged the changes in women's lives and attitudes towards cooking. Her *Si fa così* (This is the way it is done) proposed a simple but detailed guide suitable even for the most inexperienced cooks or the busiest working women.[100]

Feminist groups opened restaurants and bars. These were business enterprises aimed mainly to support cultural activities (exhibitions, theatre performances, concerts, etc.) organized in the same or adjacent spaces. Teatro del guerriero opened in Bologna in 1975, Zanzibar was established in Rome in 1978, and L'uovo opened in Turin in 1979, all feminist initiatives that combined cultural activities and food enterprises. Their objective was the creation of women-only spaces dedicated to personal development and collective experience. Their food enterprises were carefully developed with an eye to the innovations of the time, with the adoption, for example, of macrobiotic cuisine. However, cuisine was never the main interest of these feminist associations.

In 1976 *La Stampa sera* investigated the approach to cooking of women belonging to or sympathizing with the feminist movement. The interviews, with well-known names such as Lea Melandri and Natalia Aspesi, revealed diets of sandwiches and salads, justified by the desire to avoid the burden of the kitchen but also by the anti-economic aspect of cooking. However, four out of five of the women interviewed were ready to embrace cooking when experienced as a pleasurable, creative activity and around the occasion of convivial meals.[101] They differentiated between cooking as a compulsory and a creative task. In a similar vein, in autobiographical accounts of the period, women's freedom and political commitment are experienced as antithetical to cooking. Clara Sereni, revisiting her life in the late 1960s and 1970s in her *Via Ripetta 155*, narrates days of very little eating and cooking.[102] Luisa Passerini interprets the rejection of the pleasure of eating, common among her late-1960s politicized friends, as part of the more general rejection of social gratification. But she also exposes a glaring contradiction when, in convivial moments, her group of friends was ready to prepare sumptuous meals of traditional food.[103] Similarly, in *Casalinghitudine* Sereni narrates the preference in the late 1960s for tasteless food of her friends, who would then greedily devour the more sophisticated food she prepared.[104]

We can say that the process of acceptance of cooking by Italian feminists started when the feminist movement as such was coming to an end. However, the values that had been the foundations of 1960s and 1970s feminism were still carried on: the critique of patriarchal powers through a language of food that emphasizes the senses and the emotions, analysed in Maraini's *Mangiami pure* and *Il treno per Helsinki*, was expressed in new forms and with a focus on the family and the wider community in Sereni's *Casalinghitudine* in the 1980s and in the feminist practice of the Libreria delle donne di Milano (Women's Bookshop in Milan) in the following decades.

The Feminist Kitchen: From Clara Sereni to Estia

Feminism debated patriarchal power structures and made the personal and the everyday the foundations of an anti-systemic way of living. From the beginning of the 1980s, these political tenets were applied to food and cooking, now deemed a resource of creative expression. *Soffiamo sulla cicoria matta* by Ilaria Rattazzi exemplifies this trend.[105] In her book, food imaginaries pose their potential for women's expression. Hers is not simply a cookbook but a dialogue providing advice to improve daily life through cooking and homemaking. A review in the magazine *Effe* remarks on the different approach to women's food writing noticeable in the 1980s. It notes that cookbooks are no longer didactic and include the authors' memories as well as recipes, as demonstrated by the autobiographical cookbook *The Alice B. Toklas Cookbook*, which was originally published in 1954 and appeared in Italian the same year as Rattazzi's book. The reviewer concludes that, as in the case of *Soffiamo sulla cicoria matta*, cookbooks show that the author no longer needs to reject homemaking activities to feel liberated.[106] The points made in this review echo the choices behind the work of Clara Sereni, who, in her autobiographical *Casalinghitudine* (1987) but also in *Passami il sale* (2002) and *Le Merendanze* (2004), skilfully manipulates literary food.

The successful *Casalinghitudine* intertwines recipes with autobiographical narration in the style of *The Alice B. Toklas Cookbook*, Sereni's source of inspiration. As Gambaro observes, however, *Casalinghitudine* is focused on autobiography more than Toklas's book.[107] Sereni's book is structured in sections that resemble that of a cookery book, starting from baby food and moving to appetizers, first courses, second courses, eggs, vegetables, desserts, and preserves. The structure does not provide a chronological order of Sereni's life but hints at the relevance of the autobiographical focus: the first section concentrates on her motherhood, and the titles of the last two sections – "dolcezze" (sweet things) and "conservare" (preserving) – shift the emphasis from the realm of food to memory and emotions. The autobiographical materials find a suitable form of narration through their association with the recipes.

In each section, autobiographical fragments of Sereni's life are preceded by a selection of recipes. The recipes, written in the present tense, list the actions required for preparation of the dishes, without any other comments, but they appear as the building blocks in the process of giving order to her life. In fact, a group of recipes normally precedes each autobiographical section, but only the dish in the last recipe becomes significant in the autobiographical narration. The group of recipes referring to the same type of food thus functions as the materialization of a chain of thoughts, where one dish leads to another and to another that evokes a memory. In addition, the sequence of cooking actions and the choice of present tense in the recipes seem to suggest a search for a psychological order that requires listing and habitual actions. It is an attempt to keep the world at bay ("il mondo tento di tenerlo a bada con piccole invenzioni") and to create roots for her own self.[108] As she writes at the conclusion, "Cerco di radicarmi in me … Così la casa si fa radice vistosa" (I try to settle within myself … In this way my home becomes a visible root).[109]

The recipes in *Casalinghitudine* interrupt the linear consequentiality of a narrative that starts from her own self, as the author explains.[110] Sereni's book inserts itself into the critical debate on women's autobiography of the 1980s,[111] when the question of gender and the feminist debates deriving from the women's movement complicated the post-structuralist discussion on the crisis of self-representation, generating specific attention to the characteristics of women's autobiography.[112] The focus on a subject defined in relation to others, fragmented narrative, and the privileging of the private self were among the most common features of a gendered approach to autobiography.[113] While literary food contributes to the construction of a non-linear gendered autobiographical account, it also shows Sereni's interest in a form of communication that exceeds and is not limited to verbal expression. This is a creative form of narration recurrent in women, as she explained:

> "Senz'altro le donne hanno maggiormente sviluppato un linguaggio extraverbale, la capacità di esprimersi, mandare messaggi, attraverso altri codici di comunicazione: l'elaborazione del cibo, l'abbigliamento o perfino l'arredamento."
>
> (Without any doubts, women have greatly developed an extra-verbal language, the ability to express themselves, send messages, through other codes of communication: the preparation of food, clothing, and even home furnishing.)[114]

The book closes with a "Content" page, reporting the titles of the various sections as if to suggest that Sereni is summarizing her life as a subject matter of a recipe book. The recipes, therefore, translate episodes of her life into the realm of food. All the recipes mentioned in the autobiographical sections, from "arrosto con cipolle" (roast with onions) to "stracciatella" (egg and chicken soup) are relevant not as food but as memory. Each symbolizes a metonymic representation of the events narrated in the autobiographical fragments. Taste and the senses have no bearing on Sereni's reconstructions, where dishes that acquire relevance in her narrative often have not even been tasted by the narrating subject. The recipes crystallize her emotions around particular events. The sections dedicated to her relationship with her father are particularly telling because their complex and troubled relationship stands out as a crucial knot in her life.

Casalinghitudine was written after the death of Clara's father. It testifies to his daughter's difficult relationship with him and her journey of reconciliation with his memory. Emilio Sereni was an established intellectual, an anti-Fascist and member of the CLN, a politician with managerial roles within the Republican government and the Communist Party, and a very widely published scholar. His enormous public and intellectual achievements were only in part appreciated by Clara, who remembers a rigid, distant, and absent father for most of her life. In *Casalinghitudine* she revisits her sense of inadequacy caused by the pressure for perfection demanded by her father and her sense of defiance towards his authority. Two memories associated with the recipes "crema di piselli" (pea soup) and "polpettone al forno" (baked meatloaf) narrate the distance between the two in adult life. Clara does not even taste the pea soup, but the emotional charge of the occasion recalled by the recipe makes it a significant episode in her life. It relates to a restaurant lunch when father and daughter meet after a period of virtually no contact. She critically judges his bourgeois manners, unknown to her in his family life, and his appreciation of expensive food and restaurants that contradicts his parsimony at home. Clara challenges his paternal authority by smoking instead of eating, but her emotions at that confusing meeting are overwhelming: "Inondavo di lacrime impotenti la zuppa di piselli e poi il petto di vitello" (I was flooding the pea soup and then the veal breast with powerless tears).[115] A younger Clara is brought to tears by her father's approval of her own recipe for meatloaf, which interrupts a long series of critical remarks by him. It was already a complex period for Clara, who suffered from undiagnosed anorexia throughout her adolescence. Not only did she reject food within her family environment, but in cooking the meatloaf she was also trying to compete with her father's high standards. All the intricate emotions engendered by the figure of her father – sense of inadequacy, defiance, desire for approval – find a resolution on the book's last page. Sereni's manipulation of literary food is determinant in the re-elaboration of her torn emotions.

Cooking implies continuous reinvention, and likewise, with her stylistic choice of an autobiographical cookbook, Sereni emphasizes her need to reinterpret her life story or parts of it. As she writes, reinventing recipes is a necessary exercise to create new flavours and not to remain fixed on the same emotions: "Le ricette solo una base per costruire ogni volta sapori nuovi, ... reinventare per non rimasticare, reinventare per non mangiarsi il cuore" (Recipes only a basis to create new flavours every time ... reinventing in order not to consume the same food, reinventing not to eat one's own heart out).[116] *Casalinghitudine* concludes with an extract from Emilio Sereni's scholarly work on the history of food in the south of Italy. The quote pays tribute to him but also shows how the integration of his food history helps her create new meanings, allowing the daughter not to remain fixed on the same emotions. The quote from her father's academic work is absorbed within her wider project to narrate using a form of communication and a subject matter that disrupts established power structures. Clara Sereni's manipulation of recipes and memory offers new alternatives to the autobiographical subject to perceive and resolve crucial knots in her life.

The narration of her relationship with her father, better than others, conveys the transformation of emotions that literary food manages to evoke, but Sereni's book is dense with the recollection and examination of relationships with family and friends. For example, in the depiction of Ada, her sister, admired for her sophistication and taste for beautiful things, the food she prepares on special occasions is interpreted as an indication of her character: "Ada, si capiva che aveva voglia di vivere, nei giorni speciali faceva la pizza napoletana e le frittelle salate di pasta lievitata" (Ada, it was clear that she was eager for life, on special days she would make Neapolitan pizza and snacks of fried leavened dough).[117] All members of her family are narrated through their food and cooking preferences, while friends and cinema colleagues are described through their rejection of food and taste. As Maria Grazia Scrimieri asserts, food, in this book as in Sereni's autobiographical works, becomes a way to express personal conflicts, her inner contradictions, and the overlapping of her various roles, as daughter, mother, politician, partner, friend, etc.[118] The concept of family – Sereni's original family, her own, and the family of her partner – is central to the narrative and to the development of the subject. Her primary focus is the revisitation of her own relationship with her family members, her father first, and her friends, partners, and other people's relatives, who constitute her own chosen family.

The autobiographical "I" is constructed in relation to a network of relationships that move around a reconsideration or reinvention of the family. This is tied to the meaning of her neologism "casalinghitudine" (keeping house). Sereni tries to renegotiate the skills of the housewife, which she sees overly expressed in her mother-in-law, but those skills (her "casalinghitudine") are also elements of her own taking care of herself. Contrary to her mother-in-law's cooking, which reveals her need to make herself indispensable to her family, Sereni's cooking is a place of comfort that has meaning for her own self.[119] In her interpretation, cooking and homemaking are creative activities rather than duties. Gabriella De Angelis summarizes the concept of "casalinghitudine" as "espressione del ruolo insostituibile delle donne nell'arrestare il degrado del mondo" (expression of the irreplaceable role women have in stopping the degradation of the world).[120] However, the world in *Casalinghitudine*

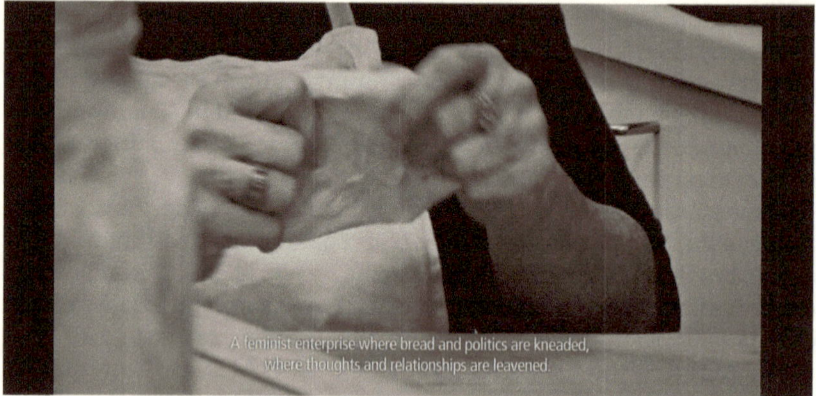

Figure 3.1 Extract from the documentary *Libreria delle donne* – a project of the Association Chiamale Storie, created in collaboration with 3DProduzioni, available on MemoMi Web TV, https://memomi.it/libreria-delle-donne. Courtesy of MemoMi 3DProduzioni.

Figure 3.2 Extract from the documentary *Libreria delle donne* – a project of the Association Chiamale Storie, created in collaboration with 3DProduzioni, available on MemoMi Web TV, https://memomi.it/libreria-delle-donne. Courtesy of MemoMi 3DProduzioni.

is represented mainly by family and close relationships. Sereni wrote an innovative form of autobiography, carrying forward the feminist slogan of the political function of the personal and giving a more complex value to the domestic dimension. Her focus is fixed on the family structure. A few decades later, the relevance of food in relation to the world outside, and not only to the family, would be further explored by the initiatives of Ida Farè at the Libreria delle donne (Women's Bookshop) in Milan.

In 1990 the Women's Bookshop in Milan, which had been founded in 1975, established the association Circolo della Rosa, a meeting and conference venue connected to the Bookshop but located on a separate site. The Circolo had a kitchen used by its members during events. Ten years later, when the Women's Bookshop had to move from its historic venue in via Dogana, the project of a venue for both the Bookshop and Circolo led to the creation of a bigger kitchen. It was at this time that a group of women cooks, named Estia after the Greek goddess of the home, came together at the Circolo. Founded by Ida Farè, the group organized dinners and cultural events and worked in synergy with the Circolo to provide catering to other event organizers.[121] Not only a catering venture, Estia defines itself as a group of political practice, showing several points of contact with the philosophy of the Diotima group of the Milan Women's Bookshop and with the practice of care.

In Greek mythology, Hestia is the goddess of the hearth and domestic life. The Milanese group described this mythological figure as the goddess who leaves the table of the gods, and hence of power and war, to live as a traveller and be close to people in need. In this sense, the group intended to replicate the anti-authoritarian spirit of the practice of care.[122] Farè refers explicitly to Letizia Paolozzi's 2013 book *Prenditi cura* (Take care) to highlight how the new millennium seems to welcome a revaluation of the concept of care. The traditional barriers between production and reproduction of the previous century are being demolished, and the practice of care is now indispensable in the public sphere in the care of human beings as well as the earth.[123] For Farè and Estia, taking care, as a woman's skill, is to be practised outside the domestic space, as an essential expertise of today's world. In the practice of cooking, care is enriched by competencies and skills that require attention to detail and the ability to solve last-minute problems.[124] The practice established by the Estia group thus also provides a form of training for what can be considered organizational skills, as well as an exploration of the self and the ethical qualities of care. In this sense, the concept of care developed by the group resonates with the analysis of sociologist Grazia Colombo, who interprets the work of care not only as an emotional and physical task but also as an organizational one.[125] Moreover, Estia is grounded on a concept of "relational cooking" that defines its structures and objectives. The group gives preference to recipes that deal with the life experience of the cooks and considers communal cooking an opportunity to share political and personal views beyond the action of cooking.[126] Cooking and eating are thought of as relational and social activities.

The group's objectives echo the notions of the practice of care explored by Italian philosophers other than the ones explicitly mentioned by Farè. Elena Pulcini, who has worked very extensively on the practice of care, highlighted that the work of care often implies going beyond the family structure and becoming aware of our own personal limits and needs, which, in a circular structure of reciprocity, become visible in others.[127] Luisa Muraro proposes the term "contiguity" – modifying Donald Winnicott's concept of continuity – to indicate the ability of the carer to empathize and welcome the other without losing their own personal identity.[128] The Estia project reaffirms many of these points related to the theorization of the practice of care, emphasizing the relational role of their practice that places individual women as both subjects and objects of care.

Contrary to what happens in a typical professional kitchen or in a traditional domestic space, the group does not attribute authority to one single individual recognized for her experience or skills. Rather, authority circulates in the group, constantly regenerated by its members through the relationship among them.[129] The objectives of the group are political, as they aim to redefine concepts of authority, relationships among women and with the external world, and self-knowledge:

> Per noi è una pratica che abbiamo definito politica perché contiene tante cose: piacere, conoscenza, relazione tra donne uomini e bambini, spirito di servizio, cura e consolazione, benessere che si espande e diventa progetto nella realizzazione delle feste.
>
> (For us it is a practice that we have defined as political because it contains many things: pleasure, knowledge, relationships among women, men, and children, an attitude to duty, care, and comfort, and well-being that enlarges and becomes a project with our party planning.)[130]

Similarities with the feminist approach of the Milan Women's Bookshop are apparent; first, in the concept of a practice established on women's relationships, as well as the relevance of women's knowledge as the basis of the practice. Although creativity is unequivocally present in their narratives, the cooks often refer to the cooking of the past and of their mothers. It is not surprising, then, that the Estia group organized a series of seminars with the philosopher of the symbolic of the Mother, Luisa Muraro.[131]

In the Estia group, cooking is also a vehicle to transform emotions. The group was born as an act of resilience after the bereavement founder Farè experienced for the loss of her son.[132] Empathy is primary in the practice of care and central to the objectives of the group. Discussions, disagreement, and bonding are part of the circulation of emotions that the relational cooking of the Estia group promotes. Despite these dynamics, the group is not an entity separated from the intellectual work carried out in the Bookshop. Stefania Giannotti co-planned the construction of the kitchen in the new venue, developing a space that communicates both with the area of the actual bookshop and with the area where the seminars are held.[133] The practice of relational cooking is thus intended also in relation to the more extended group of people who work and interact with the Bookshop.

We have seen how the mobilization of emotions was a political practice through which, in the 1970s, women expressed their uneasiness with the power structure of standard politics. In women's groups, the expression of emotions continued to be a means by which women gave voice to a new way of revisiting power relations. The manifestation of anger in the consciousness-raising groups and the analysis of blocked emotions in the *gruppi dell'inconscio* were part of the political, anti-systemic function of the women's movement. Likewise, decades later, the Estia group politicized the personal, the practice of care, and emotions through the everyday experience of cooking. The emotions Estia dealt with are different from the ones expressed in the early feminist groups; the gender contraposition and the anger that we have seen expressed in Maraini's poetry, in the cannibalistic image of the incorporation of the Other, no longer exist. In her analysis of emotions in society, Arlie Hochschild defined emotion management as the shaping of emotions dictated by the dominant culture.[134] In this perspective, the anti-systemic approach of feminism as a movement has liberated the political function of emotions. Feminism as a social movement mobilized counter-emotions, disrupting the expectations of managed emotions. As we see in Maraini's *Il treno*, literary food represents a language to express the disempowered feminine and contrast the unequal concept of politics typical of the 1968 student movement. With the waning of the feminist movement, from the 1980s, food acquired a more prominent function in the political expression of women's emotions. Clara Sereni evidences it in her choice of self-narrative, while the Estia group realizes a practice of care that carries forward feminist values in recent times. Relational cooking, with its interplay of pleasure, knowledge, and relationships among the group members, has created an experience of care valid for the group and the outside world. In the next chapter, we will see how migration and post-colonialism have re-addressed the concepts of food and emotions in relation to the global world.

Chapter Four

The Third Millennium: Food as Relationships

In the new millennium, food has become a fundamental element in the construction of "lifestyle" discourses. The pleasure of sociable eating, as well as chefs' authority and life success, are now an inextricable part of contemporary international media food discourses.[1] The increased prominence of food discourses has gone hand in hand with the change of its protagonists. Male professional chefs have eclipsed the centuries of women's work in the kitchen. Through what has been defined as the "masculine practice," male chefs have transformed the kitchen into a sphere of leisure and lifestyle rather than labour.[2] On TV the change from the traditional cookery programs presented by women to the new trend of male celebrity chefs has been similar in many countries. British food programs shifted from the skilful precision of Delia Smith to the more pleasure-seeking shows of Jamie Oliver.[3] In the United States, as Gwen Hyman vividly summarizes, new American chefs have won their mediatic space through the emphasis on male competition, rough and tough work in "a cowboy-boots-and-blue-jeans kind of way."[4] Italy followed this general trend.

While the presence of women celebrity chefs remains very limited on Italian national television, as on food networks, the most popular TV programs are presented by women, such as Antonella Clerici and Benedetta Parodi, who are not professional chefs.[5] Italian versions of international programs such as *Masterchef Italia* and *Hell's Kitchen* and the wide range of offers on food channels are distant from the kitchen-based, family-oriented formula of Clerici's and Parodi's programs. Successful lives, career changes, knowledge, experience, and authority are the ingredients of the television programs conducted by male chefs. The limited presence of women chefs does not counterbalance the dichotomy between the more domesticated sphere of the daytime kitchen-based programs led by competent but not "expert" women presenters and the fast-paced programs that often aim at taking the audience out of their home kitchen, allowing them to pursue their dreams of sharing male celebrity chefs' successful lives.

The pleasure of conviviality and the anxiety of competition are reiterated during prime-time programs with celebrity chefs. Likewise, emotions are vivid in the social media activities of individuals and food groups, who create, share, and discuss recipes and food topics. Representations of bodies and food on social media could be considered political gestures, as exemplifications of embodiment and embodied practices, but, as Deborah Lupton argues, they often re-enact binary oppositions (male/female, excess/control, civility/incivility, etc.). Moreover, the sense of agency, a typical potential of digital media, generates "intensively visceral affects," as affects are powered and multiplied by the vitalities of the media.[6] In short, social and digital media tend to be more expressive of emotions than of political attempts to disrupt binary gender oppositions. The connectedness typical of social media and the lifestyle-seeking TV cookery programs seem to be more proactive in stirring emotions than in proposing alternative and more balanced gender relationships.

In his eloquent article on the interconnected relevance of food and writing, Terry Eagleton, comparing the two, stated, "Food looks like an object but is actually a relationship, and the same is true of literary works."[7] If food can be considered a relationship, a tool that facilitates communication among people, and also a form of individual and collective communication, cookery programs that encourage respect for male authority, or digital media that facilitate narcissistic attitudes and raw expressions of affect, do not fall into this categorization. However, Eagleton's observation is apt to summarize the period from the 1990s to the present time, characterized by mass migration and consequent new relationships and interactions of human beings, affect, and material culture. Ethnic cuisines and ingredients have become more easily available. Mass migration has also engendered an array of reactions: racist anger and fear, but also hope and connectedness. Literature has been responsive to all these changes, investigating and representing the complexity of new relationships, often through the manipulation of food-related imaginaries. As we will see in this chapter, literary food strengthens the parallelism between food and writing in Eagleton's definition. Literary food in the work of Igiaba Scego calls for society's acceptance of Italian Blackness and in the translingual and transnational writing by Laila Wadia and Laura Pariani proposes hope for mended interracial relationships and intercultural subjectivities. On the contrary, at the social level, the increased presence of ethnic food enterprises in Italy has often been the catalyst of racist attacks and contrasting relationships.

Beyond Aestheticization: Racism and Traditions

As was the case with Italian food in the first immigration to the United States, or with the opening of the first Indian restaurants in Britain, in multicultural Italy the cuisine of immigrant communities has also been subjected to racial attacks. Racial boundaries are more commonly interpreted as the physical demarcation of spaces. They can be perceived, as in city areas with a high multiethnic and low-income presence, as off-limits areas for middle-class white citizens of the same city. However, the construction of a different, racially identified Other takes place through smell and taste as well. In his analysis of food and multiculturalism in East London, Alex Rhys-Taylor points out that the concept of race is discursively and visually constructed, but "racism takes on particularly visceral, dangerously invisible manifestations through its investment in the other senses."[8] Italy offers further evidence of this perspective. The presence of ethnic food enterprises in Italy has significantly increased. From 2010 to 2014 the number of foreign food entrepreneurs increased by 43.3 per cent, with the Chinese and Egyptian communities being the most represented.[9] This happens in the context of a continual expansion in immigrant entrepreneurship which, according to research of the Fondazione Leone Moressa, has increased by 31.6 per cent from 2011 to 2021.[10] As often happens in stories of immigration, new tastes are introduced and adjusted, praised by some and demonized by others, and can lead to racist attacks. Race is also constructed through taste and smell: nothing illustrates it better than the case of the kebab shops in Bergamo City. In 2008, there and in other cities in the north of Italy, the local government banned such food enterprises from historic city areas (the "anti-kebab legislation").[11] In these cases, a feeling of local and national identity rooted in the spatiality of the city's historic centre overflowed from the perception of geographic space and constructed boundaries based on gastronomic taste, the senses, and emotions.

In Italy, polarized discourses of immigration are supported by government parties and not only by extra-parliamentary groups, as in East London, studied by Rhys-Taylor. Local centre-right-wing governments have been accused of being ready to implement initiatives aimed at restricting the development of ethnic food enterprises. Their anti-kebab legislation is seen as a means to introduce anti-immigration measures, at the core of their politics. As seen in their 2010 slogan "sì alla polenta, no al couscous" (yes to polenta, no to couscous), right-wing leaders continue to make sustained use of references to national and local foods, particularly in social media. Giorgia Meloni, as leader of Fratelli d'Italia, and Matteo Salvini, as leader of Lega Nord, regularly posted selfies with gastro-nationalistic themes on their social media accounts. Seen while eating, cooking, or admiring local specialities, they present themselves as nationalists.[12] The protectionist message supported by national parties inevitably interconnects with the racist dynamics about kebab shops in city streets through a dual movement from the micro to the macro level, and vice versa. Emotions at the social level, as James Jasper highlights, can create a structure able to explain how individual and national levels connect.[13] Rage and anger are stirred at local and micro levels, then stimulated, echoed, and legitimized at the political and macro levels by the symbolic use the politicians make of food images and by local legislation. Hence, emotions can be reflected back to the micro level in a continuous exchange. Hate, Ahmed argues, is not limited to a single action but is distributed through a series of signs and bodies. It puts in "circulation" affects which determine that bodies that are labelled as hateful acquire the character of the negative.[14] The anti-kebab legislation reinforced the circulation of hate that contributes to the antagonistic relation to the Other.

However, as scholars of many disciplines have proved, immigrants have traditionally had a key role in the introduction and development of new tastes and new economies in the countries where they made their homes.[15] Italian American cuisine originated from the hybridization of the various regional food traditions that immigrants coming from different parts of Italy learned to use, once they encountered those Italian flavours in nineteenth-century America.[16] In this way, through transformations and adjustments, dishes not existing in Italy and the "red sauce cuisine" inspired by the flavours of the south of Italy became, as Simone Cinotto highlights, the first globally recognized Italian cuisine.[17] This process of modifications and adaptation is typical of several other cuisines in America, as Donna Gabaccia illustrates. The expansion of kebab shops, as well as the adjustment and modifications of the taste of the Italian clientele, seems to confirm that eating practices "originate in a paradoxical, and perhaps universal, tension between a preference for the culinary familiar and the equally human pursuit of pleasure in the form of culinary novelty, creativity, and variety."[18] In Italy, gastronomic hate discourses are counterbalanced by success stories (of adjustment and modification), such as that of the first industry of kebab meat, established in Vigevano in 2009. Owned by two Turkish families, and with trade in the whole north of Italy, the company decided to respond to the preferences of the Italian clientele by no longer using sheep meat, required in the Turkish tradition.[19]

The modification of the Italian foodscape of the third millennium is concomitant with the change of status of Italian cuisine in the world.

In the most recent decades, Italian food has transformed from a cuisine associated with lower-class Italian immigrants to an image of a lifestyle desired by upper classes all around the world.[20] Connoisseurs' knowledge of local and regional products and dishes, which are themselves a mark of "authenticity," contribute to creating this sense of class differentiation. Arjun Appadurai defines authenticity as a criterion that emerges only at the moments of significant changes in the objects whose authenticity we intend to measure.[21] The threat to authentic Italian food is to be related not to the arrival of new flavours and cuisines to the country but to the endangering of local products caused by multinational food companies. The Slow Food movement was founded in 1986 as a reaction to the opening of the first Italian McDonald's near the Spanish Steps in Rome, that is, at the time when the authenticity of local food was threatened by the burgeoning market for mass-produced food. Alison Leitch noted that this was also when new safety requirements were made compulsory by the European Union. They threatened the existence of artisanal products specific to some localities, and Slow Food perfectly interpreted those discussions on "endangered foods."[22] Slow Food and its associated enterprises are merely the most noticeable actors in the recovery of local traditions and sustainable agriculture. A radical approach is taken by independent associations of citizens, such as Genuino clandestino and Campi aperti, who oppose the neoliberal structure of the food economy, privileging biological agriculture, direct sales from producers to consumers, and traditional agriculture while rejecting EU legislation.[23] They criticize movements like Slow Food as profit-based structures, part of the neoliberal, mass food system that they are criticizing. All these movements interested in attributing new values to traditional agriculture and food are politically different from the groups that support local food in opposition to the ethnic cuisine of migrant communities. Rather than defending specific local identities, the independent food associations of citizens are interested in rediscovering local agriculture. They enact the hope for a reshaped society that moves away from a globalized, neoliberal food economy to rediscover agricultural and cooking specificities. They seem to promote what can be defined, using Jasper's analysis of social movements, as a "moral vision or ideology which suggests that the world should be different from what it is."[24] They are therefore distinct from gastro-nationalistic overtones.

From this overview, it is possible to appreciate how the contemporary Italian foodscape is alive with strong positionalities that focus on the local and the national on one side and on openness to ethnic cuisine and new flavours on the other. The literature of this period offers a window into how food imagery helps make sense of Italy's new multicultural society and configure forms of multiculturalism. As we will see, the critique of racist attitudes in contemporary society, as well as the representation of the complexity that invests the diasporic subject, materializes through the emphasis on food and taste. I contend that in the work of women writers, the approach to narratives of migration and postcoloniality through literary food accentuates ethical discussions by emphasizing the emotions needed for intercultural communication and responsibility. In their writing, the body is the unnegotiable element to express indignation, care, nostalgia, and compassion. Ian Chambers and Lidia Curti, analysing migrant literature in Italy, define writing itself as a "home," because the stories narrated piece together the migrant writers' fragmented identity.[25] It is a multicultural home where, as Tahar Lamri observes, identities can meet and build bridges.[26] Literary food is part of the structure of these bridges.

Food and Multiculturalism in Migrant Writing

In migrant literature, the trope of food expresses an array of emotions attached to the experiences of bodies across countries and continents: fear of unknown cultures and anger but also solidarity, compassion, and nostalgia. It is recurrent in novels that do not make the alimentary topic central in their story, for example, Amara Lakhous's successful *Scontro di civiltà per un ascensore in Piazza Vittorio* (*Clash of Civilization Over an Elevator in Piazza Vittorio*).[27] In this novel, the Iranian Parviz's dislike for pizza becomes an expression of his lack of integration and resentment as a refugee whose appeal has been rejected by the Italian authorities. Parviz can experience happiness and joy only when he is absorbed in the cooking of Iranian dishes.[28] The undocumented Peruvian Maria Cristina suffers from eating disorders. In contrast, the daily consumption of a typical Italian breakfast of cappuccino and croissant – together with reading the national newspaper *Corriere della sera* – marks the integration of the much-loved but mysterious Algerian Ahmed/Amedeo. Through these food-related characterizations, Lakhous depicts the immigrants' suffering and fear and an unsuccessful concept of assimilation through Amedeo's misleading integration.

The complexity of diasporic subjectivity is illuminated in Tahar Lamri's short story "Il caffè" by the representation of the protagonist's pleasure in devouring traditional Algerian dishes and drinking Italian espresso.[29] In Lamri's story, the protagonist's journey back to Algiers, after twenty years, turns into joyous, avid eating without restraint, a rediscovery of the senses. But his acquired taste for bitter coffee, so different from that of the sweet Algerian tradition, suddenly transpires and needs to be affirmed as an unnegotiable essential.[30] It is a new habit that leads to his mother's rejection of him, as, by now, he appears to her at a sidereal distance from their family traditions. The protagonist's consequent despair and his restated preference for bitter coffee materialize the complexity of diasporic subjectivity. Never fully part of the destination country, as the protagonist's voracious rediscovery of traditional flavours demonstrates, the diasporic subject has acquired tastes of the destination country that substitute some of his past traditional habits. Lamri's short story reveals that taste and instincts voice the complex identity development of the subject living between two cultures. The body is the protagonist of the perception process of the diasporic subject. It is through the instinctual reactions of taste that the main character perceives and understands his subjectivity.

The food-related scenes recurring in the narration of migration and postcoloniality are not only colourful embellishments or occasions for humorous vignettes. In the narratives mentioned above, as well as in the works by women writers that we will examine more closely, literary food illuminates diasporic identities, multiculturalism, and racism. The powerful images of diasporic or postcolonial subjects devouring, disliking, or appreciating foods of the countries of origin or destination draw the reader into the narrative by materializing the migrants' experiences and by making the Other's experience familiar. The emotional turmoil associated with these representations of diasporic or postcolonial experience – anxiety, rejection of assimilation, anger, and nostalgia – becomes lucidly evident through the evocation of the senses. Literary food converts into a powerful tool to discuss the complexities of multiculturalism and, through the narratives by women writers, a way to propose new future possibilities.

Since the 1990s, women writers have widely contributed to raising awareness of the Italian colonial past, the struggles of the modern multicultural society, and the complexity of diasporic feelings. Those who have dealt with these topics have been vocal and numerous.[31] In their work too, literary food often mediates diasporic and migrant experiences. In 2014 the literary prize Lingua Madre, a project of the Piedmont region and the International Book Fair in Turin, published a collection of twenty-five short stories by migrant women titled *Il sapore del cibo e delle parole* (The taste of food and words). With this book, the editors accentuate the function of food in the lives of migrant women, who are carers and feeders and able to establish new relationships through cooking and food knowledge transmission.[32] The short stories collected in the volume are a testimony of the intercultural function of food within migration cultures. The writing, however, seems constrained by the commissioned nature of the project. Other works by women writers seem to better illuminate the diasporic and postcolonial subjects' complexities.

In her short story "Salsicce" (Sausages), Igiaba Scego uses the alimentary trope to discuss race and citizenship. The short story marks the beginning of Scego's flourishing career, which has firmly posed her among the most influential figures in the debate of Italy's postcolonial past. Indian-born author Laila Wadia has made literary food central to her writing and concerns about multicultural experiences. Equally, the transnational writing by Laura Pariani speaks of an intergenerational communication that, from a marginal, liminal position, projects a new anti-imperialist dimension. I analyse the writing by Wadia, Pariani, and Scego to discuss how through literary food they criticize Italian society and propose a reconsideration of intercultural dynamics based on interdependence. In each of them, different concerns about modern multicultural society become evident. Theirs is a polyphonic dialogue with a political anti-hegemonic message grounded in principles of relationality and cooperation. Taste, in the case of Wadia, allows representations of openness to alterity and in both Wadia and Pariani is associated with an ethical approach to relationships, which are also intended as intergenerational and transnational. Care and responsibility, and all the emotions connected to them, emerge in the works of all three authors: the protagonist of Scego's story experiences fear for the destiny of Black immigrants without Italian citizenship; the compassion of Pariani's narrator-protagonist delineates a story of colonial reparation, while Wadia's work exudes hope for intercultural communication. In works by all three, taste, through literary food and the emotions with it, plays an active part in the development of the protagonists' understanding of interracial or postcolonial relationships. In line with neuroscience research which shows that mental status is always embodied, these authors represent the understanding of the complexity of the experience of migration as an embodied process. First, I consider how Scego turns the humble sausage into a discussion of racism, responsibility, and identity.

The Politics of Taste: Embodied Racial Anxiety and the Taste for Mediation in Scego and Wadia

In 2003, Scego's "Salsicce" won the Eks & Tra Prize for migrant writers. It was her first publication and a first recognition for her in the same year that she published *La nomade che amava Alfred Hitchcock*. The short story was successful and reprinted in the 2005 anthology *Pecore nere*, authored by four women: Gabriella Kuruvilla, Ingy Mubiayi, Laila Wadia, and

Scego herself.[33] Scego's beautifully constructed story gives voice to the uneasiness of the Black Italian protagonist in a country where racist attacks and racist attitudes are more widespread than the country cares to believe. The trigger for the protagonist's identity crisis is the news of the latest legislation on immigration, which required fingerprint records for everyone on visa permits. On the spur of the moment she buys a kilo of sausages and tries to cook and eat them. Her purchasing of the sausages provides a gesture that enacts and materializes her inner turmoil and allows a light-hearted touch in the complex discussion of racism. The story of the sausages frames the narration of the protagonist's confusion, her search for identity, and criticism of Italian society.

Pork is a forbidden food for the Muslim protagonist but also a common dish in the Italian tradition. The sausages symbolize, therefore, the protagonist's composite identity by showing that the multiple aspects of her self cannot be simply assembled. Similarly to Lamri's short story, Scego shows that some elements of our identity are instinctually unnegotiable. In the protagonists of both stories, the body, with the senses, participates in the delineation of identity. In Scego's short story too, the perception of the protagonist's sense of self appears formed through a negotiation of rational and instinctual elements. Unlike Lamri though, Scego discusses racial discrimination, rather than only the complexity of diasporic identity, and describes Italian culture, habits, and institutions. As Sandra Ponzanesi states, the writing of an author like Scego is counter-hegemonic, and not involving only the author's personal relationship to a former colony, Somalia in Scego's case: "It is more than a simple talking back, but it implies the operation of transformation and contamination that affects the different agents, organizations, and ideas involved."[34]

In "Salsicce," the protagonist's display of her Italianness is linguistic, thanks to her use of the Roman dialect from the first page of the short story, as well as cultural, thanks to her familiarity with Italian cinema, literature, and music. Moreover, as she emphasizes, her Italian identity is legally proven by her passport. But her lack of confidence, triggered by the news of the novel requirement for immigrants' fingerprints, is deeply rooted in the inner corners of her self ("Quelle maledette impronte avevano risvegliato quel demone che si era assopito da tempo immemorabile"; Those bloody fingerprints had woken up that demon within me that had been dormant for immemorable time).[35] Her desire for the forbidden Italian food, which like any food connects gastronomic culture with the inner body, symbolizes well the anxiety generated by the her dissonance between the acquired culture and her body.

The sausages reveal a moment of confusion in the otherwise solid cultural competence of the Italian protagonist because they speak of the protagonist's embodied identity that connects her to her Blackness rather than to her culturally formed Italianness. The protagonist will never eat the sausages. The smell, not the taste, of the sausages provokes a physical reaction and rejection of the perceived "filthy" food. The refusal to eat them is a bodily rather than a rational decision. In trying to establish some tranquillity, the protagonist fetches a newspaper and comes across the news of a Black teenager beaten up by white policemen. At this point, the image of the sausages aligns in the narration with the image of the fingerprints and the violence against Black people. This association of thought highlights that the food is a symbol of the protagonist's turmoil because it is a symbol of her racial difference: "Perché cavolo ci pestano sempre? E poi questo non mi aiuta a dimenticate le salsicce! Non mi aiuta a dimenticare le impronte della diversità!" (Why the hell do they always beat us up? And this doesn't help me to forget the sausages! Doesn't help me to forget the fingerprints of diversity!)[36] She mulls over all the struggles that a Black person must face, in Western countries as in Africa: there are no escape routes for the Black victims in any countries where they may be.

The resolution of her personal turmoil is given by the conclusion of a classic Italian comedy she watches, on that day, on TV. In this film, Alberto Sordi is tempted to follow his brother-in-law, who abandoned Italy to start a new life in Africa. But such a possibility is not available to the middle-class Sordi, who is obliged to come back to his conformist life. For Scego's protagonist, the film solicits a comparison to her own life: she is not obliged to live a life encapsulated in one single vision of the world, as Sordi is in the film. She still has a choice – "ho ancora me stessa" (I still have myself) – and acts on this perception by throwing the sausages in the bin.[37] Her Black Italian identity is her strength and richness. The sausages as a racial passport to the dominant white identity are not a valid option anymore for the protagonist, who embraces the complexity of her identity. She will continue to live in the difficult multicultural society she has criticized, aware of her powerful identity, therefore taking forward her message for a more inclusive society.

The self-awareness attained by the protagonist at the conclusion of the story originates from the senses – the smell of the sausages – and is articulated through both a reflective process and her empathic emotions towards the disenfranchised Black population. It is through this combination, which represents a form of embodied cognition – as the body, through the senses and emotions, is an active part in the development of the protagonist's understanding – that she reaches a resolution about her own identity. This process echoes the research by neuroscientist Vittorio Gallese, who, expanding on his discovery of mirror neurons, established that mental states and even the understanding of others are not abstract thoughts but embodied processes.[38] Relations with the world around us are at the core of the empathic process and non-verbal communication described by Gallese. This is helpful to show how the imagery around migration is deeply ingrained in images of the body that, through literary food, express racial anxiety and a desire for mediation.

The protagonist is an Italian citizen. As such, she would not be required to respect the discriminatory rule on fingerprints applied only to immigrants. Her anxiety generates from her empathic attitude towards Black people like her. She fears for them and for the destiny of suffering that Blackness has entailed and will entail. As Elena Pulcini reminds us, there "is an undisputable link between emotions and morality," as we make judgments based on emotions on what is good or bad and act accordingly.[39] Care is a moral action based on different types of emotions. Pulcini highlights that these emotions are not necessarily positive emotions, such as generosity and compassion, but also "fear for the fate of the others," which, like indignation, leads the subject to action.[40] The unfolding of the story, with its portrayal of a racist society, represents the narrator/author's moral action triggered by fear for the fate of Black immigrants.

Throughout her oeuvre, Scego has continued to address racism and Italy's oblivion of its colonial past. She has also been involved in public initiatives. She has been active in the protests for the removal of monuments of Fascist colonialists. She curated textbooks and radio programs to educate children and the general public about multicultural societies. Food has continued to feature in her work; many are the original names of African foods often cited in her writing. Italian linguists have recently coined the word "migratismi" ("migratisms") to indicate words in the original language appearing in the Italian writing of migrant or postcolonial writers. The largest use of "migratismi" appearing in Scego's oeuvre is related, as Jacopo Ferrari has established, to gastronomy.[41] Somali food words in the original language, like any other "migratismi," have the ability to contaminate the Italian language. Scego has continued then to create multicultural identities on the page through the use of gastronomic names. She has continued raising awareness of the complexity of Black Italian identities. Another writer who started publishing in the same period as Scego and has made consistent use of food imagery to discuss multicultural identities is Laila Wadia.

Eagleton's remark that food is after all a relation rather than an object is perfectly illustrated by Wadia's writing. Like Scego in "Salsicce," Wadia uses a comic tone in her early short stories. She elaborates on the concept of taste to mediate embodied identities between cultures. Silvia Contarini has pertinently underscored that much migrant literature written by women often depicts positive narratives of mediation of cultures that in part obscure the sufferings endured by migrant women, their low-paid jobs in the destination countries, and difficulties in their home countries.[42] In Scego's "Salsicce" as well as in Wadia's early narratives considered in this section, a similar tendency towards mediation and resolution in either second-generation characters or characters who have acquired a high level of competence and acculturation is apparent. I contend that through food narratives, women writers make the body crucial in their narrative of mediation. They reaffirm the body as a corporeal sign of difference in the context of migration. As seen in "Salsicce," the body acquires meaning for its racialization in contemporary society but also for its ability to produce embodied cognition, that is, an understanding and, in fact, a mediation of cultures that requires an embodied process.

A member of the Parsi community who moved from India to Trieste when she was in her twenties, Wadia has written mainly in Italian but also English. In her early fiction and poetry, literary food is a trope to discuss Italian contemporary society and develop a language beyond borders. Food is a central theme in her short stories "Spaghetti allo scoglio" (2004), "Curry di pollo" (2005), and "Il segreto della calandraca" (2007) and in her collection of poems *Kitchensutra* (2016) and is an element of the narrative in the novel *Amiche per la pelle* (2007). Wadia is also the editor of *Mondopentola*, a collection of short stories with a food theme. She too represents an Italian society that struggles with concepts of multiculturalism. However, in her writing, representations of taste extend to embrace alternative models of multiculturalism, rather than only a critique of contemporary society and a form of resistance, like in Scego's story. Katia Pizzi has defined Wadia's writing as an example of Antonio Gramsci's *traducibilità* (translatability) – that is, an illustration of dialogic translation across cultures – within the setting of the multicultural city of Trieste, historically a cradle of languages and cultures.[43] As I show, through her narrative around taste, Wadia strives to unknot the contraposition of dominant/marginal cultures in contemporary Italy. Taste denotes the encounter and clash of cultures in her earlier short stories "Spaghetti allo scoglio," published in Wadia's first collection, *Il burattinaio e altre storie extra italiane*, and "Curry di pollo," part of the co-authored collection *Pecore nere*. Both are centred on a family meal: in the former story, it is the first family dinner of the protagonist's Italian boyfriend with her Indian parents.

The narrating voice and protagonist, sixteen-year-old daughter Anandita, a second-generation Italian born and raised in Milan, defines herself through the fashion, hairstyle, and eating habits of the Italian youth of her generation. Taste marks the cultural dissonance between Anandita and her father: the daughter's cereals are seen as "sterco di coniglio" (rabbit excrements) by her father, Mr Kumar, and the Indian bread and fried vegetables are excessively oily and unhealthy to her.[44] That kind of generational gap does not exist between Anandita's father and his mother, who he left behind in India. A new country has meant financial and entrepreneurial success for him, but his lifestyle has remained the same, especially around taste. While Anandita convinced her mother to cook a pasta dish instead of a traditional curry, at the table it is evident that her father struggles more with the Italian dish. Chicken curry is his favourite food. It is a symbol not only of his Indian identity but also of his bond with his family of origin – his wife's recipe of this dish is in fact his own mother's recipe, considered the best in their village. With such a traditional take on cuisine, the father can only be in disbelief at the news that Anandita's boyfriend, Marco, tried curry on a mushroom pizza and in a bowl of precooked prawn rice. Anandita's mother proposes a resolution to the awkward situation created by the different culinary tastes of Mr Kumar and Marco by offering to add chilli to the pasta dish. Taste and sensual pleasure are for Mr Kumar the powerful forces able to win Marco over to the delights of traditional Indian cuisine, as he promises him the sublimation of the senses with a traditional curry that will send all his previous hybrid experiences into oblivion.[45]

In the short story "Spaghetti allo scoglio," an Italian lunch is the scene of another important first family meeting and another clash of cultures. The Italian protagonist, Riccardo, has wed a younger woman from Tibet, Ayjis, and has become an activist for the autonomy of Tibet, resulting in a crisis with his bourgeois sister, Ramona, and her husband, Aldo, a candidate in the regional political elections. The meal planning revolves around the domestication of Ayjis's culinary and fashion preferences. Riccardo decides that Ayjis will dress in Western clothes and pretends to his guests that she cooked the traditional Italian pasta they serve. The lunch, despite the good intentions, will be very different from the diplomatic conciliatory event that it was meant to be. The simple canapés almost reduce Ramona to tears, as Ayjis spiced them up with chilli to make them less bland, and the pasta is so salty as to be almost inedible. Aldo is the only one able to eat everything, showing the same insensitivity to the subtleties of taste that he reveals in his conversation with Ayjis, which is laden with racist overtones.[46] The alimentary crisis is resolved by Ramona's unexpected tasting of some Tibetan dumplings that in exasperation Ayjis has quickly warmed up for herself. Ramona is captured by the dish and starts eating one dumpling after the other with gusto.[47]

In "Curry di pollo," Wadia represents first-generation immigrants still rooted in their country of origin's culture but agents of a series of cultural and demographic changes in the destination country. The immigrants' presence has an impact on the country's foodways. A taste for Indian cuisine is not uncommon among the Italians in the story: Anandita's friend, Samantha, loves Mrs Kumar's chicken curry, and Marco and his family are consumers of a new food product market that has grown in the last few decades of mass migration. As the narrating voice is Anandita's, the lack of integration of her parents is clearly emphasized, but Anandita herself, with her rejection of their culture of origin, shows her limitation in not embracing part of her family culture. Marco, by associating the traditional curry with supermarket novelty products, replicates the downfalls of cultural appropriation and domestication of non-Western products, highlighted by hook's paradigm of "eating the other" in contemporary Western societies.[48] Effectively, all the main protagonists of the story experience difficulties or a lack of understanding of the culture they are living in, be it Italian culture for Anandita's parents, Indian culture for Anandita, or the perception of Indian culture in multicultural Italy for Marco. In this polyphony, Wadia projects an image of hope for the communication between cultures. As Maria Cristina Mauceri underlines, the resolutive chilli is a spice common to both the Indian and the Italian food cultures.[49] It is through taste, then, that the protagonists' limited appreciation of each other's culture is momentarily overcome.

The potent conciliatory function of taste is echoed in "Spaghetti allo scoglio," where it brings Ramona closer to a non-Western culture that she was not prepared to accept. In this context, taste functions as a translation of Tibetan culture. As Alex Rhys-Taylor has observed in his ethnographic study of food in multicultural East London, "tastes can also serve as points of translation through which intercultural association takes place, and through which 'transcultural' identities and culture emerge."[50] Ramona's eagerness and pleasure in eating the dumplings seem to imply the possibility of a new relationship, which her request for the dish's recipe projects into the future. Ramona does not acquire an understanding of non-Western culture by simply eating the dumplings, and in this sense, Elizabeth Buettner has demonstrated the limits of eating multicultural food.[51] It is, however, pertinent to read Ramona's eager eating as a new openness towards the world.

As Nicola Perullo argues following Levinas, gastronomic aesthetics always expresses an ethical value, which is secular because "il godimento, il piacere gustativo sono vissuti anche come *gioia del mondo*. Non è soltanto questione di donazione infinita all'altro, quanto di relazione dinamica con tale alterità" (enjoyment, gustative pleasure are experienced as *joie de vivre*. It is not so much an unlimited donation of oneself to the other, but a dynamic relationship with that alterity).[52] Taste, explains Perullo, cannot be seen only as a cultural construct; it is also an instinctual, primary pleasure that he calls "naked taste," a stage that is never overcome and that appears, when it does, with all its natural force.[53] In the scene of Ramona eagerly eating the Tibetan dumplings, we can read that aspect of "naked" taste that, with its instinctual nature, let her overcome her distrust of non-Western cuisine. Communication of cultures, the Gramscian *traducibilità* noted by Pizzi, is presented as experience embodied through taste.

A representation of the embodied embrace of culture and embodied multiculturalism is given in a scene in *Amiche per la pelle*. The block of flats in the centre of Trieste, the setting of the novel's events, is a rickety building but a place where the five families of different nationalities live emotionally connected lives. The smell of international food in the stairwell is a sign of their daily happy life, while its absence signals the worries caused by the imminent eviction.[54] The multicultural sensoria of that building speak of positive, convivial cohabitation despite the idiosyncrasies of its tenants. For all the efforts of the women in the families, their lives are affected by the limited integration, not unusual, among first-generation immigrants. This is perceivable through the struggle with Italian grammar, the awkward way of dressing for an afternoon at the theatre, and their awareness of their limited knowledge of Italian culture. Eating the traditional Triestine dish *jota* is presented by one of the characters, Marinka, as a fundamental element of local culture and the basic step towards integration. Yet the strong sour smell of *jota* proves distasteful to most of Marinka's migrant female friends and neighbours, who remain defined by the tastes of their country of origin, following a pattern very common to first-generation immigrants, where eating habits are the last to be modified.

As in "Curry di pollo," food scenes are a source of humorous exchange in the representation of the first generation's experience, while the second generation lays the path to a more positive cohabitation. A scene with the Indian protagonist of the novel and her daughter, Kamla, exemplifies it. The child is proud to be able to recite to her mum the poems by Giuseppe Ungaretti she has been learning with Mr Rosso, the only Italian tenant in the building, an elderly and disagreeable man who suddenly took to heart the education of little Kamla. In this scene, her mother has just prepared some *samosa* for her:

> Kamla si è messa a tavola e con la bocca piena di patate piccanti in sfoglia di grano ha declamato: "Si sta come d'autunno sugli alberi le foglie."
>
> (Kamla sat at the table and, with her mouth full of spicy potatoes in wheat-germ pastry, declaimed: "We are as in autumn on branches the leaves.")[55]

The excitement and accomplishment of the child are misunderstood by her mum, who interprets the shortness of Ungaretti's poem "Soldati" (Soldiers) as the child's failure to learn an Italian poem in its full length and wonders whether the reference to soldiers alludes to Fascism. The scene instead encapsulates both the distance between the experiences of the first and second generations and the new prospects of the second generation. While the mother is unable to comprehend the learning process her daughter has begun, the recitation of Ungaretti's poem, emblematic of Kamla's first steps towards cultural integration, is concomitant with her eager tasting of Indian cuisine, an uncompromisable element of her parents' cultural identity. The similar etymological origin of the Italian words *sapore* (taste) and *sapere* (knowledge), from the Latin *sapio* (to have a taste), comes to mind to elucidate this scene. It focuses on the mouth as the location of speech as well as the organ of taste, which has the effect of merging the culture of origin and the destination culture. It underlines again an embodied form of mediation. The choice of a transnational poet like Ungaretti – who was raised in Egypt and lived in France, Brazil, and Italy – intensifies the author's message. As a second-generation child, Kamla hints at an additional level of diversity within the multilayered Triestine society, a "super-diversity," using the term coined by Steven Vertovec to define the increased level of transformation of British immigration from the 1990s onwards.[56] In the increased complexity of society, Kamla projects the possibility of intercultural dynamics within the coexistence of cultures.

Food Nostalgia and Multiculturalism

Literary food as a means to discuss the range of emotions around the migration experiences is more extensively elaborated by Wadia in her edited collection of stories *Mondopentola* (2007) and her poetry book *Kitchensutra* (2016). *Mondopentola*, published in a series directed by Armando Gnisci, a pioneer of the study of migration literature and mentor of several migrant and second-generation writers, comprises thirteen short stories by authors who have become well known in Italy (among them Gabriella Ghermandi, Tahar Lamri, Christiana de Caldas Brito, and Mihai Mircea Butcovan), as well as a contribution co-authored by Gnisci and Wadia and the short story "Il segreto della calandraca," where Wadia explores food nostalgia. This is a recurrent emotion in narratives of food and migration. In her short story, I contend, Wadia transforms the typical interpretation of nostalgia into an image of integration and coexistence of cultures. The study of nostalgia is central to the analysis of movement and migration and, in fact, has spawned several theoretical interpretations outside the reference to food.

Considered a medical illness from the seventeenth century to the nineteenth century, nostalgia came to be considered an emotion dealing with the relationship between past and present only with the work of the American sociologist Fred Davis. The fundamental innovation of Davis's groundbreaking work was to identify that in the course of the nineteenth century, nostalgia began to be seen not only as a medical condition but as an emotion affecting the daily lives of ordinary people.[57] While the analysis of nostalgia as the relationship between past and present has often led to its conceptualization as a revaluation of the past compared to a more devalued present, other meanings are associated with it. Scott Alexander Howard argues that the relation between past and present in the inception of nostalgia must also be redefined; as the involuntary Proustian recollection shows, nostalgia does not necessarily derive from the poverty of the present. Considering nostalgia as an affective experience rather than a fascination with the past, as Howard does, leads him to conclude that nostalgia may be triggered by an unrecoverable past perceived, in that specific moment, as generating desire "for its bittersweet affective character [rather] than for the sort of past it is directed towards, or the relationship that obtains between that time and now."[58]

This same line of thought is shared by David Gerber in his work on the personal correspondence of nineteenth-century British immigrants to North America. He studied a group of letters written by three immigrants from different social milieux to their families in Britain. He argued that the nostalgic attachment expressed in these letters can be interpreted as a process, through which the immigrant subjects elaborate their relationship to their past in their home country and their new present lives in America. Nostalgia is therefore an emotion psychologically significant to the migrant subject at the moment of adjusting themselves to new identities.[59] The influential interpretation by Svetlana Boym in *The Future of Nostalgia* also draws on an idea of nostalgia as fruitful for the future, rather than being a dead-end illusory fascination. Her theorization of restorative and reflective nostalgia clarifies the relevance that the emotion can have for the subject's development, where reflective nostalgia weaves together even discarded elements of the past to create an idea of the past useful for the future.[60]

David Sutton has demonstrated how the sensuality of food is a perfect device for the elaboration of memory.[61] Nostalgia is recurrent in recollections around food. Lupton argued that nostalgia around comfort food is associated with a re-imaging, which can be real or fictitious, of a happy childhood.[62] Perullo's concept of "naked" taste as an instinctual, infantile pleasure that characterizes the first relationship with food here explains the philosophical reasons behind Lupton's sociological study. Food nostalgia plays a determinant factor in the experience of diaspora.

Foodways may be a way to reconnect with life in the homeland and express through it a sense of loss. As Cinotto states, the establishment of thriving Italian food businesses originated thanks to the fostering of diasporic nostalgia for the homeland and, in fact, "the economy of Italian immigrant food was always also an economy of emotions."[63] In contrast with such a tangible and real form of nostalgia, Monika Janowski discusses how foodways that have not been known in the first person by second generations become part of diasporic narratives able to generate memory.[64] This demonstrates, as the successful history of Italian food businesses does, that nostalgia and food memory are not only structures that reconnect a fragmented identity to their ancestral roots but are ways to engage with the construction of migrants' futures as well. As Janowski summarizes, "Food provides a sensuous and social space for drawing on the past to construct the present and imagine the future."[65] This is echoed both in Igiaba Scego and in Laila Wadia.

Scego's memoir *La mia casa è dove sono* (Home is where I am) opens with the scene of a superb chicken dish cooked by her sister-in-law in her home in Manchester, where the diasporic Somali family meet for a reunion. The exquisite taste of this dish triggers a bittersweet nostalgia, difficult to define by the author and for which she uses the Portuguese word *suadade*: "Una sorta di malinconia che si prova quando si è stati molto felici, ma nell'allegria si insinua un sottile sapore di amaro … [La] *saudade* di esiliati dalla propria madre terra" (a kind of melancholia that you feel when you have been very happy, but the joy is permeated by a subtly bitter taste … It is the *saudade* of the people in exile from their homeland).[66] The remapping of identity that, in Scego's book, is materialized by the creation of the map of Mogadiscio and Rome, originates from the sensory nostalgia elicited by her sister-in-law's special chicken dish. The sense of Scego's identity in the present, acquired throughout the memoir, is triggered then by taste. In a similar way, in her introduction to the collection *Mondopentola*, Laila Wadia mentions food nostalgia as a forward-looking perspective for a new world. Commenting on a scene from Jhumpa Lahiri's *The Namesake*, where the protagonist eats an unlikely assemblage of food to replicate the taste of an Indian snack, Wadia writes:

> A me piace pensare che questo piatto ibrido non funga solo da balsamo anti-nostalgia, ma che contenga i germogli della voglia di creare un nuovo mondo in cui si possano mediare lo ieri e l'oggi per dare vita al domani.
>
> (I like to think that this hybrid dish does not function only as an antidote against nostalgia, but that it contains the sprouts of the desire to create a new world where past and present can be mediated to give life to the future.)[67]

Wadia's own interpretation of food nostalgia is evidenced in her short story "Il segreto della calandraca."

The *calandraca* of the title is a traditional Triestine stew. It is memory food for the protagonist's husband, who unsuccessfully tries to recover in his wife's cooking the taste of the dish his mother would prepare. At the centre of the plot is the closure of Gerbini's in Trieste, a deli specializing in foodstuff from all around the world. For the protagonist, the deli represented a refuge from her homesickness for India, well before she began her search for the perfect *calandraca*'s secret ingredients. When the protagonist visits the shop, nostalgia acquires an embodied connotation. Her body and her taste buds drive her to seek a reconnection to her homeland:

> Era il mio rifugio. Il rifugio della mia anima quando essa veniva sopraffatta dal mal di patria, quando il mio corpo reclamava i sapori della mia India natia, quando le mie papille gustative imploravano una tregua dai carboidrati raffinati e dagli oli extra vergini spremuti a freddo.
>
> (It was my refuge. The refuge of my soul when it was overcome with homesickness, when my body reclaimed flavours of my country of origin, India, when my taste buds begged for a truce from refined carbohydrates and cold-pressed extra virgin olive oil.)[68]

It is an "emotional refuge," a retreat from predominant emotional norms, as Reddy would put it, and it appears as such in the above description that evokes clashing and truce. The deli is the place where several emotions and states of being can find respite. Each section of the shop has the power to soothe specific uneasiness or emotional states of being: while nostalgia can be treated through the smell of Indian spices, physical tiredness is soothed by the sight of colourful ready-mix American cakes. When mentally tired, the protagonist wanders among sauces and ready-made meals from all around the world.[69] The deli, for the protagonist, is a magic place, where one can find everything from Croatian cheese to Spanish ham, Turkish *halwa*, and Canadian maple syrup, and above all it is a place where all nationalities live one next to the other: "Gerbini non è un negozio – è le Nazioni Unite del sapore. È la prova vivente che un altro mondo è possibile." (Gerbini's is not a shop – it is the United Nations of taste. It is the living evidence that a different world is possible.)[70]

Amid that exceptional range of flavours, the protagonist finds the smells and aromas of her childhood. She re-experiences the scenes of family meals and, above all, an instinctive sense of happiness that allows her to overcome dark moments.[71] In addition to this pleasure that, like Scego's *suadade*, manifests the sense of displacement of a diasporic subject, in the shop the protagonist benefits from the aromas of other cultures, which all contribute to her well-being. Rather than a food nostalgia enclosed within a revisitation of a distant, imagined country, Wadia represents a coming together of cultures in what she calls a United Nations of tastes. This is further illustrated by what represents the resolution of the story, the secret ingredient for the *calandraca*. Thanks to Mr Gerbini, the shop owner, a Triestine man with sixty years' experience in international deli products, the protagonist obtains a packet of mixed seasoning with the addition of Hungarian sweet paprika that will transform the *calandraca* into a very close reconstruction of her mother-in-law's dish, and into a recipe for happiness. Her husband's food nostalgia, which effectively does seem to be a search for a personal childhood memory, is also recovered thanks to the Hungarian flavour, which hints at the influence of the Austro-Hungarian traditions in the local cuisine. The city of Trieste, with its intricate history and network of cultures, is the perfect setting for projecting the image of coexisting cultures.[72] In an interview I conducted with Wadia, she described her relationship with Trieste, a city of historic migration, reiterating her fascination for a place that, a bit like her native India, allows the co-sharing of cultures. It is a place where she found, in what she defined as a "culture of cultures," "the freedom to keep whatever you want as a language, as a food, as an identity, and still share it with others."[73]

Nostalgia in "Il segreto della calandraca," both as an emotion felt by a displaced subject for her distant homeland and as a longing for a reconnection to a personal and local past, as in the case of the protagonist's husband, is never removed from a myriad of other cultures.

The rendition of the coexistence and sharing of cultures through food echoes Levinas's interpretation of the eating practice as the paradigm of ethics, given that it is always an opening up of the self or, as Perullo summarizes, it represents a dynamic relationship with the Other.[74] The shutting of the deli shop in Wadia's short story does not imply a cessation of the relationship with the Other, which continues through the *calandraca* recipe inserted at the conclusion. The replication of the *calandraca* recipe also functions as the legacy of Gerbini's shop with its ethos of cultural coexistence. The multiculturalism that Wadia proposes in this short story is facilitated by the particular history and culture of Trieste, with its multilayered and intertwined interconnections of cultures and local traditions. The same interest in cultures' coexistence is echoed in her poetic work.

In her poetry collection *Kitchensutra*, Wadia plays with words and food-related images to unearth emotions, feelings, and identities that seem not to find a definition within established structures. The concomitant use of more languages in the same poem, with the alternation of English and Italian in most, and the parallel texts in English and Italian of some poems echo that uneasiness with communication. Multilingualism, wordplay, and neologism are recurrent elements in this collection. In "Brezmeja," food names from Germany, America, Mexico, Italy, Trieste, India, and more are joined together to form words (i.e., "jotamulligatawny," "kartoffelnhummus") that suggest the image of a world without borders. The poem's title blends two Slovenian words to accentuate the idea of the closeness of cultures.[75] In the poem "Making Minestrone," the language of food visualizes different forms of cultural coexistence. The poetic subject refuses the concept of the melting pot, which has the disadvantage of confusing identities ("Where aloo becomes French / fries"). She favours instead the minestrone as a symbol of stable identity, as each ingredient remains the same while sharing flavours ("Where every ingredient / stays the same / yet shares").

Throughout the whole collection, language is a cogent topic of investigation and reflection. In "Punteggiatura," the poetic subject questions the usefulness of languages if they can barely convey her state of being. In the poem "I speak pav bhaji," the favoured language is that of cooks, musicians, and lovers, a language without words that only the senses can translate. In "Translation," national languages are defined as the subject's medium of communication with human beings, while emotions and nature provide the language to talk, think, and dream about the intimate aspects of human and natural lives. In her poetry, more directly than in her fiction, Wadia evidences her search for a form of communication alternative to codified languages. Literary food proves to be the medium suitable for the poetic subject to express inner emotions – as she does in the love poems of the collection – and give voice to her ideas of multiculturalism.[76]

In Wadia's writing, the language of food, as a language of the senses, has represented the experience of the migrant subject and has put forward concepts of nostalgia and multiculturalism apt to inspire new visions and hope for the future. Wadia's literary food is political, as it takes a stand in the contemporary discussion of migration. Her use of literary food implicitly underlines the relevance of the medium of the senses in providing an understanding of the emotional dynamics of contemporary multicultural societies.

Laura Pariani and Transnational Care

Scego writes from the point of view of a Black Italian taking forward anti-hegemonic and postcolonial instances; Wadia discusses the coexistence of cultures as an Indian-born migrant in multicultural Trieste. Well-established Italian writers have intervened in the discussion of migration too. The marginal position of the migrant subject and the liminality of the discourse of food, as well as the ethical function of literature for the peaceful coexistence of cultures, are distinctive aspects of the short story "Il colore del silenzio" (The colour of silence) by Laura Pariani, published in the 2003 collection *L'uovo di Gertrudina* (Gertrudina's egg). In her copious, successful, and beautifully sophisticated narrative, Pariani returns several times to stories of migration, from Italy to South America and vice versa, focusing on female characters. Her work frequently constructs a fluidity of voices where the character, narrator, and author share similar experiences and emotions, often across centuries and continents. A gendered perspective is a focal point in her writing, as feminism is in her life experience. Pariani took an active part in the feminist movement of the 1970s and was a member of Lotta femminista, as well as of consciousness-raising groups and the prominent collective of via Cherubini. Gigliola Sulis summarizes the overall objective of Pariani's extensive production in her interest in the disenfranchised, the person who "per scelta o per destino, non ha avuto la possibilità di esprimersi" (for choice or destiny, could not express themselves).[77]

In "Il colore del silenzio," the setting – the southern and most inhospitable part of Chile – intensifies the liminal position of the protagonist, a nun, Suor Assunta. She is not the only protagonist. We follow the experience of a woman narrator who travels to the places where Suor Assunta lived to reconstruct her story. "Il colore del silenzio" engages with the history of colonialism and with the untold story of the Fuegians, and it creates a transnational and intergenerational mending process through a particular food image. The narration unfolds through an entwined process of mutual care: the care of the narrator for Suor Assunta's life story, the care of Suor Assunta for the Fuegian women and their freedom, the care of their descendants and the narrator for a memory of those people and events. Through this interplay, Pariani shows the relevance of mutual dependence. She repositions the subject, distancing it from the concept of the autonomous self. In this sense, her interest echoes philosopher Elena Pulcini's description of the modern subject as one constructed through "the myth of autonomy and independence," which had the effect of removing "the reality of our mutual dependence and constitutive 'neediness.'"[78] In her story Pariani shows the importance of interrelationships for the understanding of others and as a way to mend the scars of colonialism.

At the end of the nineteenth century, Suor Assunta leaves behind her comfortable life in Piedmont to join the Catholic Mission in Punta Arenas in southern Chile, and later the San Rafael Mission on the remote Dawson Island. Never understood by her family, who over the years considered her insane, Suor Assunta is a disempowered character in Piedmont and Chile as well, where she must observe the rules of the male clerical hierarchy. She becomes even more isolated on her return to Italy when she decides to confine herself to her room and live a life of silence. The figure of the narrator is also marginal: a woman from the same Piedmontese area who embarks on an arduous journey to the Brunswick Peninsula, in southern Chile, where, among the scarce tourist population, solo women travellers are rare. Her only objective is to piece together the story of a woman to whom she is not attached by any apparent bond, driven as she is just by her curiosity and willingness to understand an unusual life.

The End of the World, as the southern Chilean area is called, appears as a place at the margin, and as such it suits the narrator and her "passione per le cose estreme" (passion for extreme things).[79] For her research on the nun's life, she relies on a series of materials that she uncovers little by little: photos, letters, Suor Assunta's diary of the period spent in southern Chile, and recorded oral interviews. A fictionalized reconstruction, given in italics, completes the sources of her narration. The reconstruction of the past takes place, therefore, through an interplay of facts and fiction, equally important for the understanding of characters and events. This non-linear rendition of the past is conveyed by a language dotted with sentences in the Piedmontese dialect as well as Spanish, a form of multilingualism not uncommon in Pariani's writing.

Spanish and Piedmontese dialect accentuate the orality of communication and the coexistence of cultures in the protagonists' lives. The coloured face painting of the Fuegians is another medium of expression. Pariani describes it as a non-lingual communication, one that is more sincere than the wordy discourses of the white colonizers:

> Tutti questi disegni sono parole sincere; verità ben diversa dai discorsi confusi e complicati degli Uomini Bianchi che parlano di superstizione e non conoscono un maledetto nulla di ciò che sta al di là di quello che vedono con i loro deboli occhi.
>
> (All these paintings are sincere words, a truth which is fundamentally different from the confused and complicated dialogues of the White Men who talk about superstition and don't understand a damn about what there is beyond what they can barely see with their weak eyes.)[80]

The oppressing and limited function of the colonizers' language has no relational power, as it remains distant from the natural environment and the Other represented by the Fuegians. On the contrary, the Fuegian culture relates to both humans and animals: both are believed to be capable of communication. In her articulate story, Pariani uses a traditional Piedmontese dish as a form of communication and a symbol for a transnational mending, across centuries, of the fracture caused by colonialism.

The fifteen years spent at the Catholic Mission on Dawson Island are deeply transformative for Suor Assunta, as the narrator reconstructs: "Era una giovane piena di sogni quando partì per l'America, una donna tormentata quando lasciò la Missione" (She was a young woman full of dreams when she left for America and a tormented soul when she left the Mission).[81] Her relationship with the indigenous women, her perception of the racist views of the priests at the Mission, and their cruelty towards the Fuegians transform her attitude and understanding. In the early entries of her diary, the nun jotted down her impressions on a population indifferent to the Catholic teaching, sure that one day they would realize that "solo noi Salesiani nutriamo nei suoi confronti vero amore e volontà di sacrificio" (only we of the Salesian Catholic order have true love and willingness to sacrifice for them).[82] Progressively, her perplexity about the priests' attitude towards the native Fuegians grew as she detached from the dominant perspective of her Catholic group. The priests openly judged the indigenous language as "poco più del linguaggio delle bestie" (just something more than beast language) and talked of their alleged cruelty as animal-like.[83] She responded critically to the priests taking the Fuegians' caring attitude towards their children, which she witnessed daily, as evidence of the opposite. Echoing Suor Assunta's criticism, the narrator comments on the absurdity of Darwin's analysis, which had placed the indigenous Fuegians at the lowest level of humanity because of their uneasiness with complex conversations. A fictional section in italics, juxtaposed to the nun's and the narrator's criticism, imagines Suor Assunta with the Fuegian women busy with face painting, a form of communication and a ritual she encouraged. At a closer reading of the nun's diary, a sentiment of compassion appears evident to the narrator: "Via via che passano gli anni, l'orrore e la ripugnanza per il comportamento incomprensibile degli indios furono a poco a poco sostituiti dalla compassione" (As the years went by, the horror and the aversion for the incomprehensible behaviours of the indigenous people were substituted by compassion).[84]

A diary reference to a newly born baby daughter, named Severina Pikespul, suggests to the narrator a different perception of Suor Assunta's experience at San Rafael Mission. In the fictionalized sections, the narrator envisages her as maternal and caring. Once this intuition is perceived through the fictional section, a different reading of Suor Assunta's diary becomes accessible to the narrator, as to stress that communication is based not only on rationality and facts. The nun's relationship with the indigenous women is, unexpectedly for the narrator, connoted by a maternal attitude: "Mi stupii di trovare molte frasi in cui balzava agli occhi l'istinto materno che le indie le risvegliavano" (I was surprised to find many sentences where her maternal instinct for the indigenous women stood out).[85] It is by always following her intuition that the narrator manages to track down Asunción, the daughter of Severina, the baby girl mentioned in the diary.

Asunción's memory of Suor Assunta is linked to her language teaching, but there is only one word she can mention: "*panìscia*." A traditional dish of Novara, the area of Piedmont Suor Assunta and the narrator-protagonist come from, *panìscia* has retained a strong local characterization up until now, so much so that in the Vercelli area, adjacent to Novara, the dish is prepared following a different procedure. Suor Assunta would cook *panìscia* as a celebratory dish reserved for important festivities and would add a particular type of local mushroom, yellow and bright. The *panìscia* does not signify the colonized acculturation of the indigenous population, as is the case of another food scene we will consider later. It rather symbolizes the intercultural dynamics between the nun and the Fuegian community, as well as the empathy of the nun and the narrator towards the indigenous women. The dish, in Assunción's memory, had a relevant function in the dramatic event of the Fuegians' failed escape attempt from the Mission.

Carefully planned for Christmas Eve, it was cruelly sabotaged by the priests. Suor Assunta was unaware of the sabotage and perplexed and distressed at the priests' behaviour ("col cuore in tumulto ... desolata ... il modo di agire dei Padri ... la lascia perplessa"; in anguish, ... desolated ... the priests' behaviour leaves her perplexed).[86] A fictionalized section reconstructs her compassion and maternal care towards the children, whom she persuades to eat the *panìscia* she had prepared for the Christmas celebration. It is comfort food that eases Severina's and the other children's disappointment:

> Le porge il piatto di panìscia, insiste davanti al suo no; finché il volto di Severina si copre di rossore e all'improvviso, tutta in lagrime, la bambina capìtola ingoiando un cucchiaio dopo l'altro di quel calduccio che sta nel riso e fagioli.
>
> (She offers her a plate of *panìscia* and insists in the face of her refusal up until Severina blushes and suddenly, in a flood of tears, gives in and swallows, spoon after spoon, that little warmth that is rice and beans.)[87]

The empathic and comforting attitude imagined in this fictionalized section is a perceptive understanding of the nun's maternal attitude. Soon after, a bundle of letters the nun wrote to Severina after her return to Italy and kept by Assunción testify to the nun's attachment to the native population and her sense of guilt for not having done enough to defend them at the Mission: "So di essere colpevole nei confronti di tutti voi: non sono stata capace di difendervi abbastanza" (I am aware I am guilty towards you all: I was not able to protect you enough).[88]

Empathy and compassion explain Suor Assunta's relationship with the Fuegians and her choice of a life of silence when she returned to Europe. Philosophers have defined empathy as a fundamental emotion at the basis of relationships, a "discovering of the other."[89] Empathy puts the nun in relation with the women, for example, when she perceives their weakness and submission towards their men.[90] It is the emotion that sustains her maternal care upon the discovery of the failed escape attempt. As Pulcini explains, empathy and compassion are the emotions that allow the practice of care. Compassion is a "common feeling that implies the recognition of a common humanity."[91] It is evident in the gradual detachment of the nun from the priests' racist attitudes and her closeness to the women and the young Severina.

Suor Assunta's progressive change of attitude – from detachment and lack of understanding to compassion, care, and desire to protect the Fuegian population – weaves in a discourse of respect for the Other that seems to be accessible to the woman subject from her liminal position. It is, in fact, through a female lineage, inscribed in the language of food, that the care and respect for the indigenous population achieve a resolution. At the end of the story, the narrator, before departing for Italy, visits Severina's tomb and leaves there a packet of rice and dried beans as a gift. Her gesture reconnects Severina to the language of food that had represented for Suor Assunta a language of maternal care. The image of the nun's and the narrator's isolation seems to dissipate through the gift of the rice and beans, which establishes a bond among the three women. This introduces the woman narrator to a form of communication through food, as she finds in the *panìscia* a link between herself and the unknown woman and, in the figure of Severina, an explanation for the mysterious life of the nun. The *panìscia* codifies the support and care of the nun towards the Fuegian women, but also the care of the narrator towards the memory of Severina and through her towards the Fuegians.

The story told by the *panìscia* also has the function to counteract the forms of cultural imperialism represented in Pariani's "Il colore del silenzio." Enlightening in this sense is the reconstruction of the Colombian Exhibition, held in Genoa at the turn of the nineteenth century, on the 400th anniversary of the discovery of the Americas. There, the indigenous peoples were on display for the visitors of the exhibition. One of them, Silvestre, who had been brought up at San Rafael Mission, is given a bowl of *trenette* pasta and a fork. After a few failed attempts to use the fork, amid the dismay and excitement of the "Uomini Bianchi," Silvestre uses his hands to try what seems to him an unusual and unappealing taste.[92] This image further distances Suor Assunta's *panìscia* from colonialist practice. Pariani constructs an ethical system of values that lines up Suor Assunta, the narrator, Severina and her daughter, and the recipe of the *panìscia* modified with the additional ingredient of local mushrooms as a symbol of care. Suor Assunta developed a caring and maternal relationship with the Fuegian women, but it is the narrator who translates that supportive and reciprocal attachment in contemporary times. Pariani, through the reference to the Novarese *panìscia*, has projected a transnational bond that attempts to mend the violence and abuse of colonialism. Care, in her work, is to be intended as an ethical relationship towards the world that opposes the politics of colonial exploitation.

In the short story "L'uovo di Gertrudina," at the conclusion of the volume, the crucial ethical function of literature is made explicit. The story, while a tribute to the Manzonian Gertrude, is a skilful manipulation of the different storylines presented in the book. The life experiences of the characters, the narrator, and the author are simultaneously represented in a circular form that disrupts timeline and geographical location. Thinking of cases of isolation and abuse of power she has represented in the stories in the book, Pariani concludes by asserting the power of literature, its ability to project new paradigms for a more dignified future: "La letteratura può anche essere gesto di libertà, di salvezza, perfino di redenzione ... le donne che allora furono forzate e sconfitte ancora possono rivolgerci uno sguardo di sogno" (Literature can also be a gesture of freedom, of salvation, and even of redemption ... the women who once were constrained and defeated can now have a dreaming glance).[93]

In the authors analysed in this chapter, literature has an ethical function: for its ability to show racial stereotypes through irony and humour, as in much of Scego's and Wadia's writing; for its ability to create new visions, as in Wadia's poetic constructions; and for its power to re-imagine a life of freedom and dream, as in Pariani's women characters, who remain marginal but fundamental to a new vision of the world. For the three writers, literary food is a tool that allows openness to the world, as Perullo would say, and creates new emotional landscapes for an anti-racist, collaborative present. Local and regional identities, represented for example by the Triestine *calandraca* and the Novarese *panìscia*, are part of, and not in contraposition to, the imagined transnational present. Food and writing in these works are not objects anymore but relationships.

Conclusion

My analysis started with Virginia Woolf's and M.F.K. Fisher's references to voluptuous eating and drinking as expressions of daring actions and independence. *Food and Emotions in Italian Women's Writing* asks why food imaginaries have the power to convey such a disruptive message about women's intellectual freedom and autonomy. Through the analysis of fiction, poetry, cookbooks, magazine articles, sociocultural initiatives, and historical events, this book demonstrates that the topic of food in women's writing and in history is always political. Through activities and writing around food, over the decades women have influenced society and political and social discourses. From food protests during the war to the politics of care of the Estia group; from showing the relevance of the senses with literary food during Fascism to imagining transcultural relationships in contemporary times, women have found in the domain of food a way to express emotions and to influence the world around them.

My framework of analysis covers a period of one hundred years and interlaces the history and imagery of food in women's writing with the expression of the emotions that their stories arouse. I consider the themes of food and emotions not only as topics whose history enlightens the understanding of women's daily lives but also as areas of investigation interconnected with the body and its theorization. The thematic thread of food and emotions, with its interconnections with the corporeal, has focused attention on the lived experience and the neglected aspects of women's lives. They allow forms of disruption of dominant emotional discourses. The methodology I follow has been necessarily interdisciplinary. Literary analysis, philosophical theories of taste, theories of emotions, archival research, and historical analysis have all shaped my gender analysis. My aim has always been to reconsider women's fictional and historical writing in such a way as to establish more inclusive and gender-specific ways of narrating women's creativity and history.

My analysis focuses on three objectives. First, I attempted to construct an overview of women's engagement with the domain of food in a variety of social frameworks. Up until the third millennium, food work has been traditionally associated with domesticity and the life of women, so an outline of domestic literature offers insight into what was expected of women, as well as how women negotiated dominant social practices. Women have been involved in food work and the creation of recipes from much earlier times than the Fascist period, but the politics of the regime meant that, for the first time in peacetime, women were asked explicitly and collectively to join in the building of the empire through the shaping of eating habits. Authors of cookbooks in the Fascist period and during the war were able to pursue their interests and take an active part in the changes that Fascism brought about. But the image of women these texts projected was still framed within a model of femininity that was submissive to the dominant power structures of the time. In a similar manner, during World War II, food protests, which involved hundreds of women around the country, were presented in ambivalent tones by the anti-Fascist groups that instigated the demonstrations. The newsletters of *Noi donne* published in occupied Italy stirred women to protest, while the official issues of the same journal softened the image of aggressive women with the construction of a more traditional and compliant, motherly view. The Piedmontese partisan Marisa Ombra wrote of the sad premonition which came to her as the war ended. Her fear of the re-normalization of women's roles subverted by the war became a reality in the new consumer society of the 1950s economic boom.

Home appliances, snacks, supermarkets, and prepared food changed habits, albeit not homogeneously across the country. Women were again at the forefront of the changes around food, as advertisements and the new television ads projected them as a supreme symbol of modernity while arousing new concerns about desirable body shapes and food contaminations. In later decades, when the personal became political and voicing emotions was a structural part of the way women did politics, the search for authenticity and new cuisine was, on the contrary, motivated by a concern for well-being and personal development. Women were interested in new cuisines of the time for their alleged health benefits; indeed, some cookbooks were inspired by the desire to find solutions to illnesses in the author's family. New feminist food enterprises emerging in the 1970s were connected to women's cultural organizations, so their food work and production were not as important as their contribution to strengthening the alternative cultures of the feminist organizations. Decades later, the establishment of the Estia group at the Women's Bookshop in Milan changed that attitude and made food work a feminist practice.

My second objective in this book was to use the theme of food and emotions to re-map women's writing in the last century. Since the 1990s, Italian women writers have acquired increasing visibility, with a growing number of admired and prize-winning publications.[1] Veronica Galletta, Michela Murgia, Giulia Caminito, Viola Di Grado, and Donatella Di Pietrantonio, to mention just a few, are among recent winners of the Campiello prize, while Claudia Durastanti, Nadia Terranova, Francesca Melandri, Edith Bruck, Lia Levi, Sandra Petrignani, Maria Grazia Calandrone, and Romana Petri were recent finalists of the Strega prize, which was awarded to Helena Janeczek, Melania Mazzucco, Margaret Mazzantini, and Di Pietrantonio in the last two decades. This exponentially increased interest in women's writing in the new millennium raises questions about how to narrate this "galassia emersa" (surfacing galaxy) of women authors.[2] In the traditional male-dominated literary canon, women writers were often, albeit not always, present. Their names were, however, the expression of exceptionality. For decades figures such as Elsa Morante or Grazia Deledda were the most usually cited representatives of women's writing in anthologies or literary studies, uncritically dominated by male authors. A few names sprinkled across a well-established, tradition-conforming literary domain have consistently failed to create what Daniela Brogi defines as "lo spazio delle donne" (the space of women).

In this book, the themes of food and emotions allowed me a wide, encompassing view of women's writing, where a variety of authors from the celebrated to the hardly known are in focus in a picture that contextualizes the work that women do with food. Well-known writers like Dacia Maraini, Ada Gobetti, Laura Pariani, Clara Sereni, Igiaba Scego, and Alba de Céspedes are analysed here together with lesser-known authors like Pina Ballario, Giovanna Zangrandi, and Laila Wadia and those not normally mentioned in the study of women's writing, like Cesarina Bracco. My investigation concentrated on the representation of daily experiences around food rather than on narratives where food is the central topic of the story, thereby opening the analysis to a wide range of styles and genres. In each historical period, my analysis also interacted with the work of the many women who engaged in the codification of domestic literature, like Amalia Moretti Foggia, Ada Boni, and Anna Gosetti della Salda, and the women who, like Ida Farè and Stefania Giannotti, constructed new cultural and social enterprises around food.

As theorists and philosophers have argued, food is not a topic like any other, in particular in its relation to women. The quotations by

Virginia Woolf and M.F.K. Fisher crystallized the theoretical notion that "doing food is doing gender," while philosophers like Lisa Heldke and Dean Curtin have demanded that the topic of food be taken seriously as a way of conceptually regrounding philosophy. Thanks to this complex valence that food entails, the manipulation of its imagery in women's writing has proved suitable to voice their reactions about the world around them and their identity and subjectivity. The topic of food, as we have seen, spreads into different domains: labour first of all; the perception of the self through taste, as Perullo has argued; the relationship with other cultures, as migration has repeatedly demonstrated. The analysis of literary food as an expression of emotions supplied insight into the engagements of writers with the social emotions and politics of their times, hence revealing their standpoints. In this sense, it has offered the possibility of surveying a heterogeneous group of writers at work within a landscape very much populated by women.

My third objective in this book was to present the narrativization of the body made possible by food writing. In bringing together the senses and the emotions, my analysis of literary food has underscored the relevance of corporeal imagery in the work of women writers. Across the decades, the body as the site of experience and emotions continues to be a treasure trove for the expression of the self and the world all around it. Scholars like Victoria de Grazia, Michela De Giorgio, Marina Addis Saba, and Robin Pickering-Iazzi have long demonstrated that the Fascist "ruling" of women also led to dynamic expressions of independence among women who were experiencing the dictatorship. *Food and Emotions in Italian Women's Writing* demonstrates how literary food was able to convey the sense of freedom and the rejection of the overpowering concept of nationalistic duty. The longing for pleasure, for a more intimate sense of motherhood in Ballario, and the desire for the spoken and the written word in the description of the young women in de Céspedes's novel all reveal the power of expression of literary food and a willingness to give attention to the personal feelings that the regime was denying. The book demonstrates how emotional communities – involving both supporters and detractors of the regime – challenged the Fascist rules of duty and sobriety.

In the dramatic time of World War II and the Resistance, food and taste gained a more radical meaning. In the memoirs by Zangrandi and Bracco, through the combination of the sense of taste and the emotions, literary food articulates the elation and agency that the experience of the Resistance had for women. Through the taste of the coffee that Zangrandi sips after dealing simultaneously with a group of Nazis, partisans, and prisoners of war, we come to appreciate the joy and the defiance of power structures represented by that gesture, encapsulating the feeling of transgression and freedom that the Resistance experience brought for many women. I frame the food scenes in Zangrandi's and Bracco's memoirs as performances of emotion. They are symbols able to capture the embodied sense of self that the memory of war tried to deny to women. On the contrary, Ada Gobetti's narrative conveys a life of exceptional partisan and intellectual activities, but she avoids the expression of personal emotions.

The reconstruction of the country and its subsequent economic development were based on the negation of those independent elements of women's subjectivities that the war had generated. The uneasiness and disquiet for the gender politics of the post-war years emerged openly in the feminist search for authentic selfhood and emotions in the late 1960s and 1970s. From the disquiet of *Quaderno proibito*'s protagonist to the uneasiness with existing political structures voiced by women in the 1970s, the expression of emotions has given voice to the development of women's subjectivity. Using William Reddy's approach, I define women's declared emotions in the 1970s, their "mi sento male" (I feel unwell), which typically manifested in public discussions, as "emotives," tools to rethink the meaning of power and political debate. The personal as the political reveals its potentials for the restructuring of society. In this context, Maraini's *Mangiami pure* shows how literary food becomes a political tool to express women's anger towards patriarchy and a sophisticated means to express women's uneasiness with system-regenerating politics, as the 1968 cultural liberation turned out to be. The embodied imagination of literary food becomes an anti-systemic language that counteracts dominant power structures. Clara Sereni offers a further demonstration of the power of food imagery: as a language to renegotiate her relationships with family and close friends. Decades later, "relational cooking," the concept of care as an ability to protect and help the external world, and the circulation and sharing of power formed the basis of the activities of the Estia group, who expanded their focus outside the family structure. Estia looks sympathetically at the new trend of male chefs of the third millennium, "liete che l'importanza e il calore dei fuochi, il lavoro oscuro delle nostre madri, che ha tenuto in vita il mondo, riesca finalmente a diventare centrale nell'economia del mondo" (happy that the relevance and warmth of the kitchen, the forgotten work of our mothers that kept the world alive, finally becomes central to the economy of the world).[3]

In the new millennium, additional layers of complexity have made the topic of food more political than ever. As a trope in contemporary migrant and transnational literature, literary food discusses racial identity, postcoloniality, and multiculturalism. The sustained use of literary food by Laila Wadia, Igiaba Scego's interpretation of the racial body, and the transnational interpretation of colonialism by Laura Pariani follow this path. In their works, the senses, and the representation of the emotions that food-related senses evoke, all intertwine with the meaning-making around migration and postcoloniality of their food stories. Taste and the senses become embodied forms of mediation between cultures, and Pariani's *panìscia* a language for the disenfranchised and a symbol of transnational care. Within a contemporary sociopolitical climate that tends to exacerbate conflicts, women writers have emphasized a language of emotions focusing on the relationship between cultures. Scego's, Pariani's, and Wadia's works, like the Estia group's activities, evidence a change in the concept of care: no longer simply a woman's duty to the family – as illustrated by Petronilla's writing – but a relational and political attitude towards the world. From the mid-1920s, when women as a group started becoming visible in the codification of domestic literature, through autarky, war, economic boom, and the 1968 protests, up until the multicultural Italy of the new millennium, food has represented an imaginary that women wanted and needed to negotiate, doing so, more often than not, on their own terms.

Notes

Introduction

1 Woolf, *Diary*, 200–1.
2 Fisher, *How to Cook*.
3 Gilbert, *Culinary Imagination*, 146.
4 Fisher, *Gastronomical Me*, 191.
5 Brady et al., "Filling Our Plate," 3.
6 Kate Cairns and Josée Johnston in *Food and Femininity* use Antonio Gramsci's idea of hegemony and a focus on emotions to carry out a nuanced analysis of how feminine subjectivities are embodied in daily life through food. By analysing emotional reaction in interviews, and avoiding the binaries of assimilation and resistance, they look at how neoliberalism is reproduced and challenged through everyday food choices. Marjorie DeVault in *Feeding the Family* argued that women's responsibility around family feeding is consistently devalued. Patricia Allen and Carolyn Sachs have shown that food is pervasive in women's lives, as they are "occupied and preoccupied with food," in disadvantaged and low-paid jobs within the sector, and enacting resistance through healthy food initiatives. Yet food-related work doesn't only represent oppression and disadvantage for women, as Allen and Sachs also acknowledge when they give credit, for example, to women's success in agri-food systems. Allen and Sachs, "Women and Food Chains." Psyche William-Forson's *Building Houses Out of Chickens' Legs* contributed to a significant shift in the analysis of women's food labour. She demonstrated how, for African American women, food preparation has also represented a means to defy negative constructions of Blackness. Although from a different perspective, Carole Counihan's anthropological work has also shed light on the powerful position that food labour has conferred on women. For example, she highlighted how in a small village in Sardinia, the modernization of the

food and bread-making industry led to women's loss of influence and power within the private sphere. Counihan, *Anthropology of Food and Body.*

7 Bourk, "Pain," 495.

8 Woolf, *Room of One's Own*, 23.

9 Explaining the connection between food consumption and self-identity, Fischler individuates three values characteristic of human beings' food incorporation: the representational value, the sense of self-control, and the building of collective identity. The representational value is given by the cultural and emotional charges that we attribute to the food we decide to eat. As incorporation relates to the choice of meanings and characteristics attributed to food, it can be said that the ultimate function of the representational value of incorporation is control over the body. The third function of incorporation is, for Fischler, the reinforcement of our collective identity. He argues that cultures that have lost their language but still retain their cuisine are an irrefutable example of how food remains a fundamental expression of collective identity. Fischler, "Food, Self and Identity."

10 Counihan, *Anthropology of Food and Body*, 11.

11 Counihan, *Anthropology of Food and Body*, 11–12.

12 Lupton, *Food*, 10–12.

13 Adams, *Sexual Politics.*

14 Lupton, *Food*, 12.

15 Lupton, *Food*, 13.

16 Brogi, *Lo spazio delle donne*, 27. All translations are mine unless otherwise noted.

17 Brogi, *Lo spazio delle donne*, 28.

18 Salvatici, *Storia delle donne.*

19 Adolph, *Food and Femininity*, 14.

20 Heller and Moran, *Scenes of the Apple*, 1.

21 Heller and Moran, *Scenes of the Apple*, 2.

22 Sceats, *Food, Consumption and the Body*, 5–7.

23 Curtin and Heldke, *Cooking, Eating, Thinking.*

24 Heldke, "Unexamined Meal," 204.

25 Curtin, "Food/Body/Person," 4.

26 Korsmeyer, *Making Sense of Taste.*

27 Rigotti, *La filosofia in cucina*. On the theme of food, Rigotti has also published *Gola: La passione dell'ingordigia* (Bologna: Il Mulino, 2008) and *Manifesto del cibo liscio: Per una nuova filosofia in cucina* (Novara: Interlinea, 2015).

28 Perullo, *Taste as Experience*, 8.

29 A pivotal discussion of marginality is that of Gloria Anzaldúa, who in her seminal autobiographical work *Borderlands* (1987) presented the concept of border identity as an explanatory model for the Chicano woman living in the geographical space of the US-Mexico border. In a similar way, concepts

of borders and boundaries have been pivotal in feminist and women's studies as metaphors for going beyond pre-fixed identities; theories such as Rosi Braidotti's nomadic subject (*Nomadic Subjects*) and Donna Haraway's cyborgs (Haraway, *Simians, Cyborgs and Women*) all derive from the concept of boundary-crossing.

30 Perullo, *Taste as Experience*, 9.
31 Perullo, "Esperienza estetica," 90.
32 Perullo, *Taste as Experience*, 18.
33 Damasio, "Emotions and Feelings," 51–2. Damasio's theory influenced other disciplines. Some psychoanalysts were ready to propose the use of Damasio's theories and their emphasis on the embodied self, in clinical psychology, in order to include in psychoanalytic analysis changes in bodily reactions, feelings about one's own body, and facial gesture. Sletvold, "Neuroscience," 551.
34 Linden, *Touch*; Barrett, *How Emotions Are Made*.
35 Rosenwein and Cristiani, *What Is the History*, 107.
36 Boddice, *History of Feelings*; Boddice and Smith, *Emotion, Sense, Experience*.
37 Gatens, *Imaginary Bodies*; Grosz, *Volatile Bodies*.
38 Ahmed, *Cultural Politics*, 206.
39 Ahmed, *Cultural Politics*, 205–6. See Koivunen, "Affective Turn"; Cvetkovich, *Depression*.
40 hooks, *Talking Back*; Lorde, *Sister Outsider*; Spelman, "Anger and Insubordination"; Hochschild, *Managed Heart*.
41 Boddice, "History of Emotions," 13.
42 Boddice, "History of Emotions," 13.

1. Fascism, Food, and the Senses

1 Wodak and Richardson, *Analysing Fascist Discourse*.
2 Spackman, *Fascist Virilities*.
3 Spackman in *Fascist Virilities* discusses emotions in her analysis of homophobic economies. See also Arthurs, "Settling Accounts"; Biess, "Feelings of the Aftermath"; Goodwin, Jasper, and Polletta, *Passionate Politics*. On emotions in a contemporary perspective, see Wodak, *Politics of Fear*; Westberg, "Affective Rebirth."
4 Helstosky, *Garlic and Oil*, 63.
5 Nützenadel, "Dictating Food," 92.
6 Helstosky, "State of Meatlessness," 12. Cookbooks had risen in popularity during the unification period; no longer addressing the aristocracy, they were intended for the new middle class emerging at this time. The first published cookbook by a woman is Giulia Ferraris Tamburini, *Come posso mangiar bene?* (1900).

7 Reddy, "Against Constructionism," 335.
8 Rosenwein, *Emotional Communities*, 11. See also Rosenwein, "Worrying About Emotions in History."
9 Falasca Zamponi evidences this point by looking at the poster of the eighth Concorso per la vittoria del grano, which skilfully combined the image of two children and a religious motto. Falasca Zamponi, *Fascist Spectacle*, 155–6.
10 Falasca Zamponi, *Fascist Spectacle*, 12.
11 Nützenadel, "Dictating Food," 91–2.
12 Nützenadel, "Dictating Food," 89–91.
13 Helstosky, *Garlic and Oil*, 75.
14 Saraiva, *Fascist Pigs*, 22.
15 Ferris, "Consumption," 125.
16 Borojevic and Borojevic, "Transfer and History," 456.
17 Saraiva, *Fascist Pigs*, 35.
18 Helstosky, "Fascist Food Politics," 5.
19 Falasca Zamponi, *Fascist Spectacle*, 155–6.
20 Ascenzi and Brunelli, "Accomplishing the 'Silent Mission,'" 511.
21 Ascenzi and Brunelli, "Accomplishing the 'Silent Mission,'" 513.
22 Ascenzi and Brunelli, "Accomplishing the 'Silent Mission,'" 515.
23 Corner, "Italy," 159.
24 As a consequence of the embargo, international countries – albeit with some notable exceptions – reduced the export of goods related to the war in Italy (arms, steel, and coal); credit to the Italian government, institutes, and individuals was also forbidden.
25 Dickie, *Delizia!*, 265.
26 Addis Saba, *La corporazione delle donne*, 35–6.
27 Spackman, *Fascist Virilities*.
28 De Grazia, *How Fascism Ruled Women*; De Giorgio, *Le italiane*; Addis Saba, *La corporazione delle donne*; Pickering-Iazzi, *Mothers of Invention*.
29 Historians remark that the adjective "muliebre" suits the preference for Latinism typical of the Fascist period as it "traspone sul femminile l'elevatezza morale attribuita al virile" (transfers on femininity the moral high standards attributed to masculinity). Emma Scaramuzza, quoted in Addis Saba, *La corporazione delle donne*, 34.
30 For the role of Massaie Rurali within Fascist nationalistic politics, see Willson, "Cooking the Patriotic Omelette."
31 Quoted in Re, "Fascist Theories of 'Woman,'" 82.
32 Quoted in Chang, *Crisis-Woman*, 54.
33 Chang, *Crisis-Woman*, 55.
34 Ghezzo, "Topographies of Disease," 202–3.
35 Ghezzo, "Topographies of Disease," 205–6.

36 Palmieri, "A casa le madri," 183.
37 Cantono, "Il lavoro della donna," 189.
38 Gozzini, "La donna," 41–2.
39 Gozzini, "La donna," 42. The *Almanacco della donna italiana*, however, with its regular overview of women's writing in the column Rassegna femminile, did provide a wide range of alternative images. See Balestra, "Writing Women in 1930s Italy," 63.
40 Ottello, "Scrittrici," 500.
41 Canuti, "Cronache sociali," 286.
42 Sandra Ponzanesi traces the development of interracial relationships in the Italian colonies, identifying a shift from the propaganda image of the virile conquest of Africa, epitomized by the Italian man conquering African women, to the construction of the colonies as a land of married men once Italian wives were encouraged to join their husbands there. Ponzanesi, "Colour of Love."
43 Poggiali, "La donna italiana in A.O.," 65.
44 Poggiali, "La donna italiana in A.O.," 65.
45 Perricone Violà, *Ricordi somali*, 172.
46 Helstosky, *Garlic and Oil*; Ferris, "Consumption"; Anderson, *Control and Resistance*; Garvin, *Feeding Fascism*. See also, on food and power in different contexts, Martschukat and Simon, *Food, Power, and Agency*, and Avieli, *Food and Power*.
47 Garvin, *Feeding Fascism*.
48 Together with the already mentioned research by grain geneticists, the Fascist government promoted "scientific" research on nutrition and other aspects of the alimentary discourse. Well known is the dubious research by Giuseppe Tallarico, which correlated the consumption of wheat germ in wholemeal bread to human fertility. Helstosky, "Fascist Food Politics," 12. Modernization of the kitchen space in the name of efficiency was another sector where much work was being done, also by authors like Lidia Morelli.
49 Randi, *La cucina autarchica*, 21.
50 Randi, "Come si mangia," 319.
51 Randi, "Come si mangia," 307–12.
52 For a discussion of the concept of disease in the Ascension Day speech, see Spackman, *Fascist Virilities*, 146.
53 Morelli, *Le massaie. Dalla cucina al salotto*, the successful book of manners by Lidia Morelli, alias Donna Clara, originally published in 1905, was republished in 1925 with the addition of a section dedicated to recipes: Clara, *Dalla cucina al salotto*.
54 Morelli, *Le massaie*, 64–6.
55 Zamara, *La cucina italiana*, 349–50.

56 Petronilla, "Vitello al limone," 10.
57 Bonfiglio Krassich, *L'Almanacco della cucina*.
58 Capuzzo, "Food and Locality," 69–70.
59 Capuzzo, "Food and Locality," 71.
60 Bonfiglio Krassich, *L'Almanacco della cucina*, 5.
61 Dickie, *Delizia!*, 285–6.
62 Boni, *Il talismano*, 5.
63 Boni, *Il talismano*, 10.
64 She wrote, "Il Fascismo tra le sue benemerenze ha avuto anche quella di abbattere ogni vincolo campanilistico affratellando in un unico grande ideale ogni regione, e completando nel modo più reale e fattivo la grande unità d'Italia attraverso l'unità degli spiriti" (Fascism, among its many qualities, has had the ability to demolish any parochial culture by uniting each region in a common idea, and completing in the most pragmatic way the great unity of the country through a unity of souls). Boni, *Il talismano*, 17.
65 Boni, *Il talismano*, 17.
66 Adorni and Magagnoli, "La 'cucina italiana,'" 20–31.
67 Adorni and Magagnoli, "La 'cucina italiana,'" 24–5. Futurist activities were publicized throughout the magazine.
68 Adorni and Magagnoli, "La 'cucina italiana,'" 24.
69 Pautasso, *Cucina Futurista*, 11–14.
70 Pautasso, *Cucina Futurista*, 15–16.
71 Pautasso, *Cucina Futurista*, 21–5.
72 Futurist dining occasions were also organized as part of theatre pieces. During the interval of the last performed comedy by Marinetti, "Simultanina," Futurist food was served, and the performance concluded with Marinetti's appearance on stage passionately advocating for the abolishment of pasta from Italian cuisine. Pautasso, *Cucina Futurista*.
73 Griffiths, "Marisa Mori's Edible Futurist Breast," 25.
74 Ghiazza, "La letteratura rosa," 146.
75 Rorandelli, "Nascita e morte."
76 Re, "Fame, cibo e antifascismo."
77 The modernist aesthetics of Masino's short story "Fame" has been also analysed by Enrico Cesaretti in conjunction with Massimo Bontempelli's theatre piece "Fame" of the same period. Cesaretti, *Fictions of Appetite*, 169–208.
78 Already in the 1920s, the government established a literary prize for the new genre of the colonial novel. Supporting this genre meant fostering colonial desire and ambition in the population. The reception of colonial literature was, however, rather ambivalent. As a genre, it was both much appreciated and much condemned by the critics of

the time. Indeed, in 1931 a survey organized by the magazine *L'Azione coloniale* and addressing writers, intellectuals, and colonizers aimed at establishing whether a colonial literature really existed. Venturini, *Fuori campo*, 22–3. Many lamented a lack of interest among the general public and a lack of a real colonial conscience, while supporters of colonial literature, such as Filippo Tommaso Marinetti, stressed its importance for Fascist colonialization. Fascism promoted children's literature as a privileged way to shape the new Italians. See Colin, *I bambini di Mussolini*.

79 Anonymous, "Il premio Bologna," 3.

80 Ballario, *Come ho visto la Russia e altri paesi del mondo* and *Il figlio che mi hai dato*.

81 Around the world, many were the women travel writers who covered long distances in the British and French empires. As Michela De Giorgio clarifies, in Italy from the 1880s, segregation in the house starts being considered a lack of modernity and the more independent life of British and Northern European women was seen as a model. De Giorgio, *Le italiane*, 89–90. Among the women travel writers of the end of the nineteenth century and the beginning of the twentieth, we remember Carla Serena, Angela Bettoni, Cesarina Lupati, Amy Bernardy, and Irene de Robilant. Before them Cristina Trivulzio di Belgioioso and Amalia Nizzoli provided great examples of travel writing.

82 Burdett in *Journeys Through Fascism* discusses the travel writing of women like Alba Felter Sartori, Louise Diel, and Margherita Sarfatti.

83 Rizzi, "Una donna giramondo," 193.

84 Rizzi, "Una donna giramondo," 195.

85 Ballario, *Come ho visto*, 97.

86 Ballario, *Come ho visto*, 105.

87 Ballario, *Come ho visto*, 242.

88 Ballario, *Come ho visto*, 165.

89 Ballario, *Come ho visto*, 156.

90 Ballario, *Come ho visto*, 166.

91 Ballario, *Come ho visto*, 226–7.

92 Ballario, *Come ho visto*, 155–6.

93 Ballario, *Come ho visto*, 128.

94 Ballario, *Come ho visto*, 197.

95 Ballario, *Come ho visto*, 116.

96 Ballario, *Come ho visto*, 209.

97 Lupton, *Food*, 36.

98 Ballario, *Fortuna sotto vento*.

99 Pickering-Iazzi, "Labors of Love," 79.

100 Even the male hero, Veniero, who is a model of Fascist colonial ideals and, at the conclusion of the novel, predicably becomes Azizia's husband-to-be, can only order his male cook to prepare lobster and *insalata russa* for his guest Gian. It is a meal based on prepared, tinned food with minimal personal involvement or cultural contact. In Ballario's second novel on Libya, *I giardini dell'oblio*, food references assume a comic dimension, with jokes invariably relating to the indigenous cooks' inability to work at high standards. African cuisine and expertise are systematically devalued.
101 hooks, "Eating the Other," 21.
102 Pickering-Iazzi, "Labors of Love," 84.
103 Ballario, *Il figlio*, 92.
104 Ballario, *Il figlio*, 108.
105 Ballario, *Il figlio*, 71.
106 Sorgoni, "Racist Discourses," 51.
107 Sorgoni, "Racist Discourses," 52.
108 De Napoli, "Origin of the Racist Laws," 111.
109 Lucidi, "L'alimentazione del bambino," 16.
110 Lucidi, "L'alimentazione del bambino," 16.
111 Ballario, *Il figlio*, 78.
112 Ballario, *Il figlio*, 46.
113 Ballario, *Il figlio*, 146.
114 Ballario, *Il figlio*, 46.
115 Ballario, *Il figlio*, 34.
116 Ballario, *Il figlio*, 71.
117 Ahmed, *Cultural Politics*, 4.
118 Ahmed, *Cultural Politics*, 24.
119 Fasullo, "Vivere per scrivere."
120 Boemia, "'Come un salto nel buio.'"
121 Åkerström, "Revisione critica," 806.
122 For a detailed discussion of the genesis of this novel, see Andreoni, "*Io, suo padre. Romanzo sportivo.*"
123 Carletti, "'La sponda dell'attesa'"; Ferme, "Against Marriage and Child-Rearing"; Gallucci, "De Céspedes's *There's No Turning Back*"; Zancan, "Introduzione"; Zancan, *Alba de Céspedes.*
124 Gallucci, "De Céspedes's *There's No Turning Back*," 201.
125 De Grazia, *How Fascism Ruled Women*, 233.
126 Pickering-Iazzi, "Sexual Politics," 90.
127 De Céspedes, *Nessuno*, 100.
128 Both Pickering-Iazzi, "Sexual Politics," and Zancan, *Alba de Céspedes*, indicate the image of the bridge as a suggestion of new possibilities.
129 De Céspedes, *Nessuno*, 15.

130 De Céspedes, *Nessuno*, 10.
131 De Céspedes, *Nessuno*, 30.
132 De Céspedes, *Nessuno*, 26, 63.
133 De Céspedes, *Nessuno*, 119.
134 Pickering-Iazzi, "Sexual Politics," 89–94.
135 De Céspedes, *Nessuno*, 39.
136 De Céspedes, *Nessuno*, 137.
137 De Céspedes, *Nessuno*, 302–3.
138 De Céspedes, *Nessuno*, 44.
139 De Céspedes, *Nessuno*, 412.
140 De Céspedes, *Nessuno*, 156.
141 In Milly's description of her reading, haptics is also emphasized as a non-verbal and embodied form of communication. The visually impaired Milly describes the written words of her beloved entering her pores, blood, and body through her fingers (88).
142 De Céspedes, *Nessuno*, 106.
143 Babini, *Parole armate*, 155.
144 In the appendix to a subsequent edition of her 1949 *Dalla parte di lei*, de Céspedes explicitly comments on the loss of autonomy and illusion of freedom of democratic Italy. De Céspedes, *Romanzi*, 833–4.
145 De Céspedes, "Lettera a Natalia Ginzburg," 137.

2. World War II, Food, and Women's Bodies

1 Bruzzone and Farina, *La Resistenza taciuta*; Guidetti Serra, *Compagne*; Alloisio and Beltrami, *Volontarie della libertà*; Bravo and Bruzzone, *In guerra senz'armi*; Slaughter, *Women and the Italian Resistance*; Addis Saba, *Partigiane*; Gagliani et al., *Donne, Guerra, politica*; Porzio, *Arrivano gli Alleati!*; Ponzani, *Guerra alle donne*.
2 Petronilla, *Ricette di Petronilla per tempi eccezionali*, 1.
3 Petronilla, *Ricette di Petronilla per tempi eccezionali*, 94.
4 Legnani, "Consumi di guerra," 110.
5 Bertolo, *Donne e cucina*, 45.
6 Legnani, "Consumi di guerra," 111. For a discussion of the black market and women's experience of it, see my "Dynamics, Experiences, and Political Meaning."
7 Legnani, "Consumi di guerra," 111.
8 Petronilla, *Desinaretti per … questi tempi*, 5.
9 Zagatti, "Il problema dell'alimentazione," 229.
10 Lovallo, "Società e giustizia: i reati annonari attraverso le sentenze del tribunale di Bologna,"256, 263.
11 Anonymous, "Tribunale di Pescara," 6.

12 La Massaia, "Benvenuta Autarchia," 15.
13 La Massaia, "In cucina," 11.
14 Petronilla, *200 suggerimenti*, 252.
15 Petronilla, *Ricette di Petronilla*, 33; emphasis in original.
16 Salvatici, *Storia delle donne*, 129.
17 Nuboli, *Fasciste di Salò*, 66.
18 Nuboli, *Fasciste di Salò*, 66.
19 Marisa Ombra, quoted in Gabrielli, Cicognetti, and Zancan, *Madri della Repubblica*, 72.
20 Quoted in Gabrielli, Cicognetti, and Zancan, *Madri della Repubblica*, 73.
21 Addis Saba, *Partigiane*, 27–8.
22 Addis Saba, *Partigiane*, 158–9.
23 Ellwood, "Trauma of Liberation," 133–4.
24 Venturoli, "La violenza taciuta." According to Venturoli, the decision to ignore Fascist violence on partisan women was supported by the desire to reconciliate the country after the civil war and the reiteration of the value of male honour.
25 Fantozzi, "L'onore violato," 92.
26 Ellwood, "Trauma of Liberation," 136.
27 Fantozzi, "Raccontare Tombolo," 422.
28 Fantozzi, "L'onore violato," 101.
29 Fantozzi, "Raccontare Tombolo," 421.
30 Patrizia Gabrielli sees the constitution of the GDD as the result of the initiatives of the Communist Party, which in November 1943 published the future developments of women's politics in the *Direttive per il lavoro tra le masse femminili*. Gabrielli, Cicognetti, and Zancan, *Madri della Repubblica*, 11. Marina Addis Saba detects the strict link between the Partito Comunista Italiano (PCI) and the GDD also in the choice of the name. *Partigiane*, 40. Laura Orlandini, piecing together the accounts given by Ada Prospero Gobetti and Lina Merlin, suggests that the GDD was probably created at the intersection of directives by the Comitato di Liberazione Nazionale (CLN) and the initiatives of anti-Fascist women. *La democrazia delle donne*, 16. The women of the founding group were already involved in the political parties of the CLN: Giuliana Barcellona, Giulietta Fibbi, and Rina Picolato were members of the PCI; Laura Conti and Lina Merlin were Socialist; Elena Dreher and Ada Gobetti were part of the Partito d'Azione. Addis Saba, *Partigiane*, 40. However, Orlandini and other sources note a slightly different list of founding members. *La democrazia delle donne*, 14n9.
31 "Atto costitutivo: Programma d'azione dei GDD," Archivio Digitale UDI, folder C75/1.
32 *Noi donne* (Veneto), "I compiti dei gruppi," 2.
33 *Noi donne* (Veneto), "I compiti dei gruppi," 2.

34 Istituto per la Storia della Resistenza di Modena, Fondo Adamo Pedrazzi 1943–45, box 3, vol. viii.
35 Prior to its publication in Italy, *Noi donne* was the title of the anti-Fascist monthly magazine of the Union of the Italian Women, an association of Italian migrant women in France. It was first published in 1936 in Paris. Gavioli, "Parliamo di Noi (donne)."
36 *Noi donne* (Emilia Romagna), no. 2 (May 1944): 5.
37 *Noi donne* (Tuscany), no. 5 (July 1944): 1.
38 *Noi donne* (Tuscany), no. 5 (July 1944): "Un bell'esempio di lotta," 1.
39 *Noi donne* (Emila Romagna), "Manifestazione di donne per l'aumento delle razioni," no. 3 (June 1944): 9.
40 *Noi donne* (Veneto), "Manifestazioni di donne," 2. The representations of determined and fighting women facing weaker Nazis are not unusual in the clandestine press of *Noi donne*. In issue 5 of July 1944 (with an unidentified place of publication), the story of a revolt in Omegna, in Piedmont, led by women to obtain the liberation of four partisans offers an example of the overtones used: "La popolazione … le donne in testa, … assale i tedeschi i quali rimangono sconcertati dalla furia delle donne che imprecano e li prendono per i capelli" (The population … captained by women … attacks the Germans, who remain disconcerted by the fury of the women who, insulting them, grab them by their hair). *Noi donne*, "Soldati partigiani strappati alla morte," 8.
41 *Noi donne* (Veneto), "Agitazioni femminili nel veronese," 2.
42 *Noi donne* (Lombardy), "Le lavoratrici milanesi," 1.
43 *Noi donne* (Liguria), "Basta con le ruberie tedesche!," 6.
44 *Noi donne*, "Le donne di Reggio," 2.
45 *Noi donne*, "Abbiamo ricevuto Noi donne," 13.
46 *Noi donne* emphasized the certain attainment of women's vote in the post-war Parliament: "Non vi è dubbio che a guerra finita verrà dato alle donne italiane il diritto di votare e di essere elette alle cariche di direzione del paese" (Undoubtedly, at the end of the war women will be granted the right to vote and to be elected to government office). *Noi donne*, "Il nostro movimento," 5. The war and Fascism were presented as a direct consequence of women's absence from the political life of the country: "Ma è proprio perché il popolo italiano, e le donne in particolare, non si sono interessate sufficientemente di politica che il governo dell'Italia è caduto nelle mani di una banda di avventurieri e di profittatori, con Mussolini alla testa" (But it is just because the Italian people, and women in particular, did not get sufficiently interested in politics that the Italian government has fallen into the hands of a band of unscrupulous cowboys with Mussolini as head"). *Noi donne*, "Il nostro movimento," 5.
47 *Noi donne*, "Una madre italiana," 3.
48 *Noi donne*, "Una madre italiana," 3.

49 For women's legitimization through the familial role, see Bravo, "Armed and Unarmed," 480.
50 *Noi donne*, "Manifestazione di donne," 13.
51 *Noi donne*, "Epurazione, lavoro e pane," 14.
52 *Noi donne*, "Epurazione, lavoro e pane," 14.
53 The Gruppi d'Azione Patriottica (GAP) were small groups of partisans engaged in guerilla fighting in cities. *Noi donne* describes GAP women in this way: "Ed infine c'erano le azioni dove le donne non meno degli uomini giustiziavano i traditori, senza sadismo e senza leggerezza, rendendosi ben conto della gravità di quello che facevano, ma sicure di agire secondo giustizia … Donne che hanno saputo affrontare il loro dovere di esseri 'morali' e viventi in una determinata situazione storica" (And finally there were the attacks where women, just like men, would kill traitors, without sadism and with no light-heartedness, being aware of what they were doing, but sure to act according to justice … Women who were able to face their duty of "moral" human beings in a specific historical situation). *Noi donne*, "Le ragazze nei GAP," 10.
54 For the reference to women's Resistance amounting to two million women, see Willson, "Women, War and the Vote," 619.
55 Gabrielli, *Scenari di guerra*, 20.
56 Bruzzone and Farina, *La Resistenza taciuta*; Guidetti Serra, *Compagne*.
57 On the influence of political parties on the official commemorations of the Resistance see Gundle, "'Civic Religion.'" Evidence of late official commemorations is provided by the region Abruzzi, where, only in 2018, local women partisans were officially commemorated for the first time with the renaming of city streets.
58 Semelin, *Sans armes face à Hitler*.
59 Addis Saba, *Partigiane*, x–xi.
60 Bravo and Bruzzone, *In guerra senza armi*.
61 Bravo, "Armed and Unarmed," 480.
62 Bravo, "Armed and Unarmed," 476.
63 Bravo, "Armed and Unarmed," 479.
64 Bravo and Bruzzone, *In guerra senza armi*, 19.
65 De Silva, *In Memory's Kitchen*; and Georget, *Imaginary Feasts*.
66 Le Breton, *Sensing the World*, 11.
67 Le Breton, *Sensing the World*, 11.
68 Levinas, *Totality and Infinity*.
69 Lennon and Wilde, "Alienation and Affectivity," 44.
70 Colombetti, "Affective Incorporation," 239.
71 Archivio dell'Istituto per la storia della Resistenza e della società contemporanea nel Biellese, nel Vercellese e in Valsesia (Istorbive), fondo Gladys Motta, envelope 141, box 4.

72 Bracco, *La staffetta*, 65.
73 Bracco, *La staffetta*, 68.
74 Bracco, *La staffetta*, 89.
75 Bracco, *La staffetta*, 12.
76 Feher, Naddaff, and Tazi, *Fragments;* Scheer, "Bourdieuian Approach; "Feeling Faith"; Pernau and Rajamani, "Emotional Translations."
77 Bracco, *La staffetta*, 83.
78 Bracco, *La staffetta*, 83.
79 Bracco, *La staffetta*, 19.
80 Bracco, *La staffetta*, 20.
81 Bracco, *La staffetta*, 80.
82 Bracco, *La staffetta*, 80.
83 Le Breton, *Sensing the World.*
84 Colombetti, "Affective Incorporation," 239.
85 Colombetti, "Affective Incorporation," 242.
86 Bravo and Bruzzone, *In guerra senza armi*, 19.
87 Trevisan, *L'archivio di Giovanna Zangrandi*, 16.
88 Morris, "Giovanna Zangrandi," 94.
89 Morris, "Giovanna Zangrandi," 120–1.
90 Zangrandi, *I giorni veri*, 15; emphasis in original.
91 Zangrandi, *I giorni veri*, 16; "Il clan dei bolognesi ed emiliani con i loro cenini e le loro tagliatelle" (The clan of the Italians from Bologna and Emilia with their habit of dinners and tagliatelle).
92 Zangrandi, *I giorni veri*, 17; emphasis in original.
93 Zangrandi, *I giorni veri*, 12.
94 Zangrandi, *I giorni veri*, 14.
95 Zangrandi, *I giorni veri*, 27.
96 Zangrandi, *I giorni veri*, 28.
97 Zangrandi, *I giorni veri*, 31.
98 Zangrandi, *I giorni veri*, 41.
99 Zangrandi, *I giorni veri*, 145.
100 Zangrandi, *I giorni veri*, 216.
101 Zangrandi, *I giorni veri*, 51.
102 Zangrandi, *I giorni veri*, 216.
103 Zancan, "Parole vere," 273.
104 Zangrandi, *I giorni veri*, 216.
105 Zangrandi, *I giorni veri*, 127.
106 Zancan, "Parole vere," 273.
107 Zangrandi, *I giorni veri*, 56, 160, 177, 199. For more food stories of civilians' support see Carrara and Salvini, *Partigiani a tavola.*
108 Zangrandi, *I giorni veri*, 145.
109 Zangrandi, *I giorni veri*, 197, 212.

110 Zangrandi, *I giorni veri,* 242.
111 Levinas, *Totality and Infinity.*
112 "E' il libro di una donna, non una delle tante semplici donne italiane che in quel periodo furono spinte da un istintivo desiderio di pace e di giustizia a una superiore coscienza civile, ma d'una donna la cui vita era già stata segnata dalla lotta antifascista: Ada Prospero, la vedova di Pietro Gobetti ... Ma questa tempra di combattente s'accompagna, è una cosa sola, con lo spirito della donna laboriosa e pratica e tenace e di buon senso, e della madre, la madre di dovunque e di sempre, sollecita e ansiosa soprattutto per la sua prole." (It is the book of a woman, not one of the many simple Italian women who, in that period, were moved to a superior civil conscience by an instinctive desire of peace and justice, but a woman whose life had already been marked by the anti-Fascist fight: Ada Prospero, widow of Pietro Gobetti ... But her fighting character is accompanied, and in fact is one thing, with the laborious, pragmatic, tenacious, and common-sense woman, with the mother, the mother wherever and always, attentive and anxious for her own offspring.) Calvino, "Nota," xvii.
113 Credaro, "Ada Gobetti Marchesini Prospero," 218–19, 219.
114 Pieri, "Souvenir d'une militante," 124–5.
115 Fofi, "Introduzione," viii.
116 Moorehead, *House in the Mountains.*
117 Alano, "Introduction," 9.
118 Pezzini, "La concreta utopia"; Pezzini, "Memoria, esperienza, sconfitta."
119 Pezzini, "Memoria, esperienza, sconfitta," 404.
120 Gobetti, *Diario,* 31.
121 Gobetti, *Diario,* 171–2.
122 Gobetti, *Diario,* 184.
123 Gobetti, *Diario,* 221.
124 Gobetti, *Diario,* 143–4.
125 Gobetti, *Diario,* 354.
126 Gobetti, *Diario,* 354.
127 Gobetti, *Diario,* 361.
128 Gobetti, *Diario,* 33.
129 Gobetti, *Diario,* 211.
130 Alano, "Introduction," 11.

3. The Politicization of the Everyday

1 Balestracci, "Il PCI," 997.
2 Balestracci, "Il PCI," 998.

3 Bracke, *Women*, 35–6. Although the two groups were interested in different aspects of women's life – UDI focused on women's labour and CIF on family – their requests became similar at the turn of the decade. As Bracke notes, CIF discussed the reconciliation of work and family and UDI gave more emphasis to the role of woman in the family, criticizing the patriarchal view of the Communist Party. It was on the discussion of state-funded childcare that the two organizations came together. Finally the long-debated divorce law brought both groups to detach from the main parties. Bracke, *Women*, 36–7.
4 Crainz, *Storia del miracolo italiano*, 29.
5 On the Merlin law see Azara, *L'uso "politico" del corpo femminile*; Bellassai, *La legge del desiderio*.
6 See Scarpellini, *Material Nation*; Asquer, *La rivoluzione candida* and *Storia intima dei ceti medi*.
7 Bottinelli, "Tradition and Modernity."
8 Sollazzo, "Il lavastoviglie," 17.
9 On the effects of the economic growth on the middle classes see Asquer, *Storia intima dei ceti medi*.
10 Harris, *Italian Women's Experiences*.
11 Scarpellini, *Food and Foodways*, 124.
12 Italian Parliament, "Inchiesta parlamentare sulla miseria."
13 De Berardi, "I Consumi in Italia," 493.
14 Corvino and Renato, *Consumi e industria alimentare*, 96.
15 Corvino and Renato, *Consumi e industria alimentare*, 96.
16 Scarpellini, *Food and Foodways*, 132.
17 See Piccone Stella, *La prima generazione*; and Saraceno, *Pluralità e mutamento*.
18 Crainz, *Il paese mancato*; Piccone Stella, *La prima generazione*; Passerini, *Storie di donne e femministe*.
19 See Morris, *Women in Italy*.
20 Gambaro, "Interno borghese," 232.
21 Gambaro, "Interno borghese," 233.
22 Morris, "From Private to Public," 14.
23 Quoted in Morris, "From Private to Public," 19.
24 Signorelli, "Women in Italy," 51.
25 Signorelli, "Women in Italy," 46.
26 Signorelli, "Women in Italy," 46.
27 Lussana, "Le donne e la modernizzazione," 499; Lussana, "Lezione."
28 De Céspedes, *Quaderno proibito*, 233.
29 De Céspedes, *Quaderno proibito*, 233.
30 De Céspedes, *Quaderno proibito*, 63.
31 Geoff Eley, in Therborn et al., "1970s and 1980s," 15–17.

32 Hajek, "Despite or in Debt to 1968," 39. On this topic see also Bracke, "One-Dimensional Conflict"; von der Goltz, *Talkin' 'Bout My Generation.*
33 Bravo, *A colpi di cuore*, 57.
34 Bravo, *A colpi di cuore*, 48–50. For Bravo, the Beat generation and the student movement differentiated first of all in the image they projected: miniskirts, long hair, and casual dresses for the Beat generation, jackets and pleated skirts for the first groups of students who took the streets to protest. But also, a lower-class origin was more common among the Beat generation, as well as being different in their choice of music and readings. Moreover, the student movement was strongly politically committed and supported the protests of factory workers. Bravo, *A colpi di cuore*, 42–4.
35 Lussana, "Le donne e la modernizzazione," 488. It is also evident that feminism, as Lussana summarizes, is a metahistorical movement that will never end, unlike the student movement, which is limited to a historical moment (491).
36 The first divorce bill was brought to parliament in 1878 by the Socialist Salvatore Morelli, who supported women's equality. In 1902 Giuseppe Zanardelli presented another proposal, but it was only in 1970 that the bill promoted by Lois Fortuna and Antonio Baslini was approved and became law. The political forces that supported the church immediately started a campaign for the abrogation of the 1970 divorce law. The referendum in 1974, with 59% of the votes in favour of divorce, finally made divorce legal in Italy. See Lussana, *L'Italia del divorzio*; Lombardi, *Storia del matrimonio.*
37 Gruppo Anabasi, *Donna è bello.*
38 These enterprises preceded the 1975 legislation for the state-managed *consultori* and asserted the right to an autonomous woman-only institution.
39 A report of the fourth conference of the British feminist movement, held in London in November 1972 and attended by Italian feminists, offers the Italian feminists' judgments of the British movement. Shared in the magazine *Sottosopra*, published in Milan with the aim of bringing together the experiences of the numerous women's groups present in Italy, the report underscored the contrast with British feminist groups at the conference on the question of political autonomy. Unlike them, Italian feminists had excluded from their movement all groups belonging to political parties. *Sottosopra*, "Convegno a Londra," 23.
40 Anna Rossi-Doria reminds us that a sense of uneasiness was often felt by several feminists who had first been active within extreme left-wing political parties. Caught up in the dilemma of the "double militancy" (doppia militanza), they experienced their moving away from their political parties to enter the feminist groups as a rejection of their political self to focus on women's liberation. Rossi-Doria, "Ipotesi," 23.

41 An extensive collection of materials about this group, donated by Mariarosa Dalla Costa, is now available at the Archivio Mariarosa Dalla Costa.
42 Lotta femminista's project was articulate and promoted free nursery schools and cafeterias, as well as women's health clinics autonomously managed by women.
43 Lotta femminista, *Quaderni di Lotta Femminista*, 7–8.
44 Leccardi, "La reinvenzione," 117.
45 Boler, *Feeling Power*, xi.
46 Heldke, "Unexamined Meal," 204; Curtin, "Food/Body/Person," 4.
47 Bracke, *Women*, 44.
48 Archivio Primo Moroni, "Primo Moroni e Ida Farè."
49 Reddy, *Navigation of Feeling*, 105.
50 Jasper, "Emotions of Protest," 408.
51 Hochschild, *Managed Heart*.
52 Leccardi, "La reinvenzione," 108.
53 Alcune femministe milanesi, "Pratica," 12.
54 Alcune femministe milanesi, "Pratica," 15.
55 *Sottosopra*, "Noi pratichiamo," 19.
56 Anderlini, "Prolegomeni."
57 Cesari, "La cipolla," 47.
58 Cesari, "La cipolla," 28.
59 Cesari, "La cipolla," 30.
60 Cesari, "La cipolla," 29.
61 Rivolta femminile, "Manifesto," 18.
62 Curtin, "Food/Body/Person," 5.
63 Guida, "Ricostruzione dell'io," 77.
64 Maraini, *Mangiami pure*, 3–4.
65 "Il vivente fratello che mi divora … si è abolita la posizione del 'dirimpetto' e si è trapassati nella posizione interiore" (The living brother who devours me … we have abolished the facing position and moved to the interior position). "Intervista con Dacia Maraini."
66 Maraini, *Mangiami pure*, 43–4.
67 Lillith, "Mater mortifera," 10.
68 Maraini, *Mangiami pure*, 9. For an analysis of the theorization of the mother-daughter relationship within the history of Italian feminism, see chapter 1 of my *Corporeal Bonds*.
69 "Intervista con Dacia Maraini."
70 Maraini, *Il treno*, 13.
71 Gabriele, *Dacia Maraini's Narratives*; Lazzaro-Weis, "Subject's Seduction"; Sumeli Weinberg, *Invito alla lettura*; Amoia, *Twentieth-Century Italian Women Writers*.
72 Maraini, *Il treno*, 3.
73 Gabriele, *Dacia Maraini's Narratives*, 3, 5.

74 Lillith, "Mater mortifera," 10.
75 Maraini, *Il treno*, 8.
76 Maraini, *Il treno*, 12–13.
77 Maraini, *Il treno*, 230.
78 Maraini, *Il treno*, 124–5.
79 Maraini, *Il treno*, 120.
80 Maraini, *Il treno*, 255.
81 Maraini, *Il treno*, 89.
82 Maraini, *Il treno*, 24.
83 Lupton, *Food*, 31.
84 Häberlen and Keck-Szajbel illustrate how the search for authenticity and a truer self was the central motor of 1968 protests and the changes derived from them. They note that in Czechoslovakia, Václav Havel labelled Communism as a lie and "thus called for 'living in the truth' to resist the communist regime." In Western Europe, listening to rock and punk music, as well as being open about sexuality, were all part of the attempts "to live more 'authentically.'" Moreover, from the mid-1970s, Michel Foucault's analysis in *Discipline and Punishment* and *The History of Sexuality* clarified how our sense of self is shaped in power relationships determined by institutions and social discourses. Häberlen, Keck-Szajbel, and Mahoney, *Politics of Authenticity*, 2–9.
85 Carson, *Silent Spring*; Lappé, *Diet for a Small Planet*.
86 Carstairs, "Granola High," 308.
87 Zancani, *How We Fell in Love*, 178.
88 Robertson, Flinders, and Godfrey, *Laurel's Kitchen*.
89 Bloodroot Collective, *Political Palate*.
90 Hartman, "Political Palate," 33.
91 McGrath, "Recipes," 174–5. Katzen, *Moosewood Cookbook*; Thomas, *Vegetarian Epicure*.
92 McGrath, "Recipes," 173; Brown, *Tassajara Bread Book* and *Tassajara Cooking*.
93 Belasco, *Appetite for Change*.
94 Sclauzero, *La cucina macrobiotica*.
95 "Ecologia in cucina," 12.
96 Buonfino, *La cucina integrale*.
97 "La cucina, i vini, sono argomenti affascinanti. Il loro revival, dopo alcuni anni oscuri, è legato secondo me, a motivi ecologici. E' in altri termini, un ritorno alla naturalezza, alla semplicità, a quei valori contadini che bene o male sono parte integrante della nostra cultura." (Food and wine are fascinating topics. Their revival, after a few dark years, is connected to ecological reasons, I think. It is, I mean, a coming back to simplicity, to those peasant values that, in a way or the other, are an integral part of our culture.) Veronelli, "A tavola alle sette."
98 Gosetti della Salda, *Le ricette regionali italiane*.
99 Gavotti, *Menù per un anno*.

100 Vera, *Si fa così.*
101 Gallotti, "Le impegnate in cucina," 13.
102 Sereni, *Via Ripetta 155.*
103 Passerini, *Autoritratto di gruppo*, 64–5.
104 Sereni, *Casalinghitudine.*
105 Rattazzi, *Soffiamo sulla cicoria matta.*
106 Cichi, "La minestra degli stupidi." For the categorization of food writing by women as autobiographical cookbooks, culinary memoirs, and autoethnographic cookbooks, see Kelly, "Voodoo Priestess."
107 Gambaro, *Diventare autrice*, 252.
108 Sereni, *Casalinghitudine*, 164.
109 Sereni, *Casalinghitudine*, 164.
110 Gaglianone, *Conversazione*, 19–20.
111 Cf. Brodzki and Schenck, *Life/Lines*; Mason, "Other Voice"; Smith, *Poetics of Women's Autobiography*; Stanton, *Female Autograph.*
112 Neuman, "Autobiography," 2.
113 Neuman, "Autobiography," 2. Cf. Benstock, *Private Self.*
114 Gaglianone, *Conversazione*, 7.
115 Sereni, *Casalinghitudine*, 40.
116 Sereni, *Casalinghitudine*, 165.
117 Sereni, *Casalinghitudine*, 114.
118 Scrimieri, "Around the Table," 153.
119 Sereni, *Casalinghitudine*, 165.
120 De Angelis, "Clara Sereni," 337.
121 A member of the extra-parliamentary party Avanguardia operaia in the late 1960s, Ida Farè went on, at the beginning of the 1980s, to make significant contributions in architecture, promoting ideas of urban and house spaces able to reflect women's competencies and lives. She was a long-standing member of the Women's Bookshop in Milan.
122 Giannotti, "¿Qué se cuece?," 116.
123 Farè, "Nel nome di Estia," 24.
124 Farè, "Nel nome di Estia," 25–6.
125 Colombo, "Per una definizione."
126 Giannotti, "La cucina," 35.
127 Pulcini, *Il potere di unire.*
128 Muraro, "Sull'essere in relazione."
129 Giannotti, "¿Qué se cuece?," 116–17.
130 Cuoche Varie, *Fuochi*, 117.
131 Essential readings on the symbolic of the Mother include Muraro, *L'ordine simbolico della madre*; Diotima, *Mettere al mondo il mondo*; Diotima, *Oltre l'uguaglianza*; Cavarero and Restaino, *Le filosofie femministe.*
132 In fact, another Estia member, Stefania Giannotti, expressed her grief for the loss of her son in her culinary memoir *Troppo sale: Un addio in ricette* (2017).

133 Giannotti, "La cucina," 40.
134 Hochschild, *Managed Heart.*

4. The Third Millennium: Food as Relationships

1 On this point see Bell and Valentine, *Consuming Geographies;* Ashley et al., *Food and Cultural Studies.*
2 Ashley et al., *Food and Cultural Studies,* 184.
3 Ashley et al., *Food and Cultural Studies,* 181–3.
4 Hyman, "Taste of Fame," 44.
5 Benedetta Parodi, a journalist turned cook, from 2011 acquired popularity for her recipe-based programs and associated cookery books. The well-known presenter Antonella Clerici dominated the midday television slot with her *La prova del cuoco,* which, with its BBC-adapted format (daily competition, food experts, and sections dedicated to children), engaged a wide audience. In fact, not only recipe books but also music CDs and a Nintendo game have spawned from the program. It is perhaps not surprising that Clerici's departure in 2018 was followed by a drop in the program popularity that reached its closure in 2020, to be substituted by a new program always presented by her.
6 Lupton, "Vitalities and Visceralities," 164.
7 Eagleton, "Edible ecriture."
8 Rhys-Taylor, *Food and Multiculture,* 121.
9 Mascarello et al., "Ethnic Food Consumption."
10 Fondazione Leone Moressa, "Rapporto annuale."
11 For a discussion of the protest to the kebab shop in Bergamo Alta that took place on Facebook, see Cavanaugh, "Il y a kébab." Local governments' initiatives to limit ethnic shops in historic centres have also been taken in Verona, Genoa, Padua, Milan, the province of Bergamo, and in 2020 in Vicenza.
12 Salvini's preference for selfies of gastronomic theme has been analysed in a course of communication at the Luiss School of Journalism in Rome. Ceccarelli, "La gara gastro-elettorale."
13 Jasper, "Emotions and Social Movements: Twenty Years," 295.
14 Ahmed, *Cultural Politics,* 57.
15 Buettner, "Going for an Indian"; Cinotto, *Italian American Table;* Gabaccia, *We Are What We Eat;* Zanoni, *Migrant Marketplaces.*
16 Cinotto, "Culture and Identity," 182.
17 Cinotto, "Culture and Identity," 182.
18 Gabaccia, *We Are What We Eat,* 6.
19 Maniaci, "Il kebab."

20 Parasecoli, "Invention of Authentic Italian Food."
21 Appadurai, "How to Make."
22 Leitch, "Slow Food," 440.
23 Both Genuino clandestino and Campi aperti use radical tones for their political stand regarding protection of traditions and methods of cultivation. Genuino clandestino states their intentions to take forward their fights "con o senza il consenso della legge" (within or outside legislation). See Genuino clandestino's manifesto: Genuino clandestino, "Comunità in lotta per l'autodeterminazione alimentare," https://genuinoclandestino.it/il-manifesto/. Campi aperti describes their active role through their "Palestra di Autodifesa Alimentare" (Training in alimentary self-defence). See Campi aperti, "Le origini di Campi Aperti," www.campiaperti.org/chi-siamo/le-origini/.
24 Jasper, "Emotions and Social Movements: Twenty Years," 291.
25 Chambers and Curti, "Migrating Modernities," 394.
26 Lamri, quoted in Chambers and Curti, "Migrating Modernities," 394.
27 Lakhous, *Scontro di civiltà*.
28 On the relevance of food imagery in this novel, see Parati, "Where Do Migrants Live?"; Mauceri, "Dalla bocca al cuore"; Horn, "Assaporare la tradizione."
29 Lamri, "Il caffè."
30 Lamri's depiction of the joy of food as joy of communal life, as reconnection to culture of origin, in addition to and not excluding the new flavours and cultures acquired through migration, echoes the work of Carmine Abate, who made these topics recurrent in his narrative of migration.
31 Among this group of authors are Erminia Dell'Oro, Gabriella Ghermandi, Cristina Ali Farah, Gabriella Kuruvilla, Ornela Vorpsi, Viola Chandra, Christian de Caldas Brito, Ribka Sibhatu, Ingy Mubiayi, Shirin Ramzanali Fazel, Igiaba Scego, and Laila Wadia.
32 Finocchi, *Il sapore*.
33 Scego, "Salsicce."
34 Ponzanesi, "Postcolonial Turn," 61.
35 Scego, "Salsicce," 26.
36 "Salsicce," 33.
37 "Salsicce," 35.
38 Gallese, "Brain, Body, Habit," 379.
39 Pulcini, "What Emotions," 65.
40 Pulcini, "What Emotions," 65.
41 Ferrari, "Parole migranti," 889.
42 Contarini, "Narrazioni migrazioni e genere."
43 Pizzi, "Translation Interrupted," 403.

44 Wadia, "Curry di pollo," 43.
45 Wadia, "Curry di pollo," 51.
46 Aldo addresses Ayjis as if she was Chinese, making use of a series of Western-centred and racist remarks: "'Voi cinesi siete proprio un popolo intraprendente ... Cinese, tibetano, giapponese, per noi sono tutti uguali,' Aldo ride scioccamente, 'se non mangiassero tante mandorle sarebbe più facile distinguerli forse'" ("You Chinese people are truly enterprising ... Chinese, Tibetan, Japanese, for us you are all the same," Aldo laughs stupidly, "if they did not eat so many almonds perhaps it would be easier to distinguish them"). "Ma voi siete comunisti allora? ... Ma allora li odi quanto noi?" ("But you are Communist then? ... But then, you will hate them as much as we do?") Wadia, "Spaghetti allo scoglio," 104–5, 106.
47 Wadia, "Spaghetti allo scoglio," 110.
48 hooks, "Eating the Other."
49 Mauceri, "Cultural Encounters," 268.
50 Rhys-Taylor, *Food and Multiculture*, 30.
51 Buettner, 'Going for an Indian."
52 Perullo, "Esperienza estetica," 90.
53 Perullo, *Taste as Experience*, 26.
54 Wadia, *Amiche*, 86, 93.
55 Wadia, *Amiche*, 29. The translation of Ungaretti's poem is by Colarossi, "Soldati/Soldiers."
56 Vertovec, "Super-Diversity."
57 Hutton, "Preface," 2.
58 Howard, "Nostalgia," 647.
59 Gerber, "Moving Backward," 310.
60 Boym, *Future of Nostalgia*, 41–5.
61 Sutton, *Remembrance of Repasts*.
62 Lupton, "Food, Memory and Meaning"; Lupton, *Food*.
63 Cinotto, "Italian Diasporic Identities," 58.
64 Janowski, "Introduction," 182.
65 Janowski, "Introduction," 183.
66 Scego, *La mia casa*, 13.
67 Wadia, "Introduzione," 11.
68 Wadia, "Il segreto," 131.
69 Wadia, "Il segreto," 132.
70 Wadia, "Il segreto," 132–3.
71 Wadia, "Il segreto," 132.
72 On Triestine culture see Ara and Magris, *Un'identità di frontiera*; Pizzi, *City in Search*; Pizzi, *Trieste*.
73 Sambuco, "Laila Wadia in Conversation."

74 Perullo, "Esperienza estetica," 89–90.
75 Wadia, *Kitchensutra*.
76 Playing with the images of food, the poetic subject states her desire with confidence in poems such as "No seconds," "Brevity," "Rolls," "Umami," and "Addiction," while expressing also rejection ("No tempura"), detachment ("Menu"), and disappointment ("Gifts") for her loving partner. Wadia, *Kitchensutra*.
77 Sulis, "Il racconto come militanza," 310.
78 Pulcini, "What Emotions," 68.
79 Pariani, *L'uovo*, 26.
80 Pariani, *L'uovo*, 68.
81 Pariani, *L'uovo*, 53.
82 Pariani, *L'uovo*, 43.
83 Pariani, *L'uovo*, 66.
84 Pariani, *L'uovo*, 71.
85 Pariani, *L'uovo*, 71.
86 Pariani, *L'uovo*, 77.
87 Pariani, *L'uovo*, 77–8.
88 Pariani, *L'uovo*, 79.
89 Boella, *Sentire l'altro*, quoted in Pulcini, "What Emotions," 66.
90 "Le indie dovrebbero odiare la loro vita tradizionale … freddo, fame, ignoranza, dipendenza totale dal maschio, tutto le tribola e le tormenta. Eppure sembrano amarla, o perlomeno la affrontano con coraggio." (The Fuegian women should hate their traditional life … cold, hunger ignorance, total dependence on the men, everything is a torment to them. And yet they seem to like it, or at least they face it with courage.) Pariani, *L'uovo*, 70.
91 Pulcini, "What Emotions," 68.
92 Pariani, *L'uovo*, 51.
93 Pariani, *L'uovo*, 220.

Conclusion

1 Dacia Maraini, who had been publishing since the 1960s, in this decade won two major national literary prizes: the Campiello prize for *La lunga vita di Marianna Ucria* and the Strega prize for *Buio*. The success of books like Susanna Tamaro's *Va dove ti porta il cuore* (1994), Maria Teresa Di Lascia's Strega-prize-winning novel *Passaggio in ombra* (1995), and the works by authors such as Silvia Ballestra, Melania Mazzucco, and Margaret Mazzantini, together with books by established authors like Fabrizia Ramondino, all contributed to the increased visibility of women's writing in the 1990s.

2 Here I play with the definition coined by Antonia Arslan, who described the vast number of post-Unification women writers who remained marginal to the mainstream Italian literary canon as a "galassia sommersa" (submerged galaxy). Arslan and Chemotti, *La galassia sommersa*.

3 Cuoche Varie, *Fuochi*, 117.

Bibliography

Archival Materials

Archivio dell'Istituto per la storia della Resistenza e della società contemporanea nel Biellese, nel Vercellese e in Valsesia (Istorbive). Fondo Gladys Motta, b. 141, fasc. 4.

Archivio Primo Moroni. "Ida Farè intervista Primo Moroni sul movimento delle donne." 20 February 2015. https://archive.org/details/PrimoMoroniIdaFareMovimentodelleDonne.

"Atto costitutivo. Programma d'azione dei GDD." Archivio Digitale UDI, Folder C75/1.

Istituto per la Storia della Resistenza di Modena. Fondo Adamo Pedrazzi 1943–45. Box 3, vol. viii. https://gdd.anpi.it/media/uploads/2016/12/Pedrazzi_Vol_08_Fascicolo_07_0014_r.jpg.

Noi donne. "Abbiamo ricevuto Noi donne." No. 3, September 1944. Archivio storico Noi Donne. https://www.noidonnearchiviostorico.org/archivio-storico.php.

– "Epurazione, lavoro e pane: Rivendicati dalle donne di Macerata." No. 7, December 1944. Archivio storico Noi Donne. https://www.noidonnearchiviostorico.org/archivio-storico.php.

– "Il nostro movimento: Non c'è tempo da perdere." No. 1, July 1944. Archivio storico Noi Donne. https://www.noidonnearchiviostorico.org/archivio-storico.php.

– "Le donne di Reggio e provincia sempre in lotta." No. 2, March 1945. Archivio storico Noi Donne. https://www.noidonnearchiviostorico.org/archivio-storico.php.

– "Le ragazze nei GAP." No. 2, August 1944. Archivio storico Noi Donne. https://www.noidonnearchiviostorico.org/archivio-storico.php.

– "Manifestazione di donne." No. 3, September 1944. Archivio storico Noi Donne. https://www.noidonnearchiviostorico.org/archivio-storico.php.

– "Soldati partigiani strappati alla morte." No. 5, July 1944. Archivio storico Noi Donne. https://www.noidonnearchiviostorico.org/archivio-storico.php.

– "Una madre italiana: Caterina Martinelli." No. 2, August 1944. Archivio storico Noi Donne. https://www.noidonnearchiviostorico.org/archivio-storico.php.

Noi donne (Emilia Romagna). Letter signed "Una donna cattolica." No. 2, May 1944. Archivio storico Noi Donne. https://www.noidonnearchiviostorico.org/archivio-storico.php.

– "Manifestazione di donne per l'aumento delle razioni." No. 3, June 1944. Archivio storico Noi Donne. https://www.noidonnearchiviostorico.org/archivio-storico.php.

Noi donne (Liguria). "Basta con le ruberie tedesche!" No. 8, November 1944. Archivio storico Noi Donne. https://www.noidonnearchiviostorico.org/archivio-storico.php.

Noi donne (Lombardy). "Le lavoratrici milanesi all'avanguardia nella lotta per il pane e la libertà." No. 5, October 1944. Archivio storico Noi Donne. https://www.noidonnearchiviostorico.org/archivio-storico.php.

Noi donne (Tuscany). Letter signed "Una contadina." No. 5, July 1944. Archivio storico Noi Donne. https://www.noidonnearchiviostorico.org/archivio-storico.php.

Noi donne (Veneto). "Agitazioni femminili nel veronese." No. 1, May 1944. Archivio storico Noi Donne. https://www.noidonnearchiviostorico.org/archivio-storico.php.

– "I compiti dei gruppi di difesa della donna." No. 1, May 1944. Archivio storico Noi Donne. https://www.noidonnearchiviostorico.org/archivio-storico.php.

– "Manifestazioni di donne contro la scrematura del latte." No. 1, May 1944. Archivio storico Noi Donne. https://www.noidonnearchiviostorico.org/archivio-storico.php.

Books and Journal Articles

Adams, Carol. *The Sexual Politics of Meat: A Feminist-Vegetarian Critical Theory*. New York: Continuum, 1990.

Addis Saba, Marina. *La corporazione delle donne: Ricerche e studi sui modelli femminili nel ventennio*. Florence: Vallecchi, 1988.

– *Partigiane: Tutte le donne della Resistenza*. Milan: Mursia, 1998.

Adolph, Andrea. *Food and Femininity in Twentieth-Century British Women's Fiction*. Farnham: Ashgate, 2009.

Adorni, Daniela, and Stefano Magagnoli. "La 'cucina italiana': Modelli di Femminilità Fascista." *Italia contemporanea*, no. 286 (April 2018): 11–33. https://doi.org/10.3280/ic2018-286001.

Ahmed, Sara. *The Cultural Politics of Emotion*. Edinburgh: University of Edinburgh Press, 2014.

Åkerström, Ulla. "Revisione critica dell'opera di Alba de Céspedes." In *Actes du XVIIIe congrès des romanistes scandinaves, Romanica Gothoburgensia 69*, edited by Eva Ahlstedt, Ken Benson, Elisabeth Bladh, Ingmar Söhrman, and Ulla Åkerström, 801–12. Gothenburg, Sweden: Acta universitatis Gothoburgensis, 2012.

Alano, Jomarie. "Introduction." In *Partisan Diary: A Woman's Life in the Italian Resistance*, 1–19. Oxford: Oxford University Press, 2014. https://doi.org/10.1093/acprof:osobl/9780199380541.003.0001.

Allen, Patricia, and Carolyn Sachs. "Women and Food Chains: The Gendered Politics of Food." *International Journal of Food and Agriculture* 15, no. 1 (April 2007): 1–23. https://doi.org/10.48416/ijsaf.v15i1.424.

Alloisio, Mirella, and Giuliana Beltrami. *Volontarie della libertà*. Milan: Mazzotta, 1981.

Amoia, Alba. *Twentieth-Century Italian Women Writers: The Feminine Experience*. Edwardsville: Southern Illinois University Press, 1996.

Anderlini, Serena. "Prolegomeni per una drammatugia al femminile: Intervista a Dacia Maraini." *Leggere Donna* 31 (March–April 1991): 22–4.

Anderson, Lara. *Control and Resistance: Food Discourse in Franco Spain*. Toronto: University of Toronto Press, 2020. https://doi.org/10.3138/9781487534677.

Andreoni, Annalisa. "*Io, suo padre. Romanzo sportivo*: Note sul romanzo d'esordio di Alba de Céspedes." *Quaderni d'Italianistica* 44, no. 1 (2023): 61–80. https://doi.org/10.33137/q.i..v44i1.42834.

Anzaldúa, Gloria. *Borderlands/La Frontera*. San Francisco: Aunt Lute Books, 1987.

Appadurai, Arjun. "How to Make a National Cuisine: Cookbooks in Contemporary India." *Comparative Studies in Society and History* 30, no. 1 (January 1988): 3–24. https://doi.org/10.1017/s0010417500015024.

Ara, Angelo, and Claudio Magris. *Un'identità di frontiera*. Turin: Einaudi, 2015.

Arslan, Antonia, and Saveria Chemotti. *La galassia sommersa*. Padua: Il Poligrafo, 2008.

Arthurs, Joshua. "Settling Accounts: Retribution, Emotion and Memory during the Fall of Mussolini." *Journal of Modern Italian Studies* 20, no. 5 (2015): 617–39. https://doi.org/10.1080/1354571X.2015.1096517.

Ascenzi, Anna, and Marta Brunelli. "Accomplishing the 'Silent Mission of Italian Women at War': The Fascist Pedagogy of War for Women; From the Kitchen Front to the War Garden." *History of Education and Children's Literature* 11, no. 2 (2016): 497–522.

Ashley, Bob, Joanne Hollows, Steve Jones, and Ben Taylor. *Food and Cultural Studies*. New York: Routledge, 2004. https://doi.org/10.4324/9780203646915.

Asquer, Enrica. *La rivoluzione candida: Storia sociale della lavatrice in Italia, 1945–1970*. Rome: Carocci, 2007.

– *Storia intima dei ceti medi: Una capitale e una periferia nell'Italia del miracolo economico*. Rome: Laterza, 2011.

Avieli, Nir. *Food and Power: A Culinary Ethnography of Israel*. Oakland: University of California Press, 2018. https://doi.org/10.1525/california/9780520290099.001.0001.

Azara, Liliosa. *L'uso "politico" del corpo femminile: La legge Merlin tra moralismo, nostalgia ed emancipazione*. Rome: Carocci, 2017.

Babini, Valeria. *Parole armate: Le grandi scrittrici del Novecento italiano tra Resistenza ed emancipazione*. Milan: La Tartaruga, 2018.

Balestra, Maria Enrica. "Writing Women in 1930s Italy." *The Italianist* 21, no. 1 (2001): 60–80. https://doi.org/10.1179/ita.2001.21.1.60.

Balestracci, Fiammetta. "Il PCI, il divorzio e il mutamento dei valori nell'Italia degli anni sessanta e settanta." *Studi storici* 54, no. 4 (October–December 2013): 989–1021.

Ballario, Pina. *Come ho visto la Russia e altri paesi del mondo*. Milan: La Prora, 1936.

– *Fortuna sotto vento: Palermo; Hodierna Editrice*. 1931. Reprint, Milan: La Prora, 1945.

– *I giardini dell'oblio*. Milan: Sonzogno, 1935.

– *Il figlio che mi hai dato*. Milan: La Prora, 1935.

– *La sposa bianca*. Milan: La Prora, 1933.

Barrett, Lisa Feldman. *How Emotions Are Made: The Secret Life of the Brain*. Boston: Macmillan, 2017.

Belasco, Warren. *Appetite for Change: How the Counterculture Took on the Food Industry*. Ithaca, NY: Cornell University Press, 2007.

Bell, David, and Gill Valentine. *Consuming Geographies: We Are Where We Eat*. New York: Routledge, 1997.

Bellassai, Sandro. *La legge del desiderio*. Rome: Carocci, 2006.

Benstock, Shari. *The Private Self: Theory and Practice of Women's Autobiographical Writings*. Chapel Hill: University of North Carolina Press, 1988.

Bertilotti, Teresa, and Anna Scattigno, eds. *Il femminismo degli anni settanta*. Rome: Viella, 2005.

Bertolo, Bruna. *Donne e cucina in tempo di guerra*. Sant'Ambrogio di Torino, Italy: Susalibri, 2017.

Biess, Frank. "Feelings of the Aftermath: Toward a History of Postwar Emotions." In *Histories of the Aftermath*, edited by Frank Biess and Robert Moeller, 30–48. New York: Berghahn Books, 2010. https://doi.org/10.1515/9781845459987-004.

Bloodroot Collective. *The Political Palate: A Feminist Vegetarian Cookbook*. Bridgeport, CT: Sanguinaria Publications, 1980.

Boddice, Rob. "The History of Emotions: Past, Present, Future." *Revista de Estudios Sociales* 62 (October–December 2017): 10–15. https://doi.org/10.7440/res62.2017.02.

– *A History of Feelings*. London: Reaktion Books, 2019. https://doi.org/10.1017/9781108884952.

Boddice, Rob, and Mark Smith. *Emotion, Sense, Experience*. Cambridge: Cambridge University Press, 2020.

Boella, Laura. *Sentire l'altro*. Milan: Cortina, 2006.

Boemia, Dario. "'Come un salto nel buio': La promozione editoriale di Nessuno torna indietro (1938–40)." Fondazione Arnoldo e Alberto Mondadori. https://www.fondazionemondadori.it/come-un-salto-nel-buio-la-promozione-editoriale-di-nessuno-torna-indietro-1938-1940/.

Boler, Megan. *Feeling Power: Emotions and Education*. London: Routledge, 1999.

Bonfiglio Krassich, Ada. *Almanacco della cucina regionale italiana*. Milan: Sonzogno, 1937.

– *La cucina economica in tempo di sanzioni*. Milan: Sonzogno, 1936.

– *Le gioie della mensa: Manuale di economia domestica e di cucina per le famiglie*. Milan: Sonzogno, 1934.

Boni, Ada. *Il talismano della felicità*. Rome: Edizioni della rivista *Preziosa*, 1937.

Borojevic, Katarina, and Ksenija Borojevic. "The Transfer and History of 'Reduced Height Genes' (RHG) in Wheat from Japan to Europe." *Journal of Heredity* 96, no. 5 (July–August 2005): 455–9. https://doi.org/10.1093/jhered/esi060.

Bottinelli, Silvia. "Tradition and Modernity: Industrial Food, Women and Visual Culture in 1950s and 1960s Italy." *Food Studies* 5, no. 1 (December 2014): 1–17. https://doi.org/10.18848/2160-1933/cgp/v05i01/40590.

Bourk, Joanne. "Pain: Metaphor, Body, and Culture in Anglo-American Societies Between the 18th and 20th Centuries." *Rethinking Histories* 18, no. 4 (2014): 475–98. https://doi.org/10.1080/13642529.2014.893660.

Boym, Svetlana. *The Future of Nostalgia*. New York: Basic Books, 2001.

Bracco, Cesarina. *La staffetta garibaldina*. Borgosesia, Italy: Istituto per la Storia della Resistenza in provincia di Vercelli, 1976.

Bracke, Maud Anne. "One-Dimensional Conflict? Recent Scholarship on 1968 and the Limits of the Generation Concept." *Journal of Contemporary History* 47, no. 3 (July 2012): 638–46. https://doi.org/10.1177/0022009412441755.

– *Women and the Reinvention of Politics: Feminism in Italy, 1968–1983*. New York: Routledge, 2014. https://doi.org/10.4324/9781315771014.

Brady, Jennifer, Barbara Parker, Susan Belyea, and Elaine Power. "Filling Our Plate: Spotlight on Feminist Food Studies." *Canadian Food Studies* 5, no. 1 (February 2018): 1–7. https://doi.org/10.15353/cfs-rcea.v5i1.308.

Braidotti, Rosi. *Nomadic Subjects: Embodiment and Sexual Difference in Contemporary Feminist Theory*. New York: Columbia University Press, 1994.

Bravo, Anna. *A colpi di cuore: Storie del sessantotto*. Rome: Laterza, 2008.
– "Armed and Unarmed: Struggles Without Weapons in Europe and in Italy." *Journal of Modern Italian Studies* 10, no. 4 (2005): 468–84. https://doi.org/10.1080/13545710500314694.
Bravo, Anna, and Anna Maria Bruzzone. *In guerra senz'armi: Storie di donne 1940–1945*. Bari: Laterza, 1995.
Brodzki, Bella, and Celeste Schenck, eds. *Life/Lines: Theorizing Women's Autobiography*. Ithaca, NY: Cornell University Press, 1988.
Brogi, Daniela. *Lo spazio delle donne*. Turin: Einaudi, 2022.
Brown, Edward Espe. *The Tassajara Bread Book*. San Francisco: Zen Centre, 1970.
– *The Tassajara Cooking*. San Francisco: Zen Centre, 1973.
Bruzzone, Anna Maria, and Rachele Farina. *La Resistenza taciuta*. Milan: La Pietra, 1976.
Buettner, Elizabeth. "'Going for an Indian': South Asian Restaurants and the Limits of Multiculturalism in Britain." *Journal of Modern History* 80, no. 4 (December 2008): 865–901. https://doi.org/10.1086/591113.
Buonfino, Liliana. *La cucina integrale*. Milan: Nicola Vincitorio, 1976.
Burdett, Charles. *Journeys Through Fascism: Italian Travel Writing Between the Wars*. New York: Berghahn, 2007. https://doi.org/10.3167/9781571815408.
Cairns, Kate, and Josée Johnston. *Food and Femininity*. London: Bloomsbury, 2015. https://doi.org/10.5040/9781474255158.
Calvino, Italo. "Nota." In Gobetti, *Diario partigiano*, xvii–xix.
Capuzzo, Paolo. "Food and Locality: Heritagization and Commercial Use of the Past." In *Food Heritage and Nationalism in Europe*, edited by Ilaria Porciani, 65–82. London: Routledge, 2019. https://doi.org/10.4324/9780429279751-4.
Carletti, Sandra. "'La sponda dell'attesa': Journeys and Rites of Passage in *Nessuno torna indietro*." *Italian Culture* 16, no. 2 (January 1998): 173–89. https://doi.org/10.1179/itc.1998.16.2.173.
Carnacina, Luigi, and Luigi Veronelli. *La cucina rustica regionale*. Milan: Rizzoli, 1974.
Carrara, Lorena, and Elisabetta Salvini. *Partigiani a tavola: Storie di cibo resistente e ricette di libertà*. Bologna: Fausto Lupetti Editore, 2015.
Carson, Rachel. *Silent Spring*. Boston: Houghton Mifflin, 1962.
Carstairs, Catherine. "The Granola High: Eating Differently in the Late 1960s and 1970s." In *Edible Histories, Cultural Politics: Towards a Canadian Food History*, edited by Marlene Epp, Valerie J. Korinek, and Franca Iacovetta, 305–25. Toronto: University of Toronto Press, 2012. https://doi.org/10.3138/9781442661509-020.
Cavanaugh, Jillian. "Il y a kébab et kébab: Conflict local et alimentation global in Italie du nord." *Anthropologie et Société* 37, no. 2 (August 2013): 193–212. https://doi.org/10.7202/1017912ar.

Cavarero, Adriana, and Franco Restaino. *Le filosofie femministe*. Turin: Paravia, 1999.

Cesaretti, Enrico. *Fictions of Appetite: Alimentary Discourses in Italian Modernist Literature*. Brussels: Peter Lang, 2013. https://doi.org/10.3726/978-3-0353-0499-2.

Cesari, Severino. "La cipolla era un sogno celeste: Intervista con Dacia Maraini." In *Dedica a Dacia Maraini*, edited by Claudio Cattaruzza, 19–48. Pordenone, Italy: Associazione provinciale per la prosa, 2000.

Chambers, Ian, and Lidia Curti. "Migrating Modernities in the Mediterranean." *Postcolonial Studies* 11, no. 4 (2008): 387–99. https://doi.org/10.1080/13688790802456077.

Chang, Natasha V. *The Crisis-Woman: Body Politics and the Modern Woman in Fascist Italy*. Toronto: University of Toronto Press, 2015. https://doi.org/10.3138/9781442621190.

Cinotto, Simone. "Culture and Identity on the Table: Italian American Food as Social History." In *The Routledge History of Italian Americans*, edited by William J. Connell and Stanislao G. Pugliese, 179–92. New York: Routledge, 2018. https://doi.org/10.4324/9780203501856-14.

– *Gastrofascismo e impero: Il cibo nell'Africa orientale italiana, 1935–1941*. Milan: Mimesi Edizioni, 2022.

– *The Italian American Table: Food, Family and Community in New York City*. Champaign: University of Illinois Press, 2013. https://doi.org/10.5406/illinois/9780252037733.001.0001.

– "Italian Diasporic Identities and Food." In Sassatelli, *Italians and Food*, 43–70. https://doi.org/10.1007/978-3-030-15681-7_3.

Colin, Mariella. *I bambini di Mussolini: Letteratura, libri, letture per l'infanzia sotto il fascismo*. Brescia: Editrice La Scuola, 2012.

Colombetti, Giovanna. "Affective Incorporation." In *Phenomenology for the Twenty-First Century*, edited by J. Edward Hackett and J. Aaron Simmons, 231–48. London: Palgrave Macmillan, 2016. https://doi.org/10.1057/978-1-137-55039-2_12.

Colombo, Grazia. "Per una definizione del lavoro di cura." *Animazione Sociale* 12 (1995): 11–23.

Contarini, Silvia. "Narrazioni migrazioni e genere." In *Certi confini*, edited by Lucia Quaquarelli, 119–59. Milan: Morellini, 2010.

Corner, Paul. "Italy." In *The Working Class and Politics in Europe and America 1929–1945*, edited by Stephen Salter and John Stevenson, 154–71. Abingdon: Routledge, 1990.

Corvino, Francesco, and Chiapparino Renato. *Consumi e industria alimentare in Italia dall'unità a oggi*. Perugia: Giada, 2002.

Counihan, Carole M. *The Anthropology of Food and Body: Gender, Meaning, and Power*. London: Routledge, 1999.

Crainz, Guido. *Il paese mancato: Dal miracolo economico agli anni ottanta*. Rome: Donzelli, 2005.

– *Storia del miracolo italiano*. Rome: Donzelli, 2005.

Cuoche Varie. *Fuochi: La cucina di Estia, supplement to Quaderni di Via Dogana no. 111*. Milan: Libreria delle donne di Milano, 2014.

Curtin, Deane. "Food/Body/Person." In Curtin and Heldke, *Cooking, Eating, Thinking*, 3–22.

Curtin, Deane, and Lisa Heldke, eds. *Cooking, Eating, Thinking: Transformative Philosophies of Food*. Bloomington: Indiana University Press, 1992.

Cvetkovich, Ann. *Depression: A Public Feeling*. Durham, NC: Duke University Press, 2012. https://doi.org/10.2307/j.ctv11smrx4.

Dalla Costa, Mariarosa, and Selma Jones. *The Power of Women and the Subversion of the Community*. Bristol: Falling Wall Press, 1972.

Damasio, Antonio. *Descartes' Error: Emotion, Reason, and the Human Brain*. New York: Putnam, 1994.

– "Emotions and Feelings: A Neurobiological Perspective." In *Feelings and Emotions: The Amsterdam Symposium*, edited by Antony S.R. Manstead, Nico Frijda, and Agneta Fisher, 49–57. Cambridge: Cambridge University Press, 2004. https://doi.org/10.1017/CBO9780511806582.004.

De Angelis, Gabriella. "Clara Sereni, ovvero l'indecente differenza." *Cahiers d'études italiennes* 7 (2008): 335–45. https://doi.org/10.4000/cei.941.

De Berardi, Alberto. "I Consumi in Italia: Uno specchio del cambiamento." In *L'Italia e le sue regioni: L'Italia Repubblicana*, edited by Mariuccia Salvati and Loredana Sciolla, 487–509. Rome: Istituto dell Enciclopedia Italiana Treccani, 2015.

de Céspedes, Alba. *Dalla parte di lei*. Milan: Mondadori, 1949.

– *Io, suo padre: Romanzo sportivo*. Lanciano: Rocco Carabba, 1935.

– "Lettera a Natalia Ginzburg." In *Scrittrici nella politica culturale del fascismo, Quaderni del '900 V*, edited by Francesca Romana Andreotti and Silvia D'Ortenzi, 137–9. Pisa: Istituti Editoriali e Poligrafici Internazionali, 2005.

– *Nessuno torna indietro*. Milan: Mondadori, 1939.

– *Quaderno proibito*. Milan: Il Saggiatore, 2006.

– *Romanzi: I Meridiani*. Milan: Mondadori, 2011.

De Giorgio, Michela. *Le italiane dall'Unità a oggi*. Bari: Laterza, 1992.

de Grazia, Victoria. *How Fascism Ruled Women*. Berkeley: University of California Press, 1992. https://doi.org/10.1525/9780520911383.

De Napoli, Olindo. "The Origin of the Racist Laws under Fascism: A Problem of Historiography." *Journal of Modern Italian Studies* 17, no. 1 (2012): 106–22. https://doi.org/10.1080/1354571x.2012.628112.

De Silva, Cara. *In Memory's Kitchen: A Legacy from the Women of Terezin*. Lanham, MD: Rowman and Littlefield, 2006.

DeVault, Marjorie. *Feeding the Family*. Chicago: University of Chicago Press, 1991.

Dickie, John. *Delizia!* London: Hodder and Stoughton, 2007.

Diotima. *Mettere al mondo il mondo*. Milan: La Tartaruga, 1990.

– *Oltre l'uguaglianza: Le radici femminili dell'autorità*. Naples: Liguori Editore, 1995.

Donna Clara. *Dalla cucina al salotto, enciclopedia della vita domestica*. Turin: Biblioteca del Forum, 1905; reprint, Turin: Lattes, 1925.

Eagleton, Terry. "Edible ecriture." *Times Higher Education*, 14 October 1997. https://www.timeshighereducation.com/features/edible-ecriture/104281.article.

Ellwood, David. "The Trauma of Liberation: Rape, Love and Violence in Wartime Italy." In *Transmissions of Memory: Echoes, Traumas, and Nostalgia in Post-WWII Italian Culture*, edited by Patrizia Sambuco, 125–42. Teaneck, NJ: Fairleigh Dickinson University Press, 2018.

Falasca Zamponi, Simonetta. *Fascist Spectacle: The Aesthetics of Power in Mussolini's Italy*. Berkeley: University of California Press, 1997. https://doi.org/10.1525/9780520926158.

Fantozzi, Chiara. "L'onore violato: Stupri, prostituzione e occupazione alleata (Livorno 1944–47)." *Passato e presente* 99 (October 2016): 87–111. https://doi.org/10.3280/pass2016-099005.

– "Raccontare Tombolo: Prostituzione di guerra e confini della cittadinanza nella transizione alla democrazia." *The Italianist* 38, no. 3 (2018): 418–32. https://doi.org/10.1080/02614340.2018.1515880.

Farè, Ida. "Nel nome di Estia." In Cuoche Varie, *Fuochi*, 7–26.

Feher, Michel, Ramona Naddaff, and Nadia Tazi. *Fragments for the History of the Human Body*. New York: Zone Books, 1989.

Ferme, Valerio. "Against Marriage and Child-Rearing: Alba de Céspedes' *Nessuno torna indietro* vis-à-vis the Social Framework of Mussolini's Pro-Natal, Pro-Marriage Campaigns of the Ventennio." *Italian Quarterly* 43 (Winter–Spring 2006): 45–57.

Ferrari, Jacopo. "Parole migranti: I migratismi di Igiaba Scego." *Italiano LinguaDue* 14, no. 2 (July 2022): 879–928. https://doi.org/10.54103/2037-3597/18332.

Ferris, Kate. "Consumption." In *The Politics of Everyday Life in Fascist Italy*, edited by Joshua Arthurs, Michael Ebner, and Kate Ferris, 123–49. New York: Palgrave Macmillan, 2017. https://doi.org/10.1057/978-1-137-58654-4_6.

Finocchi, Daniela, ed. *Il sapore del cibo e delle parole: 25 racconti delle autrici di "Lingua Madre."* Turin: Edizioni SEB27, 2014.

Fischler, Claude. "Food, Self and Identity." *Social Science Information* 27, no. 2 (June 1988): 275–92. https://doi.org/10.1177/053901888027002005.

Fisher, Mary Frances Kennedy. *The Gastronomical Me*. San Francisco: North Point Press, 1989.

– *How to Cook a Wolf*. New York: Duell, Sloan, and Pearce, 1942.

Fofi, Goffredo. "Introduzione." In Gobetti, *Diario partigiano*, v–xv.

Foucault, Michel. *Discipline and Punishment*. New York: Pantheon, 1977.

– *The History of Sexuality*. Vol. 1, *An Introduction*. London: Penguin, 1990.

Gabaccia, Donna. *We Are What We Eat: Ethnic Food and the Making of Americans*. Cambridge, MA: Harvard University Press, 1998.

Gabriele, Tommasina. *Dacia Maraini's Narratives of Survival*. Madison, NJ: Fairleigh Dickinson University Press, 2016.

Gabrielli, Patrizia. *Scenari di guerra, parole di donne: Diari e memorie nell'Italia della seconda guerra mondiale*. Bologna: Il Mulino, 2007.

Gabrielli, Patrizia, Luisa Cicognetti, and Marina Zancan. *Madri della Repubblica: Storie, immagini, memorie*. Rome: Carocci, 2007.

Gagliani, Dianella, Elda Guerra, Laura Mariani, and Fiorenza Tarozzi, eds. *Donne guerra, politica*: Esperienze e memorie della Resistanza. Bologna: Clueb, 2000.

Gaglianone, Paola. *Conversazione con Clara Sereni*. Rome: Il libro che non c'è, 1996.

Gallese, Vittorio. "Brain, Body, Habit, and the Performative Quality of Aesthetics." In *Habits: Pragmatist Approaches from Cognitive Science, Neuroscience, and Social Theory*, edited by Fausto Caruana and Italo Testa, 379–94. Cambridge: Cambridge University Press, 2020. https://doi.org/10.1017/9781108682312.019.

Gallucci, Carole C. "Alba De Céspedes's *There's No Turning Back*: Challenging the New Woman's Future." In Pickering-Iazzi, *Mothers of Invention*, 200–19.

Gambaro, Elisa. *Diventare autrice*. Milan: Edizioni Unicopli, 2018.

– "Interno borghese anni cinquanta: Quaderno proibito di Alba de Céspedes al crocevia di generi romanzeschi." *Enthymema* 13 (2015): 228–41. https://doi.org/10.13130/2037-2426/6704.

Garvin, Diana. *Feeding Fascism: The Politics of Women's Food Work*. Toronto: University of Toronto Press, 2022. https://doi.org/10.3138/9781487528195.

Gatens, Moira. *Imaginary Bodies*. London: Routledge, 1996.

Gavotti, Erina. *Menù per un anno*. Milan: Aldo Garzanti Editore, 1970.

Gerber, David A. "Moving Backward and Moving On: Nostalgia, Significant Others, and Social Reintegration in Nineteenth-Century British Immigrant Personal Correspondence." *History of the Family* 21 (2016): 291–314. https://doi.org/10.1080/1081602x.2015.1089413.

Ghezzo, Flora. "Topographies of Disease and Desire: Mapping the City in Fascist Italy." *MLN* 125, no. 1 (January 2010): 195–222. https://doi.org/10.1353/mln.0.0227.

Ghiazza, Silvana. "La letteratura rosa negli anni venti-quaranta." In *I best-seller del ventennio: Il Regime e il libro di massa*, edited by Gigliola De Donato and Vanna Gazzola Stacchini, 129–51. Rome: Editori Riuniti, 1991.

Giannotti, Stefania. "La cucina è una fissazione." In Cuoche Varie, *Fuochi*, 27–61.

– "¿Qué se cuece entre los pucheros?" *Duoda* 55 (2018): 106–37.

– *Troppo sale: Un addio in ricette*. Milan: Feltrinelli, 2017.

Gilbert, Sandra M. *The Culinary Imagination: From Myth to Modernity*. New York: W.W. Norton, 2014.

Gobetti, Ada. *Diario Partigiano*. Turin: Einaudi, 2014.

Goodwin, Jeff, James Jasper, and Francesca Polletta, eds. *Passionate Politics: Emotion and Social Movements*. Chicago: University of Chicago Press, 2001. https://doi.org/10.7208/chicago/9780226304007.001.0001.

Gosetti della Salda, Anna. *Le ricette regionali italiane*. Milan: La cucina italiana, 1967.

Griffiths, Jennifer. "Marisa Mori's Edible Futurist Breast." *Gastronomica* 12, no. 4 (Winter 2012): 20–6. https://doi.org/10.1525/gfc.2012.12.4.20.

Grosz, Elizabeth. *Volatile Bodies*. London: Routledge, 1994.

Gruppo Anabasi. *Donna è bello*. Milan: Gruppo Anabasi, 1972.

Guida, Patrizia. "Ricostruzione dell'io nell'itinerario poetico di Maraini." *Italica* 77, no. 1 (Spring 2001): 74–89. https://doi.org/10.2307/480223.

Guidetti Serra, Bianca. *Compagne*. Turin: Einaudi, 1977.

Gundle, Stephen. "The 'Civic Religion' of the Resistance in Post-War Italy." *Modern Italy* 5, no. 2 (November 2000): 113–32. https://doi.org/10.1080/713685680.

Häberlen, Joachim C., Mark Keck-Szajbel, and Kate Mahoney, eds. *The Politics of Authenticity: Countercultures and Radical Movements Across the Iron Curtain, 1968–1989*. New York: Berghahn Books, 2019. https://doi.org/10.2307/j.ctvw04d3p.

Hajek, Andrea. "Despite or in Debt to 1968? Second-Wave Feminism and the Gendered History of Italy's 1968." In *Women, Global Protest Movements, and Political Agency*, edited by Sarah Colvin and Katharina Kalcher, 33–49. London: Routledge, 2018. https://doi.org/10.4324/9781351203715-3.

Haraway, Donna. *Simians, Cyborgs and Women: The Reinvention of Nature*. New York: Routledge, 1991.

Harris, Jessica L. *Italian Women's Experiences with American Consumer Culture, 1945–1975*. Cham: Palgrave Macmillan, 2020. https://doi.org/10.1007/978-3-030-47825-4.

Hartman, Stephanie. "The Political Palate: Reading Commune Cookbooks." *Gastronomica* 3, no. 2 (May 2003): 29–40. https://doi.org/10.1525/gfc.2003.3.2.29.

Heldke, Lisa. "The Unexamined Meal Is Not Worth Eating." *Food, Culture and Society* 9, no. 2 (2006): 201–19. https://doi.org/10.2752/155280106778606035.

Heller, Tamar, and Patricia Moran, eds. *Scenes of the Apple: Food and the Female Body in Nineteenth- and Twentieth-Century Women's Writing*. New York: State University of New York Press, 2003.

Helstosky, Carol. "Fascist Food Politics: Mussolini's Policy of Alimentary Sovereignty." *Journal of Modern Italian Studies* 9, no. 1 (2004): 1–26. https://doi.org/10.1080/1354571042000179164.

– *Garlic and Oil*. Oxford: Berg Publishers, 2004. https://doi.org/10.5040/9781350044852.

– "State of Meatlessness: Voluntary and Involuntary Vegetarianism in Early Twentieth-Century Italy." In *Veg(etari)an Arguments in Culture, History and Practice*, edited by C. Hanganu-Bresch and K. Kondrilk, 3–24. New York: Palgrave Macmillan, 2021. https://doi.org/10.1007/978-3-030-53280-2_1.

Hochschild, Arlie Russell. *The Managed Heart: Commercialization of Human Feeling*. Berkeley: University of California Press, 1983.

hooks, bell. "Eating the Other: Desire and Resistance." In *Black Looks*, 21–39. Boston: South End, 1992.

– *Talking Back: Thinking Feminist, Thinking Black*. Boston: South End, 1989.

Horn, Vera. "Assaporare la tradizione: Cibo, identità e senso di appartenenza nella letteratura migrante." *Revista de Italianistica* 19–20 (2010): 155–75. https://doi.org/10.11606/issn.2238-8281.v0i19-20p155-175.

Howard, Scott Alexander. "Nostalgia." *Analysis* 72, no. 4 (October 2012): 641–50. https://doi.org/10.1093/analys/ans105.

Hutton, Patrick. "Preface: Reconsideration of the Idea of Nostalgia in Contemporary Historical Writing." *Historical Reflections* 39 (December 2013): 1–9. https://doi.org/10.3167/hrrh.2013.390301.

Hyman, Gwen. "The Taste of Fame: Chefs, Diners, Celebrity, Class." *Gastronomica* 8, no. 3 (2008): 43–52. https://doi.org/10.1525/gfc.2008.8.3.43.

Janowski, Monica. "Introduction: Consuming Memories of Home in Constructing the Present and Imagining the Future." *Food and Foodways: Explorations in the History and Culture of Human Nourishment* 20, nos. 3–4 (2012): 175–86. https://doi.org/10.1080/07409710.2012.715960.

Jasper, James M. "The Emotions of Protest: Affective and Reactive Emotions in and around Social Movements." *Sociological Forum* 13, no. 3 (September 1998): 397–424. https://doi.org/10.1023/A:1022175308081.

– "Emotions and Social Movements: Twenty Years of Theory and Research." *Annual Review of Sociology* 37 (August 2011): 285–303. https://doi.org/10.1146/annurev-soc-081309-150015.

Katzen, Mollie. *Moosewood Cookbook*. Berkeley, CA: Ten Speed Press, 1974.

Kelly, Traci Marie. "If I Were a Voodoo Priestess: Women's Culinary Autobiography." In *Kitchen Culture in American: Popular Representations of Food, Gender, and Race*, edited by Sherrie A. Inness, 251–70. Philadelphia: University of Pennsylvania Press, 2001. https://doi.org/10.9783/9781512802887-012.

Koivunen, Ann. "The Affective Turn?" In *Conference Proceedings for Affective Encounters: Rethinking Embodiment in Feminist Media Studies*, edited by Ann Koivunen and S. Paasonen, x–xx. Turku, Finland: University of Turku, 2001.

Korsmeyer, Carolyn. *Making Sense of Taste*. Ithaca, NY: Cornell University Press, 1999.

Kuruvilla, Gabriella, Ingy Mubiayi, Igiaba Scego, and Laila Wadia, eds. *Pecore nere*. Rome: Laterza, 2005.

Lakhous, Amara. *Scontro di civiltà per un ascensore in Piazza Vittorio*. Rome: Edizioni e/o, 2006.

Lazzaro-Weis, Carol. "The Subject's Seduction: The Experience of Don Juan in Italian Feminist Fiction." *Annali d'Italianistica* 7 (1989): 382–93.

Le Breton, David. *Sensing the World*. London: Bloomsbury, 2017.

Leccardi, Carmen. "La reinvenzione della vita quotidiana." In Bertilotti and Scattigno, *Il femminismo degli anni Settanta*, 99–117.

Legnani, Massimo. "Consumi di Guerra: Linee di ricerca sull'alimentazione in Itali nel 1940–43." In *Guerra vissuta, guerra subita*, edited by Dipartimento di Discipline Storiche Università di Bologna, 109–17. Bologna: Clueb, 1991.

– "La Guerra totale: Per un'indagine su progetto e realtà della Guerra fascista." *Italia contemporanea* 213 (1998): 751–60.

Leitch, Alison. "Slow Food and the Politics of Pork Fat: Italian Food and European Identity." *Ethnos* 68, no. 4 (2003): 437–62. https://doi.org/10.1080/0014184032000160514.

Lennon, Kathleen, and Anthony Wilde. "Alienation and Affectivity: Beauvoir, Sartre and Levinas on the Aging Body." *Sartre Studies International* 25, no. 1 (June 2019): 35–51. https://doi.org/10.3167/ssi.2019.250104.

Levi, Primo. *Se questo è un uomo*. 1958. Reprint, Turin: Einaudi, 2014.

Levinas, Emmanuel. *Totality and Infinity: An Essay in Exteriority*. Translated by Alphonso Lingis. Pittsburgh: Duquesne University Press, 1969.

Linden, David J. *Touch: The Science of Hand, Heart, and Mind*. New York: Viking, 2015.

Lombardi, Daniela. *Storia del matrimonio dal medioevo a oggi*. Bologna: Il Mulino, 2008.

Lombardi-Diop, Cristina, and Caterina Romeo, eds. *Postcolonial Italy: Challenging National Hegemony*. New York: Palgrave Macmillan, 2012. https://doi.org/10.1057/9781137281463.

Lorde, Audre. *Sister Outsider: Essays and Speeches*. Berkeley, CA: Crossing Press, 1984.

Lotta femminista. *Quaderni di Lotta Femminista*. Vol. 1, *L'offensiva*. Turin: Musolini Editore, 1972.

Lovallo, Antonio. "Società e giustizia: I reati annonari attraverso le sentenze del tribunale di Bologna." In *Bologna in Guerra 1940–1945*, edited by Brunella Della Casa and Alberto Preti, 253–72. Milan: FrancoAngeli, 1995.

Lupton, Deborah. "Food, Memory and Meaning: The Symbolic and Social Nature of Food Events." *Sociological Review* 42, no. 4 (November 1994): 664–85. https://doi.org/10.1111/j.1467-954x.1994.tb00105.x.
– *Food, the Body and the Self*. London: Sage, 1996.
– "Vitalities and Visceralities: Alternative Body/Food Politics in Digital Media." In *Alternative Food Politics from the Margins to the Mainstreams*, edited by Michelle Phillipov and Katherine Kirkhood, 151–68. New York: Routledge, 2019. https://doi.org/10.4324/9780203733080-9.
Lussana, Fiamma. "Le donne e la modernizzazione: Il neofemminismo degli anni settanta." In *Storia dell'Italia repubblicana*, vol. 3, book 2, 471–565. Turin: Einaudi, 1997.
– *L'Italia del divorzio: La battaglia fra Stato, Chiesa e gente comune (1946–1974)*. Rome: Carocci, 2014.
Mafai, Miriam. *Pane nero*. Milan: Mondadori, 1987.
Maraini, Dacia. *Il treno per Helsinki*. Milan: RCS Libri, 2000.
– *La lunga vita di Marianna Ucrìa*. Milan: Rizzoli, 1990.
– *Mangiami pure*. Turin: Einaudi, 1978.
Marinetti, Filippo Tommaso, and Fillìa. *La cucina futurista*. Milan: Sonzogno, 1932.
Martschukat, Jürgen, and Bryant Simon, eds. *Food, Power, and Agency*. London: Bloomsbury, 2017. https://doi.org/10.5040/9781474298773.
Mascarello, Giulia, Anna Pinto, Silvia Marcolin, Stefania Crovato, and Licia Ravarotto. "Ethnic Food Consumption: Habits and Risk Perceptions in Italy." *Journal of Food Safety* 37, no. 4 (November 2017): e12361. https://doi.org/10.1111/jfs.12361.
Masino, Paola. *Io, Massimo e gli altri*. Milan: Rusconi, 1995.
Mason, Mary G. "The Other Voice: Autobiographies of Women Writers." In *Autobiography: Essays Theoretical and Critical*, edited by James Olney, 207–35. Princeton, NJ: Princeton University Press, 1980. https://doi.org/10.1515/9781400856312.207.
Mauceri, Maria Cristina. "Cultural Encounters and Clashes Around the Table." In *Food in Postcolonial and Migrant Literature*, edited by Michela Canepari and Alba Pessini, 257–70. Brussels: Peter Lang, 2012.
– "Dalla bocca al cuore: Cibo e emozioni in alcuni scrittori migranti in Italia." In *Dialoghi sulle Migrazioni: Letteratura, Storia e lingua*, edited by Grazia Biorci and Roberto Sinigallia, 15–22. Genoa: Genoa University Press, 2012.
McGrath, Maria. "Recipes for a New World." In *Eating in Eden: Food and American Utopias*, edited by Etta M. Madden and Martha L. Finch, 162–83. Lincoln: University of Nebraska Press, 2006.
Menozzi, Giuliana. "Food and Subjectivity in Clara Sereni's *Casalinghitudine*." *Italica* 71, no. 2 (Summer 1994): 217–27. https://doi.org/10.2307/480007.
Momigliano, Fernanda. *Vivere bene in tempi difficili: Come le donne affrontano le crisi economiche*. Milan: Hoepli, 1933.
Monelli, Paolo. *Il ghiottone errante: Viaggio gastronomico attraverso l'Italia*. Milan: Treves, 1935.

Moore Lappé, Frances. *Diet for a Small Planet*. New York: Ballantine Books, 1971.
Moorehead, Caroline. *A House in the Mountains: The Women Who Liberated Italy from Fascism*. New York: HarperCollins, 2019.
Morelli, Lidia. *Le massaie contro le sanzioni*. Turin: S. Lattes and C. Editori, 1935.
Morris, Penelope. "From Private to Public: Alba de Céspedes' Agony Columns in 1950 Italy." *Modern Italy* 9, no. 1 (May 2004): 11–20. https://doi.org/10.1080/13532940410001677467.
– "Giovanna Zangrandi: Negotiating Fascism." *Italian Studies* 53, no. 1 (1998): 94–121. https://doi.org/10.1179/its.1998.53.1.94.
– *Women in Italy 1945–1960: An Interdisciplinary Study*. Basingstoke: Palgrave Macmillan, 2006. https://doi.org/10.1057/9780230601437.
Muraro, Luisa. *L'ordine simbolico della madre*. Rome: Editori Riuniti, 1991.
– "Sull'essere in relazione come capacità di essere." In *Amore ed Empatia: Ricerche in corso*, edited by Francesca Brezzi, 13–22. Milan: FrancoAngeli, 2003.
Neuman, Shirley. "Autobiography and Questions of Gender: An Introduction." *Prose Studies: History, Theory, Criticism* 14, no. 2 (1991): 1–11. https://doi.org/10.1080/01440359108586428.
Nuboli, Cecilia. *Fasciste di Salò*. Bari: Laterza, 2016.
Nützenadel, Alexander. "Dictating Food: Autarchy, Food Provision, and Consumer Politics in Fascist Italy, 1922–1943." In *Food and Conflict in Europe in the Age of the Two World Wars*, edited by Frank Trentmann and Fleming Just, 88–108. Basingstoke: Palgrave Macmillan, 2006. https://doi.org/10.1057/9780230597495_5.
Ombra, Marisa. *La bella politica*. Turin: Laissez-passer, 2009.
Orlandini, Laura. *La democrazia delle donne: I Gruppi di Difesa della Donna nella costruzione della Repubblica*. Rome: BraDypUS Editore, 2018.
Paolozzi, Letizia. *Prenditi cura*. Milan: Et al./Edizioni, 2013.
Parasecoli, Fabio. "The Invention of Authentic Italian Food: Narratives, Rhetoric and Media." In Sassatelli, *Italians and Food*, 17–41. https://doi.org/10.1007/978-3-030-15681-7_2.
Parati, Graziella. "Where Do Migrants Live? Amara Lakhous's *Scontro di civiltà per un ascensore in Piazza Vittorio*." *Annali d'Italianistica* 28 (2010): 431–46.
Pariani, Laura. *L'uovo di Gertrudina*. Milan: Rizzoli, 2003.
Passerini, Luisa. *Autoritratto di gruppo*. Florence: Giunti, 1988.
– *Storie di donne e femministe*. Turin: Rosenberg and Seller, 1991.
Pautasso, Guido Andrea, ed. *Cucina Futurista: Manifesti teorici, menu e documenti*. Milan: Abscondita, 2015.
Pernau, Margrit, and Imke Rajamani. "Emotional Translations: Conceptual History Beyond Language." *History and Theory* 55, no. 1 (February 2016): 46–65. https://doi.org/10.1111/hith.10787.

Perricone Violà, Augusta. *Ricordi somali.* Bologna: Cappelli, 1935.

Perullo, Nicola. "Esperienza estetica, cucina, gastronomía." *estetica: studi e ricerche,* no. 1 (2011): 73–92.

– *Taste as Experience: The Philosophy and Aesthetics of Food.* New York: Columbia University Press, 2016. https://doi.org/10.7312/peru17348.

Petronilla. *Desinaretti per … questi tempi.* Milan: Sonzogno, 1944.

– *Ricette di Petronilla.* Milan: Sonzogno, 1943.

– *Ricette di Petronilla per tempi eccezionali.* Milan: Sonzogno, 1941.

– *200 suggerimenti per … questi tempi.* Milan: Sonzogno, 1943.

Pezzini, Serena. "La concreta utopia del 'nuovo ordine di domani' nel diario partigiano di Ada Prospero." In *Nascere, rinascere, ricominciare: Immagini del nuovo inizio nella cultura italiana,* edited by Laura Benedetti and Gianluigi Simonetti, 189–204. L'Aquila: L'Aquila University Press, 2017.

– "Memoria, esperienza, sconfitta: Strategie narrative di Diario partigiano." In *Il dialogo creativo: Studi per Lina Balzoni,* edited by Maria Pia Ellero, Matteo Residori, Massimiliano Rossi, and Andrea Torre, 396–406. Lucca: Maria Pacini Fazzi Editore, 2017.

Picchietti, Virginia. *Relational Spaces: Daughterhood, Motherhood and Sisterhood in Dacia Maraini's Writings and Films.* Madison, NJ: Fairleigh Dickinson University Press, 2002.

Piccone Stella, Simonetta. *La prima generazione: Ragazze e ragazzi nel miracolo economico italiano.* Milan: FrancoAngeli, 1993.

Pickering-Iazzi, Robin. "Labors of Love and Fascism in the Colonial Novel *Fortuna sotto vento.*" *Forum Italicum* 38, no. 1 (March 2004): 66–90. https://doi.org/10.1177/001458580403800103.

– *Mothers of Invention: Women, Italian Fascism, and Culture.* Minneapolis: University of Minnesota, 1995.

– "The Sexual Politics of the Migrational City." In *Writing Beyond Fascism: Cultural Resistance in the Life and Works of Alba de Céspedes,* edited by Carole C. Gallucci and Ellen Victoria Nerenberg, 85–109. London: Associated University Presses, 2000.

Pieri, Piero. "Souvenir d'une militante du Parti d'Action." Review of *Diario Partigiano,* by Ada Gobetti. *Revue d'historie de la Deuxième Guerre Mondiale* 7, no. 26 (April 1957): 121–6.

Pizzi, Katia. *A City in Search of an Author: The Cultural Identity of Trieste.* Sheffield: Academic Press Continuum, 2001.

– "Translation Interrupted: Memorial Dissonance in Trieste." In *The Routledge Handbook of Translation and the City,* edited by Tong King Lee, 394–406. Abingdon: Routledge, 2021. https://doi.org/10.4324/9780429436468-29.

– *Trieste: Una frontiera letteraria.* Trieste: Vita Activa, 2019.

Ponzanesi, Sandra. "The Colour of Love: *Madamismo* and Interracial Relationships in the Italian Colonies." *Research in African Literature* 43, no. 2 (Summer 2012): 155–72. https://doi.org/10.2979/reseafrilite.43.2.155.

– "The Postcolonial Turn in Italian Studies: European Perspectives." In Lombardi-Diop and Romeo, *Postcolonial Italy*, 51–69. https://doi.org/10.1057/9781137281463_4.

Ponzani, Michela. *Guerra alle donne*. Turin: Einaudi, 2012.

Porzio, Maria. *Arrivano gli Alleati! Amori e violenze nell'Italia liberata*. Bari: Laterza, 2011.

Probyn, Elspeth. *Carnal Appetites*. New York: Routledge, 2000.

Pulcini, Elena. *Il potere di unire: Femminile, desiderio, cura*. Turin: Bollati Boringhieri, 2003. https://doi.org/10.1177/1754073915615429.

– "What Emotions Motivate Care?" *Emotion Review* 9, no. 1 (January 2017): 64–71. https://doi.org/10.1177/1754073915615429.

Randi, Elisabetta. *La cucina autarchica*. Florence: L. Cionini Editore, 1942.

Rattazzi, Ilaria. *Soffiamo sulla cicoria matta*. Milan: La Tartaruga, 1981.

Re, Lucia. "Fame, cibo e antifascismo nella Massaia di Paola Masino." In *Il cibo e le donne nellacultura e nella storia*, edited by Giuseppina Muzzarelli and Lucia Re, 165–81. Bologna: Clueb, 2005.

– "Fascist Theories of 'Woman' and the Construction of Gender." In Pickering-Iazzi, *Mothers of Invention*, 77–99.

Reddy, William M. "Against Constructionism: The Historical Ethnography of Emotions." *Current Anthropology* 38, no. 3 (June 1997): 327–51. https://doi.org/10.1086/204622.

– *The Navigation of Feeling: A Framework for the History of Emotions*. Cambridge: Cambridge University Press, 2001. https://doi.org/10.1017/CBO9780511512001.

Rhys-Taylor, Alex. *Food and Multiculture: A Sensory Ethnography of East London*. London: Bloomsbury, 2017. https://doi.org/10.5040/9781474204347.

Rigotti, Francesca. *La filosofia in cucina: Piccola pratica della ragion culinaria*. Bologna: Il Mulino, 1999.

Rivolta femminile. "Manifesto." In *Sputiamo su Hegel, La donna clitoidea e la donna vaginale e altri scritti*, edited by Carla Lonzi, 11–18. Milan: Scritti di Rivolta femminile, 1974.

Rizzi, Fortunato. "Una donna giramondo." *Minerva* 47, no. 7 (1937): 193–5.

Robertson, Laurel, Carol Flinders, and Bronwen Godfrey. *Laurel's Kitchen: A Handbook for Vegetarian Cookery and Nutrition*. Tomales, CA: Nilgiri Press, 1976.

Rorandelli, Tristana. "Nascita e morte della massaia di Paola Masino e la questione del corpo materno nel fascismo." *Forum Italicum* 37, no. 1 (Spring 2003): 70–102. https://doi.org/10.1177/001458580303700105.

Rosenwein, Barbara H. *Emotional Communities in the Early Middle Ages*. Ithaca, NY: Cornell University Press, 2006.

– "Worrying about Emotions in History." *American Historical Review* 107, no. 3 (June 2002): 821–45. https://doi.org/10.1086/532498.

Rosenwein, Barbara H., and Riccardo Cristiani. *What Is the History of Emotions?* Cambridge: Polity Press, 2019.

Rossi-Doria, Anna. "Ipotesi per una storia che verrà." In Bertilotti and Scattigno, *Il femminismo degli anni settanta*, 1–23.

Rossi Lodomez, Vera. *Far presto*. Milan: Longanesi, 1953.

Rossi Lodomez, Vera, and Franca Matricardi. *Il Cucchiaio d'Argento*. Milan: Domus, 1950.

Salvatici, Silvia. *Storia delle donne nell'Italia contemporanea*. Rome: Carocci, 2022.

Sambuco, Patrizia. *Corporeal Bonds: The Daughter-Mother Relationship in Twentieth-Century Italian Women's Writing*. Toronto: University of Toronto Press, 2012. https://doi.org/10.3138/9781442699496.

– "Dynamics, Experiences, and Political Meaning of the Black Market in Second World War Italy." *Modern Italy* 29, no. 1 (February 2024): 38–50. https://doi.org/10.1017/mit.2023.56.

– "Pina Ballario's Colonial and Travel Writing: Desserts, Breastfeeding and Pleasure as Opposition to Fascism." *Italian Studies* 73, no. 3 (2018): 257–73. https://doi.org/10.1080/00751634.2018.1487104.

Sambuco, Patrizia, and Lisa Pine. "Food Discourses and Alimentary Policies in Fascist Italy and Nazi Germany: A Comparative Analysis." *European History Quarterly* 53, no. 1 (January 2023): 135–55. https://doi.org/10.1177/02656914221140274.

Saraceno, Chiara. *Pluralità e mutamento: Riflessioni sull'identità femminile*. Milan: FrancoAngeli, 1991.

Saraiva, Tiago. *Fascist Pigs: Technoscientific Organism and the History of Fascism*. Cambridge, MA: MIT Press, 2016. https://doi.org/10.7551/mitpress/9780262035033.001.0001.

Sassatelli, Roberta, ed. *Italians and Food*. Cham: Palgrave Macmillan, 2019. https://doi.org/10.1007/978-3-030-15681-7.

Scarpellini, Emanuela. *Food and Foodways in Italy from 1861 to the Present*. New York: Palgrave Macmillan, 2016. https://doi.org/10.1057/9781137569622.

– *Material Nation: A Consumer's History of Modern Italy*. Oxford: Oxford University Press, 2011.

Sceats, Sarah. *Food, Consumption and the Body in Contemporary Women's Fiction*. Cambridge: Cambridge University Press, 2003.

Scego, Igiaba. *La mia casa è dove sono*. Milan: RCS Libri, 2010.

– "Salsicce." In Kuruvilla et al., *Pecore nere*, 23–36.

Scheer, Monique. "Are Emotions a Kind of Practice (and Is That What Makes Them Have a History)? A Bourdieuian Approach to Understanding Emotions." *History and Theory* 51, no. 2 (May 2012): 193–220. https://doi.org/10.1111/j.1468-2303.2012.00621.x.

– "Feeling Faith: The Cultural Practice of Religious Emotions in Nineteenth-Century German Methodism." In *Out of the Tower: Essays on Culture and Everyday Life*, edited by Monique Scheer, Thomas Thiemeyer, Reinhard Johler, and Bernhard Tschofer, 217–47. Tübingen: Tübinger Vereinigung für Volkskunde, 2013.

Sclauzero, Mariarosa. *La cucina macrobiotica in Italia*. Rome: Arcana, 1973.
Scrimieri, Maria Grazia. "Around the Table: Gender and Generational Conflict in Clara Sereni's Autobiographical Writing." In *Food and Literature in Italian Literature, Culture and Society*, edited by Claudia Bernardi, Francesca Calamita, and Daniele De Feo, 153–64. London: Bloomsbury, 2020. https://doi.org/10.5040/9781350137813.0020.
Semelin, Jacques. *Sans armes face à Hitler*. Paris: Payot, 1989.
Sereni, Clara. *Casalinghitudine*. 1987. Reprint, Turin: Einaudi, 2005.
– *Le Merendanze*. Milan: Rizzoli, 2004.
– *Passami il sale*. Milan: Rizzoli, 2002.
– *Via Ripetta 155*. Florence: Giunti, 2015.
Signorelli, Amalia. "Women in Italy in the 1970s." In *Speaking Out and Silencing: Culture, Society and Politics in Italy in the 1970s*, edited by Anna Cento Bull and Adalgisa Giorgio, 42–68. London: Legenda, 2006.
Slaughter, Jane. *Women and the Italian Resistance 1943–45*. Denver: Arden, 1997. https://doi.org/10.4324/9781315087764-4.
Sletvold, Jon. "Neuroscience and the Embodiment of Psychoanalysis – With an Appreciation of Damiano's Contribution." *Psychoanalytic Inquiry* 39, no. 8 (2019): 545–56. https://doi.org/10.1080/07351690.2019.1671067.
Smith, Sidonie. *A Poetics of Women's Autobiography: Marginality and the Fictions of Self-Representation*. Bloomington: Indiana University Press, 1987.
Solnit, Rebecca. *Wanderlust: A History of Walking*. London: Granta Books, 2014.
Sorgoni, Barbara. "Racist Discourses and Practices in the Italian Empire Under Fascism." In *The Politics of Recognizing Difference: Multiculturalism Italian-Style*, edited by Ralph Grillo and Jeff Pratt, 41–58. Aldershot: Ashgate, 2002.
Spackman, Barbara. *Fascist Virilities: Rhetoric, Ideology, and Social Fantasy in Italy*. Minneapolis: University of Minnesota Press, 1996.
Spelman, Elizabeth. "Anger and Insubordination." In *Women, Knowledge and Reality: Explorations in Feminist Philosophy*, edited by Ann Garry and Marilyn Pearsall, 263–74. New York: Routledge, 1989.
Stanton, Domna. *The Female Autograph: Theory and Practice of Autobiography from the Tenth to the Twentieth Century*. Chicago: University of Chicago Press, 1987.
Sulis, Gigliola. "Il racconto come militanza: Sulle radici femministe dell'opera di Laura Pariani." *Cahiers d'études italiennes* 16 (2013): 303–24. https://doi.org/10.4000/cei.1299.
Sumeli Weinberg, Grazia. *Invito alla lettura di Dacia Maraini*. Pretoria: University of South Africa, 1993.
Sutton, David. *Remembrance of Repasts: An Anthropology of Food and Memory*. Oxford: Berg, 2001. https://doi.org/10.5040/9781350044883.
Tahar, Lamri. "Il caffè." In Wadia, *Mondopentola*, 109–14.
Therborn, Göran, Geoff Eley, Hartmut Kaelble, Philippe Chassaigne, and Andreas Wirsching. "The 1970s and 1980s as a Turning Point in European

History?" *Journal of Modern European History* 9, no. 1 (April 2011): 8–26. https://doi.org/10.17104/1611-8944_2011_1_8.

Thomas, Anna. *The Vegetarian Epicure*. New York: Alfred A. Knopf, 1972.

Toklas, Alice Babette. *The Alice B. Toklas Cookbook*. New York: Harper, 1954.

Trevisan, Myriam. *L'archivio di Giovanna Zangrandi: Inventario*. Pisa: Ministero per i Beni e le Attività Culturali, 2005.

Venturini, Monica. *Fuori campo: Letteratura e giornalismo nell'Italia coloniale 1920–1940*. Perugia: Morlacchi Editore, 2013.

Venturoli, Cinzia. "La violenza taciuta: Percorsi di ricerca sugli abusi sessuali fra il passaggio e l'arrestarsi del fronte." In Gagliani et al., *Donne guerra politica*, 111–30.

Vera. *Annabella in cucina*. Milan: Rizzoli, 1955.

– *Si fa così*. Milan: Rizzoli, 1974.

Veronelli, Luigi. *Alla ricerca dei cibi perduti*. Milan: Feltrinelli, 1966.

Vertovec, Steven. "Super-Diversity and Its Implications." *Ethnic and Racial Studies* 30, no. 6 (2007): 1024–54. https://doi.org/10.1080/01419870701599465.

von der Goltz, Anna, ed. *Talkin' 'Bout My Generation: Conflicts of Generation Building and Europe's 1968*. Göttingen: Wallstein Verlag, 2011.

Wadia, Laila. *Amiche per la pelle*. Rome: Edizioni e/o, 2007.

– "Curry di pollo." In Kuruvilla et al., *Pecore nere*, 39–52.

– *Il burattinaio e altre storie extra italiane*. Isernia: Cosmo Iannone Editore, 2004.

– "Il segreto della calandraca." In Wadia, *Mondopentola*, 131–8.

– "Introduzione." In Wadia, *Mondopentola*, 9–13.

– *Kitchensutra*. Self-published, 2016. Kindle.

–, ed. *Mondopentola*. Isernia: Cosmo Iannone Editore, 2007.

– "Spaghetti allo scoglio." In *Il burattinaio e altre storie*, 99–110.

Westberg, Gustav. "Affective Rebirth: Discourses Gateway to Contemporary National Socialism." *Discourse & Society* 32, no. 2 (March 2021): 214–30. https://doi.org/10.1177/0957926520970380.

William-Forson, Psyche. *Building Houses Out of Chickens' Legs*. Chapel Hill, NC: University of North Carolina Press, 2006.

Willson, Perry. "Cooking the Patriotic Omelette: Women and Italian Fascist Ruralization Campaign." *European History Quarterly* 27, no. 4 (October 1997): 531–47. https://doi.org/10.1177/026569149702700404.

– "Women, War and the Vote: Gender and Politics in Italy." *Women's History Review* 7, no. 4 (1998): 617–23. https://doi.org/10.1080/09612029800200190.

Wodak, Ruth. *The Politics of Fear: What Right-Wing Populist Discourses Mean*. Los Angeles: Sage, 2015. https://doi.org/10.4135/9781446270073.

Wodak, Ruth, and John Richardson, eds. *Analysing Fascist Discourse: European Fascism in Talk and Text*. New York: Routledge, 2013. https://doi.org/10.4324/9780203071847.

Woolf, Virginia. *The Diary of Virginia Woolf, Diary 3*. New York: Harcourt, 1980.

– *A Room of One's Own*. London: Grafton Books, 1977.

Zagatti, Paola. "Il problema dell'alimentazione." In *Bologna in Guerra 1940–1945*, edited by Brunella Della Casa and Alberto Preti, 223–52. Milan: FrancoAngeli, 1995.

Zamara, Emilia. *La cucina italiana della resistenza*. Milan: Edizioni "A. Barion," 1936.

Zancan, Marina. *Alba de Céspedes*. Milan: Il Saggiatore, 2005.

– "Introduzione." In *Alba de Céspedes: Romanzi*, xi–lxii. Milan: Mondadori, 2011.

– "Parole vere per raccontare i giorni veri." In Zangrandi, *I giorni veri*, 257–75.

Zancani, Diego. *How We Fell in Love with Italian Food*. Oxford: Bodleian Library, 2019.

Zangrandi, Giovanna. *I giorni veri*. Milan: Isbn Edizioni, 2012.

Zanoni, Elizabeth. *Migrant Marketplaces: Food and Italians in North and South America*. Champaign: University of Illinois Press, 2018. https://doi.org/10.5622/illinois/9780252041655.001.0001.

Documentaries

Fasullo, Simona. "Vivere per scrivere." *Passato e presente: Alba de Céspedes*, video, 2017, 40:00, https://www.raiplay.it/video/2018/01/Passato-e-presente---ALBA-DE-CESPEDES-una-vita-dentro-la-storia-e6fae64f-3ec7-4ccb-87fa-f45e5a5fcae8.html?wt_mc=2.www.cpy.raiplay_vid_PassatoePresente.

Georget, Anne. *Imaginary Feasts*. Documentary film. New York: Icarus Films, 2014.

Libreria delle donne: Una storia che continua. Documentary, 2016. Association Chiamale Storie in collaboration with 3DProduzioni. MemoMi web TV. https://memomi.it/libreria-delle-donne.

News and Magazine Articles

Alcune femministe milanesi. "Pratica dell'inconscio e movimento delle donne." *L'erba voglio*, nos. 18–19 (October 1974–January 1975): 12–23.

Anonymous. "Il premio Bologna a Pina Ballario e a Daria Banfi Malaguzzi." *Corriere della sera* (Milan), 13 November 1939.

Anonymous. "Tribunale di Pescara." *L'Adriatico*, 1 June 1942, p. 6.

Cantono, A. "Il lavoro della donna: Nuovi lavori femminili." *Il Solco*, April 1936, pp. 189–90.

Canuti, Giovanna. "Cronache sociali." *Il Solco*, June 1936, pp. 286–8.

Ceccarelli, Filippo. "La gara gastro-elettorale dei sovranisti: Meloni a tavola sorpassa Salvini." *Repubblica*, 16 September 2020. https://www.repubblica.it/cronaca/2020/09/16/news/meloni-301117590/.

Cichi, Silvana. "La minestra degli stupidi, sabbia d'argento e la cicoria matta." *Effe*, January 1982. http://efferivistafemminista.it/2014/11/la-minestra-degli-stupidi-sabbia-dargento-e-la-cicoria-matta/.

Credaro, Nella. "Ada Gobetti Marchesini Prospero, Diario Partigiano." *Il Politico*, 22 May 1957, pp. 218–19.

Gallotti, Adele. "Le impegnate in cucina: Femministe ma cuoche." *La Stampa sera*, 3 March 1976, p. 13.

Gozzini, Luigi. "La donna nel quadro del Regime." *Almanacco della donna italiana* 19 (1939), pp. 39–45.

La Massaia. "Benvenuta Autarchia." *La donna fascista*, no. 22, 3 November 1940, p. 15.

– "In cucina: Perché nulla vada sprecato." *La donna fascista*, no. 13, 30 April 1942, p. 11.

Lillith (Demau Group). "Mater mortifera." *L'Erba Voglio*, no. 15 (1974), pp. 60–1.

Lucidi, Giuseppe. "L'alimentazione del bambino in colonia." *La Difesa della Razza* 11 (5 April 1939), pp. 14–16.

Maniaci, Davide. "Il kebab 'Made in Italy.'" *Corriere della sera* (Milan), 23 October 2020, p. 10.

Ottello, Giacomo. "Scrittrici." *Il Solco*, November 1936, pp. 499–502.

Palmieri, Nello. "A casa le madri." *Il Solco*, March 1933, pp. 173–83.

Petronilla. "Vitello al limone." *Domenica del Corriere*, no. 28, 14 July 1935, p. 10.

Poggiali, Ciro. "La donna italiana in A.O." *Almanacco della donna italiana* 19 (1939), pp. 53–73.

Randi, Elisabetta. "Come si mangia in Colonia." *Almanacco della donna italiana* 19 (1939), pp. 307–19.

Sollazzo, Lucia. "Il lavastoviglie tra lui e lei." *Corriere della sera*, 16 April 1966, p. 11.

Sottosopra. "Convegno a Londra." No. 1, 1973, pp. 21–6.

– "Noi pratichiamo l'auto-in-coscienza." No. 3, March 1976, pp. 12–31.

V.B. "Ecologia in cucina." *Corriere letterario* supplement, *Corriere della sera*, 17 June 1973, p. 12.

Websites

Campi aperti. "Le origini di Campi Aperti." Accessed 25 September 2024. https://www.campiaperti.org/chi-siamo/le-origini/.

Colarossi, Matilda. "Soldati/Soldiers by Giuseppe Ungaretti." *Parallel Texts: Words Reflected* (blog), 11 February 2017. https://paralleltexts.blog/2017/02/11/soldatisoldier-by-giuseppe-ungaretti/.

Fondazione Leone Moressa. "Rapporto annuale sull'economia dell'immigrazione 2022." FLM, 14 November 2022. https://www.fondazioneleonemoressa.org/2022/11/14/rapporto-2022-flm/.

Gavioli, Micaela. "Parliamo di Noi (donne)." Rivista IBC 26, no. 1 (2018). http://rivista.ibc.regione.emilia-romagna.it/xw-201801/xw-201801-a0021.

Genuino clandestino. "Manifesto." Accessed 25 September 2024. https://genuinoclandestino.it/il-manifesto/.

"Intervista con Dacia Maraini." *Fermenti*, February 1979. http://www.fermenti-editrice.it/archivio/Intervista_DaciaMaraini_Fermenti.htm.

Italian Parliament. "Inchiesta parlamentare sulla miseria in Italia." Archivio Luce, 2 March 1953. https://patrimonio.archivioluce.com/luce-web/detail/IL3000088346/1/inchiesta-parlamentare-sulla-miseria.

Lussana, Fiamma. "Lezione di Fiamma Lussana." Fondazione Gramsci Emilia Romagna. 14 May 2021. https://youtu.be/ozaP9Bp9NOE?si=FLn36JOOqJcKvzFL.

Sambuco, Patrizia. "Laila Wadia in Conversation with Patrizia Sambuco, respondent Katia Pizzi." Italian Cultural Institute London. 4 December 2020. Vimeo video, 35:53. https://vimeo.com/487178885.

Veronelli, Luigi. "A tavola alle sette: Elogio della cucina semplice." Accessed 25 September 2024. https://www.ilveronelli.it/interviste/a-tavola-alle-sette-elogio-della-cucina-semplice/. The interview by Paolo Forcolin was originally published in *Il Settimanale*, 9 June 1976.

Index

Note: Page numbers in *italics* indicate a figure.

Adams, Carol, 6
Addis Saba, Marina, 20, 56, 63, 150
Adolph, Andrea, 7, 10, 11
Adorni, Daniela, 29
Ahmed, Sara, 11, 43, 122
Alice B. Toklas Cookbook, The (Toklas), 110
Almanacco della cucina regionale (Krassich), 26–7
Almanacco della donna italiana, 21, 24, 157n39
Andreoni, Annalisa, 160n122
Annabella in cucina (Vera), 108
anti-kebab legislation, 121, 122, 172n11
Anzaldúa, Gloria, 154–5n29
Appadurai, Arjun, 123
Arslan, Antonia, 176n2
Arthurs, Joshua, 155n3
Ascenzi, Anna, 19
authenticity: as criterion of change, 123; as form of protest, 98; in mother-daughter relationship, 101; search for, 14, 105, 148, 170n84

Babini, Valeria, 49
Ballario, Pina, 13, 31–8, 41, 44, 45, 49, 73, 149, 150, 160n100; *Come ho visto la Russia e altri paesi del mondo*, 31, 32–6; Fascism and, 31, 32; *Fortuna sotto vento*, 36–7, 43; *I giardini dell'oblio*, 160n100; *Il figlio che mi hai dato*, 37–44
Barrett, Lisa Feldman, 10
battaglia del grano. *See* Battle for Wheat
Battle for Wheat, 13, 18, 24, 31
Beat generation, 92, 102, 168n34
Belasco, Warren, 106
Bloodroot Collective, 106
Boddice, Rob, 10, 11–12
body, 15, 51, 59, 72, 78, 94, 96, 97, 98, 99, 124, 127, 129, 147, 150, 155n33; affective/emotions and, 11, 14, 65, 70, 78, 128, 150; food and, 5–6, 26, 154n9; female body, 14, 21, 30, 43, 78, 97, 98, 148; healthy body, 25, 41; mind and, 7, 8, 9, 10, 11, 65, 98; racial/racialized body, 25, 43, 130, 152; the senses and, 5, 10, 65, 72, 125, 127, 128, 137, 161n141. *See also* embodiment
Bonfiglio Krassich, Ada, 26–8, 30
Boni, Ada, 28–9, 30, 38, 149, 158n64
Bourk, Joanne, 5

Boym, Svetlana, 135
Bracco, Cesarina, 14, 51, 52, 65, 66, *67*, *68*, *69*, 73, 76, 77, 78, 79, 82, 83, 149, 150, 151; *La staffetta garibaldina*, 66–72; Resistance experience, 66
Bravo, Anna: on women's Resistance, 63–4, 71, 72, 83, 164n49; on student and feminist movements, 92, 102, 105, 168n34
Brogi, Daniela, 6, 149
Brunelli, Marta, 19
Bruzzone, Anna Maria, 63
Buonfino, Liliana, 107
Burdett, Charles, 159n82

Campi aperti, 123, 173n23
Carson, Rachel, 105
Centro italiano femminile (CIF), 85
Cinotto, Simone, 122, 136
Circolo della Rosa, 115
Colombetti, Giovanna, 65, 72
colonialism, 15, 36, 141, 142, 145, 152; colonial literature/novel, 31, 41, 158n78. *See also* race: racial legislation/laws
Contarini, Silvia, 130
Cristiani, Riccardo, 10
Counihan, Carole, 5, 6, 153–4n6
Curtin, Deane, 8, 95, 98, 150
Cvetkovich, Ann, 11

Dalla Costa, Mariarosa, 93–4, 169n41
Dalla cucina al salotto, enciclopedia della vita domestica (Donna Clara), 157n53
Damasio, Antonio, 10
de Céspedes, Alba, 13, 31, 44–50, 89, 90, 91, 149, 161n144; *Dalla parte di lei*, 90, 161n144; Fascism and, 44; *Io, suo padre: Romanzo sportivo*, 44, 160n122; *Nessuno torna indietro*, 13, 44–9; *Quaderno proibito*, 89–92, 151
De Giorgio, Michela, 20, 150, 159n81
de Grazia, Victoria, 17, 20, 45, 150
Demau Group, 95, 100, 103
De Silva, Cara, 64–5
Desinaretti per ... questi tempi (Petronilla), 53
Dickie, John, 19, 28
Dini, Fanny, 29, 30
Diotima, 115, 171n131

Eagleton, Terry, 120, 129
economic boom, 12, 86, 88, 91, 148, 152. *See also* Miracle Years
embodiment, 6, 7, 10, 120; embodied anxiety, 126; embodied cognition, 15, 128, 130; embodied communication, 161n141; embodied experience of war, 6, 56, 78; embodied feminine, 104, 153n6; embodied identity, 127, 130; embodied mediation, 134, 152; embodied memories, 64; embodied process, 12, 126, 129, 130; embodied self/subject, 10, 11, 51, 65, 72, 83, 105, 151, 155n33. *See also* body
emotions, 4, 5, 24, 31, 37, 38, 43, 51, 56, 65, 66, 74, 75, 78, 79, 80, 99, 101, 102, 104, 112, 113, 120, 122, 124, 126, 129, 134, 139, 140, 144, 147, 148, 150, 151, 153n6; anger, 14, 55, 61, 74, 75, 76, 96, 99, 100, 104, 117, 120, 122, 124, 125, 151; body and, 56, 63, 70, 71, 124; brain and, 10; cognition and, 9; compassion, 124, 126, 143, 144, 145; empathy, 15, 79, 117, 143, 144; Fascism and, 16, 17, 23, 49, 155n3; feminism and, 11, 14, 85, 95–6, 98, 100, 103, 117, 151; food and, 10, 11, 12, 13, 31, 43, 64, 72, 81, 84, 90, 92, 105, 110, 111, 117, 118, 122, 136, 137, 139, 149; history of, 10, 11; memory of, 71, 110; nostalgia, 11, 22, 50, 81, 82, 83, 84,

124, 125, 134–8, 140; racial anxiety, 126–7, 129; racist anger, 75, 120, 122; self and, 15; senses and, 7, 10, 11, 43, 48, 72, 109, 128, 150, 152
emotional communities. *See* Rosenwein, Barbara
emotives. *See* Reddy, William
Ente Nazionale Risi, 18
Escoffier, Auguste, 29
Estia, 15, 109, 115–18, 147, 148, 151, 152

Falasca Zamponi, Simonetta, 17, 19, 156n9
Fantozzi, Chiara, 57
Far presto (Rossi Lodomez), 88
Farè, Ida, 95, 115, 116, 117, 149, 171n121
Fascism: 12, 13, 16, 17, 31, 36, 44, 45, 49, 73, 134, 147, 148, 150, 158n64, 163n46; autarky/autarkic policies, 12, 13, 16, 25, 26, 30, 33, 34, 54, 152; Comitato permanente del grano, 18; domestic literature, 4, 7, 13, 17, 19, 24, 30, 51, 88, 148, 149, 152; donna-crisi, 20; donna muliebre, 20, 32; Fascist gender politics, 19–24, 38; interracial sexual relationships, 22, 39, 43; *La difesa della razza*, 39; *Preghiera del pane*, 19. *See also* colonialism; food: Fascist policies
Fascist regime. *See* Fascism
feminism, 4, 10, 11, 14, 21, 85, 92, 109, 117, 140, 168n35; emotions and, 95–7; Italian, 93–7, 100–1, 169n68. *See also* neo-feminist groups
Fillìa, 30
Fischler, Claude, 5, 10, 11, 154n9
Fisher, Mary Frances Kennedy (M.F.K.), 3, 4, 15, 147, 150
Flinders, Carol, 106
Foggia Moretti, Amalia, 26, 27, 29, 30, 52–3, 54, 56, 79, 81, 90, 149, 152
food: consumption, 5, 6, 7, 18, 34, 42, 53, 86, 87, 88, 124, 154n9, 157n48; ethnic/cuisine, 25, 120, 121, 123; Fascist policies, 17–19, 29; Futurist activities, 29–30, 158n72; imagery, 4, 5, 11, 24, 31, 50, 123, 129, 147, 150; literature and, 7, 15, 95, 120, 123, 124; memory, 35, 64–5, 70, 71, 72, 77–8, 79, 81, 102, 110, 111, 136, 137; protests, 13, 51, 55, 56, 58–62, 63, 147, 148. *See also* anti-kebab legislation

Gabaccia, Donna, 122, 172n15
Gabriele, Tommasina, 102
Gambaro, Elisa, 90, 110
GAP, 62, 164n53
Gastronomical Me, The (Fischer), 3–4
GDD, 13, 58–9, 63, 78, 81, 83, 162n30
Genuino clandestino, 123, 173n23
Georget, Anne, 64–5
Giannotti, Stefania, 117, 149, 171n132
Gilbert, Sandra, 3
Ginzburg, Natalia, 49–50
Gobetti, Ada, 14, 65, 78, 149, 15, 162n30, 166n112; *Diario partigiano*, 51–2, 78–83
Godfrey, Bronwen, 106
Gosetti della Salda, Ada, 108, 149
Gruppi d'azione patriottica. *See* GAP
Gruppi di difesa della donna e per l'assistenza ai combattenti per la libertà. *See* GDD
Gruppo Anabasi, 93
Guida, Patrizia, 99
Guida Gastronomica d'Italia, 27
Guidetti Serra, Bianca, 63, 79

Heldke, Lisa, 8, 95, 150
Heller, Tamar, 7
Helstosky, Carol, 16, 18
Hochschild, Arlie, 11, 96, 117
How to Cook a Wolf (Fisher), 3

Il Cucchiaio d'Argento, 88, 108
Il Solco, 21, 22
Il Talismano della felicità (Boni), 28–9, 88, 158n64
Inchiesta parlamentare sulla miseria, 87

Jasper, James, 96, 122, 123
Jones, Selma, 94

Katzen, Mollie, 106
Koivunen, Ann, 11
Korsmeyer, Carolyn, 8

La cucina autarchica (Randi), 24
La cucina economica in tempo di sanzioni (Bonfiglio Krassich), 28
La cucina futurista (Marinetti and Fillìa), 30
La cucina integrale (Buonfino), 107
La cucina italiana, 29–30, 108
La cucina italiana della resistenza (Zamara), 26
La cucina macrobiotica in Italia (Sclauzero), 107
La cucina rustica regionale (Veronelli and Carnacina), 107
Lakhous, Amara, 124
Lamri, Tahar, 124–5, 127, 135, 173n30
Laurel's Kitchen (Robertson, Flinders, and Godfrey), 106
Lazzaro-Weis, Carol, 102
Le Breton, David, 65, 72
Leccardi, Carmen, 94
Legnani, Massimo, 53
Le massaie contro le sanzioni (Morelli), 25–6
Le ricette regionali italiane (Gosetti della Salda), 108
Levinas, Emmanuel, 8, 65, 78, 133, 139
Libreria delle donne di Milano, 15, 85, 109, *114*, 115, 116, 117, 149, 171n121
Linden, David, 10
Lonzi, Carla, 93, 95
Lotta femminista, 93–4, 140, 169n42
Lupton, Deborah, 6, 10, 11, 36, 105, 120, 136
Lussana, Fiamma, 91, 92, 168n35, 168n36

macrobiotic cuisine, 181
Magagnoli, Stefano, 29
male celebrity chefs, 119–20
Mangiare all'italiana (Momigliano), 28
Manifesto della cucina futurista (Marinetti), 30
Maraini, Dacia, 14, 95, 97, 98, 117, 149, 175n1; *Mangiami pure*, 85, 98, 99–101, 104, 109, 151; *Il treno per Helsinki*, 85, 98, 101–4, 105, 109, 117
Marinetti, Filippo Tommasi, 29, 30, 31, 158n72, 158–9n78
Masino, Paola, 29, 158n77
Matricardi, Franca, 88
Menù per un anno (Gavotti), 108
migration, 11, 12, 15, 118, 120, 126, 129, 130, 132, 135, 138, 140, 150, 152, 173n30; anti-kebab legislation and, 121–2, 172n11; narrative of/literature, 11, 15, 120, 124–6, 134; racism and, 121–2, 125, 126, 127, 129
Miracle Years, 86; confectionery industry and, 87; consumption (habits) and, 86–8
Moore Lappé, Frances, 105
Moosewood Cookbook (Katzen), 106
Moran, Patricia, 7
Morelli, Lidia, 19, 25–6, 27, 30, 157n48, 157n53
Mori, Marisa, 30
Moroni, Primo, 95
Movimento di liberazione della donna, 93

multiculturalism, 121, 124, 125–6, 130, 133, 134, 139–40, 151
Muraro, Luisa, 116, 117, 171n131

Negri, Ada, 29
neo-feminist groups, 14, 92, 93, 95. *See also* feminism: Italian; emotions: feminism and
neuroscience, 9–10, 11, 126; Damasio, Antonio, 10; Gallese, Vittorio, 128–9; psychoanalysis and, 155n33
Noi donne, 13, 58, 59, 61, 62, 148, 163n35, 163n40, 163n46, 164n53
Notari, Delia, 29, 30
Notari, Umberto, 29, 108
Nuboli, Cecilia, 55
Nützenadel, Alexander, 16

Ombra, Marisa, 56, 84, 85, 86, 148
Orlandini, Laura, 162n30

Pariani, Laura, 15, 120, 126, 140–6, 149, 152; feminism and, 140; "Il colore del silenzio," 140–5; *L'uovo di Gertrudina*, 140, 145
Partito Comunista Italiano (PCI), 84, 85, 162n30
Passerini, Luisa, 109
PCI. *See* Partito Comunista Italiano (PCI)
Perricone Violà, Augusta, 23, 32, 45
Perullo, Nicola: emotions, 9–10, 11; naked taste, 136; relationship with the Other, 139, 146; taste, 8–9, 12, 65, 133, 150
Petronilla, 26, 52, 53, 54, 56, 79, 81, 152. *See also* Foggia Moretti, Amalia
Pezzini, Serena, 80
Pickering-Iazzi, Robin, 20, 37, 45, 46, 150
Pizzi, Katia, 130, 133, 174n72
Plato, 7, 8
Poggiali, Ciro, 22–3
Political Palate: A Feminist Vegetarian Cookbook (Bloodroot Collective), 106
Ponzanesi, Sandra, 127, 157n42
postcoloniality, 12, 45, 124, 125, 126, 140, 151, 152
pratica dell'inconscio, 96, 100, 117
Pulcini, Elena, 116, 129, 141, 144

race: racial anxiety, 126, 128–9; racial body, 152; racial difference, 22, 36, 128; racial discrimination, 127; racialization, 130; racial legislation/laws, 22, 39, 43; racial stereotypes, 146; racism, 121–2, 125, 126, 127, 129; racist anger, 75, 120, 122; racist attacks, 121, 127; racist attitudes/views, 124, 142, 144; racist definition, 43; racist overtones/remarks, 130, 174n46; racist politics, 30; racist society, 15, 129; racist terms, 57; senses and, 121
Randi, Elisabetta, 19, 24–5, 26, 27, 30
Rattazzi, Ilaria, 109–10
Re, Lucia, 31
Reddy, William, 17, 49, 95, 137, 151; emotional regime and, 17, 49; emotives and, 95–6, 151
Resistance, 13, 14, 44, 51, 52, 55, 56, 59, 69, 70, 71, 72, 73, 74, 75, 76, 77, 78, 79, 80, 81, 82, 83, 84, 85, 86, 150, 151, 164n54; memory of, 62–6, 164n57; women in the, 56–7, 58. *See also* GAP; GDD; *Noi donne*
Ricette di Petronilla per tempi eccezionali (Petronilla), 52–3, 54–5
Rigotti, Francesca, 8, 154n27
Rivolta femminile, 93
Robertson, Laurel, 106

Rosenwein, Barbara, 10; emotional communities, 17, 23, 49
Rossi Lodomez, Vera, 88. *See also* Vera

Salvatici, Silvia, 6–7
Sarfatti, Margherita, 29, 159n82
Scarpellini, Emanuela, 87, 88
Sceats, Sarah, 7
Scego, Igiaba, 15, 120, 130, 136, 138, 140, 146, 149, 152, 173n31; *La mia casa è dove sono*, 136; "Salsicce," 126–30
Sclauzero, Mariarosa, 107
senses, 17, 21, 27, 43, 46, 47, 48, 49, 78, 83, 106, 111, 121, 124, 125, 127, 128, 131, 139; cognition and (sensory), 9, 10, 15, 65, 128; food and, 5, 7, 8, 13, 15, 27–8, 31, 45, 49, 50, 98, 109, 140, 147, 150, 152. *See also under* emotions
Sereni, Clara, 109, 110, 117, 149, 151; *Casalinghitudine*, 15, 85, 109, 110–14; *Via Ripetta 155*, 109
Signorelli, Amalia, 90
Slow Food, 123
Smith, Mark, 10
Soffiamo sulla cicoria matta (Rattanzi), 109–10
Spackman, Barbara, 16, 20, 157n52
Sumeli Weinberg, Grazia, 102, 169n71
Sutton, David, 136

Tassajara Bread Book, The (Brown), 106
Tassajara Cooking (Brown), 106
Thomas, Anna, 106
Toklas, Alice Babette, 110
Tommasi Marinetti, Filippo, 29, 30, 31, 158n72, 159n78
200 suggerimenti … per questi tempi (Petronilla), 54

Vegetarian Epicure, The (Thomas), 106
vegetarianism, 6, 14, 105, 106
Venturoli, Cinzia, 57, 162n24
Vera, 108. *See also* Rossi Lodomez, Vera
Veronelli, Luigi, 107, 170n97
Vertovec, Steven, 134
Vivere bene in tempi difficili: Come le donne affrontano le crisi economiche (Momigliano), 28

Wadia, Laila, 15, 120, 126, 129–30, 134, 136, 137, 140, 146, 149, 152, 173n31; *Amiche per la pelle*, 130, 133–4; "Curry di pollo," 130, 132, 133; *Il burattinaio e altre storie extra italiane*, 130; "Il segreto della calandraca," 130, 135, 137–9; *Kitchensutra*, 130, 134, 139–40, 175n76; *Mondopentola*, 134–5, 136; "Spaghetti allo scoglio," 131–2, 174n46
Willson, Perry, 156n30, 164n54
Wodak, Ruth, 155n3
Women's Bookshop in Milan. *See* Libreria delle donne di Milano
Woolf, Virginia, 3, 4, 5, 15, 147, 150
World War II, 3, 12, 51, 52, 55, 56, 63, 64, 78, 84, 98, 148, 150; rationing and, 53–4; Servizio Ausiliario Femminile, 55; women and, 55, 56–8. *See also* GAP; GDD; Resistance

Zamara, Emilia, 26
Zangrandi, Giovanna, 14, 51, 52, 65, 70, 72–3, 79, 82, 83, 149, 150, 151; Fascism and, 72–3; *I giorni veri*, 66, 73–8, 165n91; Resistance experience, 73

www.ingramcontent.com/pod-product-compliance
Lightning Source LLC
Chambersburg PA
CBHW020300030826
48979CB00026B/1637/J